WITHDRAWN
UTSA Libraries

BURT FRANKLIN: RESEARCH & SOURCE WORKS SERIES 664
American Classics in History and Social Science 175

THE ADMINISTRATION

OF THE

AMERICAN REVOLUTIONARY ARMY

THE ADMINISTRATION

OF THE

AMERICAN REVOLUTIONARY ARMY

BY

LOUIS CLINTON HATCH, Ph.D.

BURT FRANKLIN
NEW YORK

Published by LENOX HILL Pub. & Dist. Co. (Burt Franklin)
235 East 44th St., New York, N.Y. 10017
Originally Published: 1904
Reprinted: 1971
Printed in the U.S.A.

S.B.N.: 8337-15941
Library of Congress Card Catalog No.: 70-132678
Burt Franklin: Research and Source Works Series 664
American Classics in History and Social Science 175

Reprinted from the original edition in the Ohio State University Library.

PREFACE.

THIS monograph was originally prepared as a dissertation for the degree of Doctor of Philosophy in Harvard University. It has since been revised, some matter has been omitted, and some additions have been made. For the errors of the work the author is responsible; for such merit as it may possess he is largely indebted to his friends. Special acknowledgments are due to Professor Edward Channing and Professor Albert Bushnell Hart, under whose supervision the dissertation was prepared; to Mr. Hoyt A. Moore, who has rendered most valuable assistance during the progress of the revision; to the Harvard University Library for privileges liberally accorded; to the New England Historic Genealogical Society for permission to examine the Knox MSS.; and to Mr. A. H. Allen, chief clerk of the Department of Rolls and Library in the Department of State at Washington, for permission to make use of the papers of the Board of War. Mention should also be made of courteous assistance received from Mr. S. N. Hamilton of the Department of State.

LOUIS CLINTON HATCH.

CAMBRIDGE, MASSACHUSETTS,
May, 1903.

CONTENTS.

CHAPTER I.
FORMATION OF THE ARMY 1

CHAPTER II.
CONGRESS AND THE COMMANDER-IN-CHIEF 18

CHAPTER III.
APPOINTMENT AND PROMOTION 35

CHAPTER IV.
FOREIGN OFFICERS 47

CHAPTER V.
PAY AND HALF-PAY 71

CHAPTER VI.
SUPPLYING THE ARMY 86

CHAPTER VII.
MUTINIES OF 1781 124

CHAPTER VIII.
NEWBURG ADDRESSES 142

CHAPTER IX.
MUTINY OF 1783 AND DISBANDMENT OF THE ARMY 179

APPENDICES.

A. THE NEWBURG ADDRESSES AND PAPERS CONNECTED THERE-
WITH:—

    1. First Anonymous Address to the Officers of the Army, March 10, 1783 197
    2. Second Anonymous Address to the Officers of the Army, March 12, 1783 200
    3. Washington's Address to the Officers, March 15, 1783 . , . 201
    4. Draft of a Reply to the Anonymous Addresses, March 15, 1783   205
    5. Extract of a Letter from Armstrong to Gates, April 29, 1783 . 208

B. LIST OF AUTHORITIES CITED 210

INDEX 217

THE ADMINISTRATION OF THE AMERICAN REVOLUTIONARY ARMY.

CHAPTER I.

FORMATION OF THE ARMY.

WHEN the Second Continental Congress met, May 10, 1775, the British army was shut up in Boston by bodies of imperfectly organized and ill-trained troops from the four New England colonies. This mass of armed men which constituted the besieging force scarcely deserved the name of army, and the units of which it was composed could hardly be called soldiers. The Americans, indeed, were brave, accustomed to long and difficult journeys, and familiar with the use of firearms; but they knew little of military training or military subordination. To be sure, nearly every able-bodied man served in the militia; but under a popular or a semi-popular government, and with little immediate danger of invasion, people are ordinarily too busy sowing and reaping, buying and selling, to give much attention to drills and reviews. These conditions had brought about the usual results, and the musters had degenerated into little more than farces.

In 1745 the Rhode Island legislature voted that the militia should drill but twice a year.[1] Of the Massachusetts musters, Timothy Pickering, afterwards quartermaster-general of the Revolutionary army, wrote an amusing account. The men assembled slowly, he says, and disputed with each other for places. While marching to the training field, some would break ranks to engage in the chivalrous pastime of frightening young

[1] *Rhode Island Colonial Records*, v. 156.

women by surrounding them and discharging their muskets. The "training" was made up of a few short drills, at least one "elegant entertainment" for the officers, a day's musketry practice, and two sham battles, — all very simple and useless. Pickering declared that the object of his criticism was to bring about a reform, so that, if war broke out with France and the seaports were attacked, there might be a well-disciplined militia to hold the invaders in check until aid could arrive from Great Britain.[1] The Salem patriot was following the example of a Boston town-meeting, which, in 1768, advised all persons without arms to procure them, "in consequence of prevailing apprehensions of a war with France."[2]

As the danger of a conflict with England became imminent, the colonies made earnest attempts to improve their militia. In Virginia, volunteer companies drilled busily.[3] In Maryland, there was a thorough reorganization of the militia under the leadership of Charles Lee, an English half-pay officer.[4] Rhode Island, in 1774, ordered that company drills be held monthly, regimental semiannually, brigade biennially.[5] In October of the same year the Massachusetts Congress directed the field-officers of the militia to endeavor to enlist at least one-quarter of the men in a special force, ready to march at a moment's notice; and the same Congress recommended all the inhabitants to "perfect themselves in the military skill."[6] The former were the famous minute-men of Massachusetts.

Curiously enough, the initiative in improving the militia was sometimes taken by the royal governors. On January 1, 1771, Governor Wentworth of New Hampshire informed the legislature that "the present appearances of impending war leaves us no time to loose [lose] in making effectual preparations for the defence and safety of the province, particularly in forming the

---

[1] Pickering, *Pickering*, i. 16–20, from *Essex Gazette*, January 31 and February 21, 1769.
[2] Hildreth, *United States*, ii. 546.
[3] Irving, *Washington*, i. 421–422.
[4] *Lee Papers* (New York Historical Society, *Collections*, 1874), ii. 247.
[5] *Rhode Island Colonial Records*, vii. 269–270.
[6] *Massachusetts Soldiers and Sailors of the Revolutionary War*, i., pp. ix.–x.

militia into a powerful and respectable body." His Excellency proposed that the laws on the subject "be drawn together into one plain and precise act"; and the legislature accordingly appointed a committee to prepare such a revision.[1] Probably the governor was honestly alarmed at the situation of foreign affairs, and did not appreciate the danger of revolt at home; he may have hoped also to turn the reorganization to the advantage of the crown.

In New York a similar policy was adopted. In 1772 a number of excellent companies were raised in the colony on the suggestion of Governor Tryon, a staunch loyalist; but the British government, for once understanding colonial sentiment, received the news of what he had done with considerable coolness.[2]

Besides drilling on the muster-ground, hundreds of the provincials had served with the royal troops in the French and Indian War; but this experience was, perhaps, of small disciplinary value. It was often merely a training in frontier warfare, where men fought in small groups, or even singly, and where, as Pickering said, "no other discipline was necessary than being good marksmen and dexterous in skulking behind trees and bushes."[3] Knowledge of tactics and strategy was also lacking; there was no military school in the colonies, and nearly half the American generals served their apprenticeship in the war itself. Of the remainder, three — St. Clair, Montgomery, and Dayton — had held royal commissions; the others had served in the provincial forces only. With the exception of Washington, however, the veterans, if we may call them so, manifested little superiority over their more inexperienced fellows. Of the twenty-one American major-generals in the Continental army, ten had been at least company officers in earlier wars; five of these were of small ability, three were especially valuable, and two belonged to neither category. Of the eleven who had seen no previous service, three showed little military skill, three rank among the ablest of the American generals, and three, though less eminent, deserve an honorable place in the

---

[1] *New Hampshire Provincial Papers*, vii. 267.
[2] Wilson, *Memorial History of the City of New-York*, ii. 420–421.
[3] Pickering, *Pickering*, i. 19.

military history of our country. The two unclassified are Benedict Arnold, and Parsons of Connecticut, who was probably also a traitor.¹

The lack of military experience was the more alarming on account of the power of Great Britain. The Seven Years' War had greatly increased her dominion and influence. She had a considerable army, an excellent navy, and was accustomed to combining land and sea operations. British cruisers could interrupt the foreign trade of the colonies, to whom commerce was almost a necessity, since America was not a manufacturing country; British fleets could facilitate a landing in every harbor of the extended coast; and Canada furnished a base for an attack by land. Everywhere the colonies lay open to invasion; from Eastport to Savannah there was not a single fortified town.

True, the size of the country was a better guarantee against conquest than the possession of a Quebec, or even of a Gibraltar; it was much easier to overrun the colonies than to subdue them. If the Americans could avoid a pitched battle in a fair field and be content to hover round an invading army and confine its operations, there was hope that at last Great Britain would grow weary of a struggle which brought little honor and no profit; or that foreign aid or some blunder of the enemy would give an opportunity to strike a decisive blow. It would, however, be difficult for an unwarlike democracy to maintain such a system; untrained troops are ill fitted for delicate manœuvres, and frequent retreats may demoralize even veterans. Moreover, the temper of the voters must be considered as well as that of the soldiers; and America would be fortunate if the people, impatient under the burdens of war and zealous for the glory of their

---

¹ The American major-generals of the Continental army were in the order of their appointment: Artemas Ward, Charles Lee, Philip Schuyler, Israel Putnam, Richard Montgomery, John Thomas, Horatio Gates, William Heath, Joseph Spencer, John Sullivan, Nathanael Greene, Benedict Arnold, William Alexander (called Lord Stirling), Thomas Mifflin, Arthur St. Clair, Adam Stephen, Benjamin Lincoln, Robert Howe, Alexander McDougall, William Smallwood, Samuel H. Parsons, Henry Knox, William Moultrie. — Heitman, *Historical Register of the Officers of the Continental Army*, 9.

country, did not drive the government or the general to meet the enemy in the field, though at a risk of utter ruin.

Such were the conditions under which the members of the Continental Congress were obliged to answer the solemn questions: Are you ready to risk your property and person by abetting armed resistance to the royal authority? Dare you take upon your conscience the awful responsibility of a civil war, when defeat may mean loss of charters and privileges, and victory may result in the breaking of the ties which for over 150 years have bound you to the mother country? The colonists were proud to call themselves Englishmen, and even the Whigs were reluctant to consent to independence. To us the word means liberty, but to them it meant secession. To-day, with national feeling higher than ever before, and the western hemisphere too small for our ambition, it is difficult to appreciate the moral courage displayed by the Continental Congress when they gave their sanction to an appeal to arms.

Indeed, Congress at first refused to approve of a general war, and tried to confine the fighting to the vicinity of Boston. They advised that, if British troops came to New York, they should remain unmolested, provided that they behaved peaceably and did not attempt to erect fortifications.[1] Congress also expressed disapproval of colonial incursions into Canada, and promised to give back the cannon and stores which Ethan Allen had taken at Ticonderoga, "when the restoration of the former harmony between Great Britain and these colonies, so ardently wished for by the latter, shall render it prudent and consistent with the overruling law of self-preservation."[2] Congress acted on the theory that they were opposing, not the king, but the "ministerial army" under Gage. The fiction now seems rather transparent; at that time many Americans felt that they were not making war so much as defending themselves against unlawful violence, and thought that they had suffered a real injustice when, on August 23, 1775, George III. officially declared them rebels.

Though Congress hesitated to call things by their right names, and to recognize the full meaning of the siege of Boston, they

[1] *Journals of Congress*, i. 101–102, May 15, 1775.
[2] *Ibid.* 103, May 18, 1775.

nevertheless made ready for the wider conflict which they saw might follow. They resolved that the colonies be immediately put into a state of defence, and appointed committees to consider means for obtaining ammunition and military stores, and to decide what posts in New York ought to be occupied.[1]

From Massachusetts came a call to a wider field of duty. A letter asking advice about establishing a government closed with a respectful suggestion that, as the army now collecting was for the common defence, it would be well for Congress to take the "regulation and general direction of it."[2] On June 2 President Hancock laid the letter before Congress. After a week's consideration Congress advised Massachusetts to form a government, but said nothing about assuming control of the army.[3] It would seem, however, that the question had already been practically decided; for, on the day after the letter from Massachusetts was submitted to Congress, the New York delegates wrote to the Congress of their colony, asking whom they would prefer to command "the Continental army in our province, which is to be maintained at the general charge;"[4] and Congress could hardly have kept up a force in New York, which was not yet invaded, and at the same time have left the troops before Boston to be supported by the local governments. The delay of Congress in complying with the request of Massachusetts that they would undertake the management of the army, was probably due chiefly to the difficulty of agreeing on a commander-in-chief.

No other American had the military experience and reputation of Colonel George Washington. Moreover, he had been chosen a delegate to both the First and the Second Continental Congress, and was held in high regard by his colleagues. Patrick Henry had said, "If you speak of solid information and sound judgment, Colonel Washington is unquestionably the greatest man on the floor."[5] Washington had also other advantages which were con-

---

[1] *Journals of Congress*, i. 102, 105, 106, May 15, 26, 27, 1775.

[2] Massachusetts Congress to Continental Congress, May 16, 1775, Force, *American Archives*, 4th series, ii. 621.

[3] *Journals of Congress*, i. 115, June 9, 1775.

[4] June 3, 1775, Force, *American Archives*, 4th series, ii. 898.

[5] Lodge, *Washington*, i. 127.

sidered very important. He was, for example, a man of wealth and position; and Congress wished to show that the "rebel" leaders were not penniless adventurers, but persons of substance, with an interest in the maintenance of social order. The spirit of '76 was by no means so democratic as Fourth of July orators would have us believe; we have many instances of aristocratic feeling. The New York Congress wrote to their delegates at Philadelphia that a general in America should not only be brave, able, and experienced in war; but that he should be favored by fortune, a man who would rather communicate lustre to his dignities than receive it from them, and one whose property, kindred, and connections might give sure proof of faithful exercise of power, and of a readiness to lay it down when the public welfare demanded.[1] When Clinton was elected governor of New York, Schuyler said that he hoped every patriot would support him, "although his family and connections do not entitle him to so distinguished a predominance."[2] Montgomery wished that "some method could be fallen upon of engaging *gentlemen* to serve";[3] Washington advised the colonel of a cavalry regiment to "take none but gentlemen" as officers;[4] and John Adams said that a general "ought to be a gentleman of letters and general knowledge, a man of address and knowledge of the world."[5]

Furthermore, Washington was from Virginia; and to Virginia, the largest and oldest of the colonies, there was conceded, partly through policy and partly on account of the ability and advanced views of her delegates, a kind of primacy. The first president of Congress, Peyton Randolph, was a Virginian; later, Richard Henry Lee of Virginia was selected to make the motion for independence; and Thomas Jefferson, of the same colony, was chosen to write the Declaration.

On the other hand, though a majority of the members of Congress were willing to give the command of the army to Virginia,

[1] June 7, 1775, Force, *American Archives*, 4th series, ii. 1281-1282.
[2] Schuyler to Jay, July 14, 1777, Pellew, *Jay*, 92.
[3] Montgomery to Schuyler, November 13, 1775, Washington, *Writings* (Ford), iii. 250-251, note.
[4] Washington to Baylor, January 9, 1777, *Ibid.* v. 159.
[5] Adams to Greene, August 4, 1776, John Adams, *Works*, i. 252.

there were some who thought it too hazardous an experiment to send a Southerner to command a New England army on New England soil. The danger was increased by the offence which such an appointment would give to certain influential men. Hancock, who had been colonel of a Boston regiment, wished to exchange the presidency of Congress for the command of the army. The Massachusetts general, (Artemas Ward, had been allowed to exercise most of the powers of a commander-in-chief, and there was strong opposition to superseding him.)

In Massachusetts the necessity for action was better appreciated than at Philadelphia. John Adams was continually receiving letters, many of them from civilians, others from military men, including Ward himself; and the burden of them was that, without help from Congress, the army must dissolve. Adams was told that Ward was incompetent, and that the easiest way of superseding him was for Congress to intervene and appoint a commander. Elbridge Gerry wrote to the Massachusetts delegates in Congress, "I should heartily rejoice to see this way the beloved Colonel Washington, and do not doubt the New England generals would acquiesce in showing to our sister colony Virginia, the respect, which she has before experienced from the Continent, in making him generalissimo."[1] Accordingly, Adams resolved to bring matters to a decision. Early one morning he informed his cousin, Samuel Adams, of his intention; and when Congress met, he rose, set forth the dangerous condition of affairs, and moved that the army be "adopted" and a general appointed. Without mentioning any name, he indicated his own preference for "a certain gentleman from Virginia now in Congress"; whereat Washington, "from his usual modesty," as Adams remarks in telling the story, darted into the library.

President Hancock had listened with evident enjoyment to the first part of the speech, but at the reference to Washington he was at once transformed. Adams says, in his autobiography: "I never remarked a more sudden and striking change of countenance. Mortification and resentment were expressed as forcibly as his face could exhibit them. Mr. Samuel Adams seconded

[1] June 4, 1775, Austin, *Gerry*, i. 79.

the motion, and that did not soften the president's physiognomy at all."[1]

In the debate which followed, several members said that matters were going on well in Boston; that the soldiers appeared satisfied with Ward; and that, although they had no objections to Washington personally, they thought it unwise to send him to command a New England army. Against the suggestion Pendleton of Virginia and Sherman of Connecticut took the lead in opposition; Cushing of Massachusetts and others expressed similar opinions, though less positively; Paine avoided committing himself, but eulogized Ward, who had been his fellow-student at Harvard. Unanimity was important, and the subject was postponed.

Meantime, efforts were made to obtain an agreement. The local prejudices of New England were met by those of the South. Some of the supporters of Washington had shown themselves so determined that, either from sectional pride or from fear of a New Englander, they seemed ready to defeat the "adoption" of the army unless Washington were put at the head. A large majority of the delegates favored him, and the rest patriotically consented to waive their opposition.[2]

On June 15, 1775, Congress resolved to appoint a general, with an allowance of five hundred dollars a month for salary and expenses, and Washington was unanimously elected.[3] The next day President Hancock officially informed the new general of his appointment. Washington rose in his place, and with

[1] John Adams, *Works*, ii. 417. John Adams considered Hancock unfit to command the army because of his feeble health and lack of military experience; and he thought that perhaps Hancock wished merely the compliment of an offer, to which, Mr. Adams says, "he had some pretensions, for, at that time, his exertions, sacrifices, and general merits in the cause of his country had been incomparably greater than those of Colonel Washington" (John Adams, *Works*, ii. 416). Hancock, however, had a good opinion of his own abilities: he wrote to Washington that he should like a place in the army; he took part in the expedition to Rhode Island in 1778; and he would probably have accepted the command had it been offered to him.

[2] John Adams's Autobiography, in *Works*, ii. 417-418.
[3] *Journals of Congress*, i. 119, June 15, 1775.

the mingled resolution and modesty so characteristic of the man, replied that, the choice having fallen on him, he would not decline the post, but that he begged, for his own future justification, to assure Congress most sincerely that he felt unequal to his task. He added that, as no profit could have tempted him to sacrifice his "domestic ease and happiness," he would accept no pay, but would simply present an account of his expenses.[1]

Having appointed a commander-in-chief, Congress proceeded to select the other generals; but here, owing to lack of sufficient information, they were less fortunate. Two English officers living in America had indicated their willingness to accept commissions. One was Horatio Gates, a former major, who had taken part in Braddock's expedition, but had since resigned and settled in Virginia. The other, Charles Lee, had also served in the French and Indian War, and was now a lieutenant-colonel in the British army, retired on half-pay. He was a restless, unstable, untrustworthy adventurer; but his true character was not known in America, and he was believed to possess much military knowledge and skill. There was, however, some doubt of the advisability of employing foreigners.

John Adams was distracted by thoughts of the "great experience and confessed abilities" of Lee and Gates on the one hand, and of the "natural prejudices, and virtuous attachment of our countrymen to their own officers" on the other. He was finally decided in the Englishmen's favor by the wishes of Washington and of many of the warmest patriots in the South; by the thought of the moral effect which the accession of these veterans would produce, especially in Boston; and, finally, by the "real American merit of them both."[2] Influenced probably by similar reasons, Congress determined to give Gates and Lee important places in the American service. Gates was appointed adjutant-general with the rank of brigadier;[3] his duty was to act as a kind of assistant to the commander-in-chief in the management of the army. Gates had much military experience and was a friend of Washington, and the choice was therefore a natural one.

[1] *Journals of Congress*, i. 120, June 16, 1775.
[2] Adams to Gerry, June 18, 1775, John Adams, *Works*, ix. 358.
[3] *Journals of Congress*, i. 122-123, June 17, 1775.

What to offer Lee was a harder question. Several members urged that he could not accept anything less than the senior major-generalship; but John Adams declared that it was much for Ward to consent to serve under any man, and that he ought not to serve under a stranger.[1] Accordingly, the Massachusetts officer was chosen first major-general, and Lee the second. Lee gracefully accepted the position, assuring Congress that he had "the highest sense of the honor conferred upon him"; but in reality he was much mortified at being placed under a man whom he described as "a fat old gentleman, who had been a popular *church-warden.*"[2] Indeed, Lee seems to have felt that he had no small claim to the chief command. In a letter to General Thomas he said, "According then to modern etiquette, notions of a soldier's honor and delicacy, I ought to consider *at least*[3] the preferment given to General Ward over me as the highest indignity."[4]

The third major-general was taken from New York; and Schuyler, the nominee of the Congress of that colony, was chosen. The fourth and last was Putnam; he was in high favor with Congress, and his election was unanimous. The brigadiers were Pomeroy of Massachusetts, Montgomery of New York, Wooster of Connecticut, Heath of Massachusetts, Spencer of Connecticut, Thomas of Massachusetts, Sullivan of New Hampshire, and Greene of Rhode Island.[5] The reason for selecting most of the generals from New England was that the army was then mainly composed of New England soldiers.

On June 16, 1775, Richard Henry Lee, Edward Rutledge, and John Adams were appointed a committee to draw up a commission and instructions for Washington.[6] He was directed to enforce discipline and to retain in the service the men now enlisted, and was authorized to increase the army to a number not

---

[1] Adams, Autobiography, in his *Works*, ii. 418.
[2] *Journals of Congress*, i. 122–123, June 17 and 19, 1775; *Lee Papers* (New York Historical Society, *Collections*, 1874), v. 177–178.
[3] The italics are the author's.
[4] July 23, 1775, Coffin, *Thomas*, 11.
[5] *Journals of Congress*, i. 123, 125, June 19 and 22, 1775.
[6] *Ibid.* 120, June 16, 1775.

exceeding twice that of the enemy. The instructions closed with the caution, "making it your special care, in discharge of the great trust committed unto you, that the liberties of America receive no detriment."[1]

The preliminaries accomplished, Washington and Lee set out for Cambridge. They were preceded by private letters from Massachusetts delegates, bespeaking for them a cordial welcome. Adams wrote to Gerry : —

"I hope the utmost politeness and respect will be shown to these officers on their arrival. The whole army, I think, should be drawn up upon the occasion, and all the pride, pomp, and circumstance of glorious war displayed ; — *no powder burned, however.*

"There is something charming to me in the conduct of Washington. A gentleman of one of the first fortunes upon the continent, leaving his delicious retirement, his family and friends, sacrificing his ease, and hazarding all in the cause of his country! His views are noble and disinterested. He declared, when he accepted the mighty trust, that he would lay before us an exact account of his expenses, and not accept a shilling for pay."[2]

Another Massachusetts member, Thomas Cushing, though he had doubted the wisdom of the appointment of Washington, wrote to Councillor Bowdoin : "I beg leave to recommend him [Washington] to your respectful notice. He is a complete gentleman. He is sensible, amiable, virtuous, modest, and brave. I promise myself that your acquaintance with him will afford you great pleasure, and I doubt not his agreeable behavior and good conduct will give great satisfaction to our people of all denominations. General Lee accompanies him as major-general; I hope his appointment will be agreeable to our people, and that he will be received with all due respect."[3]

Due respect was certainly shown. The Massachusetts Congress appointed a committee to meet Washington and Lee at Springfield, and to pay all bills at the inns ; they also furnished

[1] *Secret Journals of Congress*, i. 18, June 20, 1775.
[2] June 18, 1775, John Adams, *Works*, ix. 358–359.
[3] June 21, 1775, *Bowdoin and Temple Papers* (Massachusetts Historical Society, *Collections*, 6th series, ix.), 384–385.

a suitable escort. Quarters were provided at Cambridge, and measures were taken to procure furniture and servants.[1] Notice of the expected arrival of the new generals was sent to camp, that they might be received with the honors due to their rank, "without, however, any expense of powder, and without taking the troops off from the necessary attention to their duty at this crisis of our affairs." On the arrival of Washington and Lee at Watertown, where the Congress was sitting, they were presented with cordial and highly laudatory addresses of welcome.[2]

On July 3 Washington formally took command of the army. He found everything in great disorder. The Rhode Islanders alone were provided with tents; the other troops lived in huts made of boards, or sail-cloth, or both, or of stone and turf, brick, or brush. Some were mere shelters; others were furnished with doors and windows, and even ornamented according to the tastes of the builders. This variety of structure was indeed of no special importance; Chaplain Emerson, who has left us a vivid and interesting description of the camp, calls it "rather a beauty than a blemish in the army."[3] It typified more serious differences, however. Thus, the Connecticut and Rhode Island men were enlisted until the first of December; others for a slightly longer term, but none beyond the first of January. Massachusetts had 59 men (including officers and soldiers) to a company, and sometimes ten, sometimes eleven, companies to a regiment; New Hampshire and Rhode Island had 590 men in their regiments, Connecticut 1,000. By Massachusetts law, a general was also a colonel of a regiment; by the law of Connecticut he was captain of a company as well, and so were the field-officers. Rhode Island allowed only the field-officers to hold two commissions, and the second of these gave no claim to pay.[4]

Discipline was very imperfect. The respect ordinarily paid by soldiers to their officers was unknown. The privates often selected their commanders, and were socially their equals or

[1] Washington, *Writings* (Ford), iii. 1-4.
[2] Force, *American Archives*, 4th series, ii. 1447, 1472-1474.
[3] Washington, *Writings* (Sparks), iii. 492.
[4] Washington to President of Congress, August 4, 1775, Washington, *Writings* (Ford), iii. 58-60; *Writings* (Sparks), iii. 487-488.

superiors. In Massachusetts not only was a man who could raise a company a captain, but one who could get ten companies to serve under him was a colonel. The subalterns were also chosen by election. Naturally, many officers were ready to sink all distinctions of rank; some even threw their pay into a common stock, officers and privates taking an equal share. Others, forgetting not only their dignity but their duty, made profit out of their positions and cheated the government out of money and rations.[1] The day of battle proved that courage was sometimes lacking, as well as dignity and honor. Some officers, though honest and brave, were deficient in mental energy and physically unable to endure the hardships of a campaign. The system of election brought into the armies of the Revolution, as into those of the Civil and Spanish wars, officers who were worthy and patriotic men, but who proved to be very incapable commanders. The privates, like all raw soldiers, neglected the laws of health, and did not take proper care of their persons or of the camp. It was said that at home the influence of their female relatives had kept them neat and clean, but that here this stimulus was lacking.[2] The hospital department was badly managed; there was no head, and the surgeons quarrelled with each other.[3]

A radical change was clearly necessary. Washington and Lee set vigorously to work, and, in spite of great difficulties, they met with considerable success. "The new generals," wrote Knox to his wife, "are of infinite service to the army. They have to reduce order almost from a perfect chaos. I think they are in a fair way of doing it."[4] Washington found that the officers had no distinctive uniform; accordingly, recognition was made possible by the announcement that the commander-in-chief, the generals, the aides, the field-officers, the captains, and the subalterns would wear ribbons, or cockades, of different colors.[5] Lessons of respect were enforced upon the men by fines, the

---

[1] Bolton, *The Private Soldier under Washington*, 127–132; Tomes, *Battles of America*, i. 221.

[2] Tomes, *Battles of America*, i. 220.

[3] Washington to President of Congress, July 21, 1775, Washington, *Writings* (Ford), iii. 35.

[4] July 11, 1775, *Ibid.* 9, note 2. [5] Hubley, *American Revolution*, 405, 439.

THE NEW ENGLAND ARMY.

pillory, the wooden horse, thirty to thirty-nine lashes, and drumming out of camp. Proper care was also taken that this respect should be deserved. Washington announced in general orders that bravery in an officer would meet with notice and reward, cowardice with certain punishment, and that "no connections, interest, or intercessions in his behalf will avail to prevent the strict execution of justice."[1] This was no vain threat. Courts-martial for all kinds of misdemeanors sat constantly, in one case the Harvard College chapel serving as the hall of justice. Within a few weeks, Washington wrote to Richard Henry Lee, "I have made a pretty good slam among such kind of officers as the Massachusetts government abound in." He had dismissed a colonel and two captains for cowardice, three captains for other offences, and had five more officers under arrest.[2]

Washington did his best to provide for the health and comfort of the soldiers. His orderly book contains repeated directions for keeping the camp clean. He forbade the sale of liquors to the soldiers without a license, and recommended that the stock of any one disobeying this prohibition should be seized for the benefit of fatigue parties and outguards.[3] Not having authority to regulate the hospital himself, Washington applied to Congress; and they promptly provided for a medical staff under a director-general.[4]

On October 22, 1775, Washington began to arrange for the reënlistment of the army for the ensuing year,[5] a task the difficulties and disappointments of which almost drove him to despair. He wrote to a friend: "Such a dearth of public spirit, and want of virtue, such stock-jobbing, and fertility in all the low arts to obtain advantages of one kind or another, in this great change of military arrangement, I never saw before, and pray God I may never be witness to again. . . . Could I have

---

[1] July 5 and 7, 1775, Washington, *Writings* (Sparks), iii. 489–490.
[2] August 29, 1775, Washington, *Writings* (Ford), iii. 98.
[3] Hubley, *American Revolution*, 540.
[4] Washington to President of Congress, July 21, 1775, Washington, *Writings* (Ford), iii. 35; *Journals of Congress*, i. 178–179, July 27, 1775.
[5] Orderly Book, October 22, 1775, Washington, *Writings* (Ford), iii. 191, note.

foreseen what I have, and am likely to experience, no consideration upon earth should have induced me to accept this command. A regiment or any subordinate department would have been accompanied with ten times the satisfaction, and perhaps the honor."[1] Some officers enlisted, expecting promotion; some waited to see if promotion would be offered them; others first declined, and then solicited appointment. Colonial feeling was very strong. Washington wrote, " Connecticut wants no Massachusetts man in their corps; Massachusetts thinks there is no necessity for a Rhode Islander to be introduced amongst them; and New Hampshire says, it's very hard, that her valuable and experienced officers (who are willing to serve) should be discarded, because her own regiments, under the new establishment, cannot provide for them."[2]

It was necessary to arrange the officers first, for the privates would not come forward until they knew who were to command them. By the consolidation of small regiments, mainly from Massachusetts, many officers had been thrown out; and they were suspected of discouraging enlistments. The generals, therefore, issued an address to the men, appealing to their hopes and fears, and to their pride as New Englanders. They said that economy required the amalgamation of the regiments, and that the officers who were to remain had been chosen without partiality. Courage, integrity, and patriotism, they explained, could not make an officer; "a certain degree of bodily vigor, and activity of mind" were also necessary. The privates, they declared, were particularly fortunate: " Never were soldiers whose duty has been so light, never were soldiers whose pay and provision has been so abundant and ample. In fact, your interest and comfort have been so carefully consulted, even to the lowest article, by the Continental Congress, that there is some reason to dread that the enemies to New England's reputation may hereafter say, it was not principle that saved them, but that they were bribed into the preservation of their liberties."[3]

[1] Washington to Reed, November 28, 1775, Washington, *Writings* (Ford), iii, 246–247.

[2] Washington to Reed, November 8, 1775, *Ibid.* 208.

[3] November 24, 1775, Force, *American Archives*, 4th series, iii. 1666–1667.

THE "CONTINENTAL" ARMY.

By such persuasions, and by promises of numerous furloughs, a force was at last recruited sufficient to continue the siege.

January 1, 1776, may be regarded as the birthday of the Continental army: from that time it was raised and governed by the direct authority of Congress; and, notwithstanding the devolving of many duties on the States later in the war, it remained a Continental force, distinct from the militia. Washington himself recognized the change, and announced in a general order of that day, "This day giving commencement to the new army, which in every point of view is entirely Continental; the general flatters himself, that a laudable spirit of emulation will now take place, and pervade the whole of it."[1]

[1] Washington, *Writings* (Ford), iii. 311, note.

CHAPTER II.

CONGRESS AND THE COMMANDER-IN-CHIEF.

CONGRESS had now an army which they must officer and support. Much will be said in the following chapters of the failures and errors in their attempts to discharge this duty; but in justice to Congress it should be remembered that their position was one of extreme difficulty. The situation is vividly, but in the main accurately, described in a letter of John Adams to his wife: "The business I have had upon my mind has been as great and important as can be intrusted to man, and the difficulty and intricacy of it prodigious. When fifty or sixty men have a constitution to form for a great empire, at the same time that they have a country of fifteen hundred miles in extent to fortify, millions to arm and train, a naval power to begin, an extensive commerce to regulate, numerous tribes of Indians to negotiate with, a standing army of twenty-seven thousand men to raise, pay, victual, and officer, I really shall pity those fifty or sixty men."[1]

The task was one to tax the energies of a stronger government, and it overwhelmed the Congress. Until the ratification of the Articles of Confederation in 1781, their authority was undefined: any State, and even any individual who was not in the United States service, could refuse obedience to their commands, on the ground that they were unable to show any right to issue them. Congress themselves were very careful to avoid assertions of authority: they "advised" and "recommended," but were reluctant to command. In their relations with the people, they

[1] July 24, 1775, C. F. Adams, *Familiar Letters of John Adams and his Wife*, 85.

POLITICAL SITUATION.

acted mainly through the State governments; and these, even when willing to help, were not always able to do so, for they in turn could exercise but a partial control over the counties and towns.

The country was suffering from a "nightmare of liberty"; the state had lost much of that "divinity" which under ordinary circumstances doth hedge, not kings alone, but all long-established governments. Executive power suffered most of all. Except in Connecticut and Rhode Island, the governors had been appointed by the king or the proprietor, and were regarded as the representatives of a distinct, if not of a hostile, interest. In the political struggles which preceded the war, nearly every governor had been a Tory leader. On the other hand, public meetings, committees of correspondence, and committees of safety, aided by the legislatures, had brought about the Revolution. Consequently, there was a strong tendency to regard executive authority as a foe to liberty, and to limit it as much as possible.

Congress shared the popular feeling; and this prejudice, a natural reluctance to part with power, and perhaps the private interests of some members, combined to prevent them from adopting measures which they had full authority to take, and which would have done much to insure an efficient management of army affairs. A War Department with extensive powers should have been promptly established; instead, Congress retained the military administration in their own hands, merely appointing committees for special purposes, and frequently giving them authority only to report, not to act.

Such a system made it impossible to avoid delay and confusion, and on January 24, 1776, a committee was appointed to consider the subject of establishing a War Office. Five months later Congress adopted a plan providing for a Board of War and Ordnance, to consist of five of their own members and a paid secretary. John Adams, Sherman, Harrison, Wilson, and Edward Rutledge were chosen members of the Board, and Richard Peters, secretary.[1] Peters remained in connection with

[1] *Journals of Congress*, ii. 37, 208-211, January 24, and June 12 and 13, 1776.

the Board, either as secretary or as member, during the five years of its existence; and his valuable and faithful service deserves a wider and more generous recognition from his country than it has yet received.

The Board was to take charge of all military stores, superintend the raising, equipping, and despatching of the land forces, keep a register of the officers, and so forth. In 1777 its place was taken by a new Board, consisting of persons who were not members of Congress. In 1781 Congress, having become convinced of the advantage of single-headed departments, abolished the Board and appointed General Lincoln Secretary at War.[1]

Congress also sent special committees to examine affairs at camp. Six different committees were despatched to Washington's army as occasion rose,—one in 1775, two in 1776, and one in each of the years 1778, 1779, and 1780. They consisted sometimes of two, sometimes of three members. Although occasionally empowered to assist Washington,—as in issuing commissions,—their duties were mainly to investigate on the spot and report to Congress. In 1780 the committee sent to camp was given unusual powers; and many members, jealous of a few men's exercising so much authority, tried to have the committee composed of a delegate from each State. There was a warm debate; but the centralizers pointed out that such a body would merely reproduce the dissensions and delays of Congress, and the proposal failed.[2] This committee gave great dissatisfaction by considering matters which Congress thought belonged to themselves, and it was abruptly recalled.[3]

The later Congresses were far less able than the earlier ones. The position of member of Congress involved much labor and inconvenience and brought little honor or profit, while the reorganization of the State governments afforded special opportunities for usefulness and distinction at home. Hamilton and Washington wrote to their friends lamenting the degeneracy of Congress, and Gouverneur Morris declared that the members

[1] *Journals of Congress*, vii. 216, October 30, 1781.
[2] Luzerne to Vergennes, April 16, 1780, Durand, *New Materials*, 219-220.
[3] *Journals of Congress*, vi. 152-153, 160, August 2 and 11, 1780.

and the currency had alike depreciated.¹ Laurens, the president of Congress, said: "A most shameful deficiency in this branch is the greatest evil, and is indeed the source of almost all our evils. If there is not speedily a resurrection of able men, and of that virtue which I thought to be genuine in seventy-five, we are gone. We shall undo ourselves." ²

Congress did little and talked a great deal. The Southern members insisted that Congress should sit but once a day, and, as there was much committee work, this might have been very well; but, although the hours were nominally from nine till two, some delegates were "so much immersed in the pursuit of pleasure or business" that it was usually impossible to form a Congress before ten or eleven. Hosmer of Connecticut wrote to Governor Trumbull: —

"Congress has no means to compel gentlemen's attendance, and those who occasionally delay are callous to admonition and reproof, which have been often tried in vain.

"When we are assembled, several gentlemen have such a knack of starting questions of order, raising debates upon critical, captious, and trifling amendments, protracting them by long speeches, by postponing, calling for the previous question, and other arts, that it is almost impossible to get an important question decided at one sitting, and if it is put over to another day, the field is open to be gone over again, precious time is lost, and the public business left undone." ³

A striking prototype of modern difficulties in counting a quorum occurred at a session prolonged till late in the evening in April, 1778. At 10 P.M. a motion to adjourn failed, whereupon Burke of North Carolina declared that "the States might vote as they pleased, he would upon his honor adjourn himself;" which he did, and broke a quorum. The messenger of Congress was sent to desire his attendance. The man

[1] Hamilton to Clinton, February 13, 1778, Hamilton, *Works* (Lodge), vii. 536–540; Washington to Mason, March 27, 1779, Washington, *Writings* (Ford), vii. 383; Roosevelt, *Gouverneur Morris*, 68.
[2] January 27, 1778, Scharf, *Maryland*, ii. 342.
[3] August 31, 1778, Sparks, *Correspondence of the Revolution*, ii. 197–198, note.

reported that Burke answered, "Devil take him if he would come; it was too late and too unreasonable." Burke was called to account next day, but defended himself stoutly. He said that he would not submit to the tyranny of a majority of Congress which wished to keep him in his seat at unreasonable hours; that he desired to know the authority of Congress over him; that he would attend at hours which he thought reasonable, but not at those he thought unreasonable, unless compelled by force on his person; that on the preceding evening he was too unwell to attend; and that, if guilty of improper behavior, he would answer to his State. Congress apparently took much the same view of their jurisdiction; for, although they declared that the manner of his withdrawal was "disorderly and contemptuous," the principle which he asserted dangerous, and the answer returned by him through the messenger "indecent," they took no action against Burke themselves, but merely sent a copy of their proceedings to the Assembly of North Carolina.[1]

In 1779 the condition was still serious. Washington says in a letter to a friend that it is notorious that Congress is rent by faction, and devotes much time to trifling or personal questions. "Where are our men of abilities?" he asks; "why do they not come forth to save their country?"[2] There was an alarming increase of foolish parliamentary quibbling. Richard Henry Lee wrote to Laurens: "I am clearly of opinion, that if Mr. '*Clearly-out-of-order*' remains much longer in Congress, the United States will have cause to rue it bitterly. I am sure, that I have heard more talk about order, and seen less attention to it, in one week in that Assembly, since he became a member, than in four years preceding his coming in."[3]

Soon, however, signs of improvement appeared, and during the last years of the war Congress manifested greater breadth of view and a clearer understanding of the problems before them. Their various failures to use with wisdom and energy such powers as they possessed caused much distress at camp;

---

[1] *Secret Journals of Congress*, i. 62–67, April 10, 11, 24, 25, 1778.
[2] Washington to Mason, March 27, 1779, Washington, *Writings* (Ford), vii. 384.
[3] August 7, 1779, Lee, *Richard Henry Lee*, i. 224.

but posterity has been ready to attribute the sufferings of the army to other causes, and has censured Congress chiefly for giving encouragement to an attempt to displace Washington. During the first year of the war, the commander-in-chief was loyally supported in Philadelphia. In July, 1775, Benjamin Harrison told him, "Everything that we can do here, to put you in the best posture possible, I think you may depend will be done."[1] In September of the same year Richard Henry Lee wrote to him that his conduct was the object of surprised admiration.[2] Congress allowed him a wide discretion, and paid great attention to his advice. The commissary-general was appointed on his recommendation, and he was himself allowed to select the quartermaster-general and the commissary of musters. Congress ordered two battalions of marines to be raised in the army; Washington remonstrated, and Congress voted that they be raised elsewhere. When news came of the disastrous repulse at Quebec, Washington immediately requested the New England colonies to raise reënforcements for the army in Canada at the Continental expense, and apologized to Congress for not first consulting them, on the ground of the necessity for immediate action; their reply was a resolution stating that his application to the colonies was "prudent, consistent with his duty, and a farther manifestation of his commendable zeal for the good of his country."[3]

Dissatisfaction with the commander-in-chief first clearly appeared in Congress in February, 1777, when that body bombastically resolved that it was their earnest desire "to make the army under the immediate command of General Washington sufficiently strong . . . by the Divine blessing totally to subdue them [the enemy] before they can be reënforced." The New England States, Virginia, and Georgia supported the resolution; and in the debate there appeared "a great desire,

---

[1] July 21, 1775, Force, *American Archives*, 4th series, ii. 1697-1698.

[2] September 26, 1775, Sparks, *Correspondence of the Revolution*, i. 51-52.

[3] *Journals of Congress*, i. 171-172, July 19, 1775; Washington to President of Congress, July 10 and November 19, 1775, and January 19, 1776, Washington, *Writings* (Ford), iii. 12-13, 13, note 1, 225-226, and note 1, 359-360, and note.

in some of the delegates from the Eastern States, and in one from New Jersey, to insult the general." [1]

The events of 1777 increased the opposition to Washington: the public usually judges by results; Washington had been beaten at Brandywine; had lost Philadelphia; lost the forts on the Delaware; and failed at Germantown. Gates, taking command after the disaster at Ticonderoga, had twice defeated Burgoyne, and then captured him and all his army. The success at Saratoga was, indeed, largely due to Schuyler, to Stark, and to Morgan; and Washington, aware of the importance of saving the line of the Hudson, had stripped himself to reënforce the Northern army. The New England men hurried from all sides to oppose Burgoyne, while the Pennsylvanians gave little aid against Howe. But Congress did not appreciate the disadvantages under which Washington labored, and the dissatisfaction manifested itself in a movement usually known as the Conway Cabal, from the name of a foreign officer, Thomas Conway, who played a conspicuous part in the affair.

This intrigue is a subject of much interest; but, since it failed entirely, most of the participants were anxious to deny their own share in it, their biographers have also done their best to gloss the matter over, and hence the inner history of the movement is but imperfectly known. It is said that there was a plan to induce the Virginia House of Burgesses and the Massachusetts Assembly to instruct their delegates to move an inquiry into the disasters of 1776, and thereupon either to dismiss Washington or to pass resolutions that would drive him out of the army.[2]

As if conscious of the weakness of their cause, the enemies of Washington did not dare to attack him in open and honorable fashion. A letter full of reflections on the commander-in-chief was sent to Patrick Henry, then governor of Virginia. The writer, however, not only left it unsigned, but warned Henry: "A hint of his name, if found out by the handwriting, must not be mentioned to your most intimate friend. Even the letter

---

[1] Burke to Governor of North Carolina, Washington, *Writings* (Sparks), iv. 327, note.

[2] Gordon, *History of the American War*, iii. 57–58.

must be thrown in the fire. But some of its contents ought to be made public."¹ Henry sent the letter to Washington, who believed that he recognized the handwriting of Dr. Benjamin Rush of Philadelphia, a man who, he wrote, had been "elaborate and studied in his professions of regard," long after the date of the letter.² Like ill success attended an anonymous diatribe sent to President Laurens with a request that it be laid before Congress, instead of which Laurens forwarded it to Washington.³

The attacks on Washington were as bitter as they were treacherous. The paper intended for Congress asserted that "the people of America have been guilty of idolatry, by making a man their god; and the God of heaven and earth will convince them by woful experience, that he is only a man; that no good may be expected from the standing army, until Baal and his worshippers are banished from the camp."⁴ The writer of the letter to Henry said that the Northern army had shown what Americans could do when they had a general to command them, and that the main army was not inferior to the Northern. "A Gates, a Lee, or a Conway," he declared, "would in a few weeks render them an irresistible body of men."

William Williams and Jonathan Trumbull were of the opinion that "a much exalted character should make way for a *general*." Jonathan D. Sargent declared, "Thousands of lives and millions of property are yearly sacrificed to the insufficiency of our commander-in-chief, . . . and yet we are so attached to this man that I fear we shall rather sink with him than throw him off our shoulders." He also accused Washington of permitting waste and destruction which "would exhaust the wealth of both the Indies and annihilate the armies of all Europe and Asia." Clark of New Jersey said, "We may talk of the enemy's cruelty as we will, but we have no greater cruelty to complain of than the

---

¹ January 12, 1778, Washington, *Writings* (Sparks), v. 495-497.
² Washington to Henry, March 28, 1778, *Ibid.* 515.
³ Washington, with his usual magnanimity, replied that, as he had no desire to stifle inquiry, and as the suppression of the letter might embarrass Laurens, he wished him to lay it before Congress (Washington to Laurens, January 31, 1778, *Ibid.* 504). Laurens, however, very properly refrained from doing so.
⁴ Washington, *Ibid.* (Sparks), v. 499.

management of our army." Richard Henry Lee was less bitter, but he thought that "Gates was needed to procure the indispensable changes in our army."[1] Stories were circulated of the want of discipline in Washington's camp. It was said that soldiers were drawn from the line to act as servants, against express orders; that absentees were not duly reported; that a visitor had penetrated to the centre of the camp without being challenged; that General Gates's army was like "a well-regulated family," General Washington's like "an unformed mob."[2]

Few of the general officers sympathized with the attack on Washington. Mifflin, however, who had retained his rank as major-general, though he had left the army, was one of the leaders. Wayne criticised Washington, and declared that he himself meant "to follow the line pointed out by the conduct of Lee, Gates, and Mifflin"; and General Sullivan's behavior raises a suspicion that he too was more or less involved in the affair.[3] Attempts were made to win over Lafayette by filling his mind with hopes of "glory and shining projects"; "and I must confess to my shame," he wrote to Washington, "that it is a too certain way of deceiving me." But Lafayette was not to be seduced: he toasted Washington at Gates's own table, and refused to accept the command of an expedition to Canada unless he were allowed to report to Washington as his immediate superior.[4] The officers of lower rank were, for the most part, loyal to the commander-in-chief. A captain wrote: "I am content if they remove almost any general except his Excellency. The country, even Congress, are not aware of the confidence the army places in him, or motions never would have been made for Gates to take the command."[5]

The machinations of the enemies of Washington were more successful in Congress. Jay told his son that the world would never know how strong the opposition to Washington was; and

---

[1] Ford, *The True George Washington*, 256–257.
[2] Gordon to Washington, September 25, 1778, *Sparks MSS.* lii. (pt. 3), 231–233.
[3] Bancroft, *United States*, v. 211.
[4] Tower, *La Fayette in the American Revolution*, i. ch. viii.
[5] Bryant and Gay, *United States*, iii. 596, note.

FORMATION OF A CABAL.

there is a tradition that at one time the absence of two New York delegates would have resulted in Washington's dismissal.[1] Rival authorities were raised up : Congress reorganized the Board of War, put Gates at its head, and directed their president to inform him of "the high sense Congress entertain of the general's abilities and peculiar fitness to discharge the duties of that important office." Gates was also told that he was to retain his rank as major-general, and to serve at the Board or in the field as circumstances might require.[2] An inspector-general for the main army was also appointed, one of whose duties was to examine carefully into the "behavior, capacity, and assiduity" of the officers, and to make reports directly to Congress.[3] Here was, as was well said, an *imperium in imperio:* officers who wished to rise would do well to oppose the commander-in-chief.

The person chosen to fill the important position of inspector-general was Thomas Conway.[4] Conway was an Irishman by birth; but he had been brought up in France, and rose to the rank of colonel in the French army. He made a specially favorable impression on Silas Deane, the American agent at Paris, who asked him to enter the American service, and promised him the position of brigadier or adjutant general.[5] Conway possessed the Irish wit and irritability, and the French readiness to flatter and to brag. He was skilful in drilling and manœuvring troops; but he had a high opinion of his own merits, he was greedy of advancement, and he sought to gain it by impudence and intrigue. Though made a brigadier, he complained to Congress that officers who were his inferiors in France had been placed over him, and that the brigade assigned to him was in bad condition and was the weakest in the army. Conway argued at some length that his own past services and the welfare of the United States required that he should be made a major-general.

"I commanded fifteen hundred men in France," he said, "and here I command five hundred under the orders of a major-gen-

---
[1] Irving, *Washington*, iii. 374, note ; Duer, *Stirling*, 183-184, note.
[2] *Journals of Congress*, iii. 541, November 27, 1777.
[3] *Ibid.* 574-576, December 13, 1777.   [4] *Ibid.* 576.
[5] Deane to Franklin, Morris, etc., November 26, 1776, *Sparks MSS.* lii. (pt. 1), 39-40.

eral [Stirling] who is not able to command one hundred although a brave man. . . . I cannot remain under the orders of a man who will not let people do good, who cannot do it himself because he knows nothing of the matter, and if he did cannot do anything reasonable after dinner. . . . Your very speedy and categorical answer will very much oblige him,
"Who is with respect,
"Gentlemen &c.   T. CONWAY."[1]

Conway may have had real grounds for dissatisfaction; but in Europe his reflection on his superior officer, and his demand for a "categorical answer," would have incurred the penalty of dismissal. Officers of the same rank take precedence of each other according to the dates of their commissions, and Conway, having been so recently appointed, was near the foot of the list of brigadiers. His promotion would therefore give great offence; and Washington, hearing a rumor that he had been or might be made a major-general, wrote to Richard Henry Lee in terms so strong that they could easily be interpreted as a threat of resignation.[2] "To sum up the whole," he said, " I have been a slave to the service; I have undergone more than most men are aware of, to harmonize so many discordant parts; but it will be impossible for me to be of any further service, if such insuperable difficulties are thrown in my way."[3] Although several members of Congress, including even Lovell, a bitter critic of Washington, commented severely on Conway's extraordinary

[1] June 6 and September 21 (?), 1777, *Sparks MSS.* lii. (pt. 3), 127-128, 131. The address of the first of these letters is not given by Sparks. It was probably written either to Congress or to the Board of War. The second one is addressed to Congress.

[2] They were not so meant. "I can assure you," Washington replied to an inquiry from Dr. Gordon, made after Conway's appointment, "that no person ever heard me drop an expression that had a tendency to resignation. . . . While the public are satisfied with my endeavors, I mean not to shrink from the cause. But the moment her voice, not that of faction, calls upon me to resign, I shall do it with as much pleasure as ever the weary traveller retired to rest."—Washington to Gordon, February 15, 1778, Washington, *Writings* (Sparks), v. 510.

[3] Washington to Lee, October 17, 1777, Washington, *Writings* (Ford), vi. 122.

letter, demanding to be made a major-general, Conway complained a second time, and offered his resignation; but, instead of accepting it, Congress in December, 1777, gave him the coveted rank.[1] There is no evidence to show whether Washington's letter to Lee was known to the members or not; if it were, the favor shown to Conway proves the strength of the opposition to the commander-in-chief.

Conway was in full sympathy with the attack on Washington, and wrote a letter to Gates containing bitter reflections upon the commander-in-chief, which Gates probably read to his military family. After Saratoga, Gates sent his aide, James Wilkinson, to carry the news of the surrender of Burgoyne to Congress. On his way, Wilkinson stopped at Reading, where, on October 28, 1777, in the freedom of a convivial evening, he told Major McWilliams, an aide of Lord Stirling,[2] that Conway had written to Gates, "Heaven has been determined to save your country, or a weak general and bad counsellors would have ruined it." McWilliams repeated to Lord Stirling what Wilkinson said, and Stirling sent the story to Washington with the remark that he should always think it his duty to expose such duplicity. Merely to show Conway that his opinions were known, Washington wrote him the extract quoted above.

Secrecy was essential to the success of the cabal, and the conspirators were aghast. Conway went to Washington and defended himself, saw Wilkinson and got a denial of the truth of the quotation,[3] and wrote to Mifflin what had happened. Mifflin in turn wrote to Gates, begging him for the sake of his friends to take care of his papers. Gates was much disturbed, but thought that he saw a way of using the incident to injure Washington. Hamilton had recently visited Gates's headquarters, he had been alone in the general's room; and Gates is said to have declared that his desk had been broken open and a letter

---

[1] Conway to Carroll, November 14, 1777, *Sparks MSS.* lii. (pt. 3), 137-140. *Journals of Congress*, iii. 576, December 13, 1777.

[2] So called on account of a claim to the lapsed earldom of Stirling.

[3] Wilkinson excused himself on the ground that the quotation was not literal, and that he had replied "in dubious terms" (Wilkinson to Stirling, February 4, 1778, Wilkinson, *Memoirs*, i. 382).

copied, but that he would disgrace both the receiver (Washington) and the thief (Hamilton).[1] Accordingly he wrote to Washington, begging his assistance in discovering the person guilty of this treachery, and sent a similar letter to President Laurens, nominally to obtain the prompt assistance of Congress in finding out who had copied Conway's letter, but really to implicate Washington in the affair. Washington replied, clearing Hamilton and leaving Gates himself in a rather unpleasant situation. Gates tried in vain to maintain his ground, resorted to disingenuous shifts, and at last plaintively begged that the subject might be dropped.[2]

Conway obtained his original letter from Gates, and wrote to Washington that he found with great satisfaction that the letter did not contain the paragraph complained of or anything like it. Conway had formerly accused Washington of being the instigator of the opposition of the officers to his promotion, and he now complained that Washington had given him a reception "such as I never met with before from any general during the course of thirty years in a very respectable army."[3] Probably the paragraph concerning a "weak general" did not occur in Conway's letter. The quotation rests on the authority of Wilkinson, and of others who may have derived their information from him. Wilkinson's reputation for veracity is poor, and when he made his original statement he was probably under the influence of liquor. President Laurens saw what was said to be the original letter, and he told an aide of Washington that the paragraph quoted by Colonel Wilkinson was not set down "verbatim"; he added, however, that "in substance it contained that and ten times more." Laurens copied the following words: "What a pity there is but one Gates! But the more I see of this army, the less I think it fit for general action under its actual chiefs and actual discipline. I speak to you sincerely and freely, and wish I could serve under you."[4]

[1] Wilkinson, *Memoirs*, i. 373.
[2] Washington, *Writings* (Sparks), v. 487-488, 491-493, 500-502, 504-507, 511-512.
[3] Conway to Washington, January 27, 1778, *Ibid.* 502-503.
[4] Fitzgerald to Washington, February 16, 1778, *Ibid.* 511.

There may also be some truth in what Conway said of the treatment he received from Washington; although the commander-in-chief would never have encouraged a cabal among the officers. Washington treated Conway with what he thought to be the courtesy due to his official position, and was ready to support him in the discharge of his duties; but the promotion under any circumstances must cause the greatest discontent. Washington considered Conway a personal enemy and a dishonorable mischief-maker, and it is possible that he made his feelings more manifest than he intended, and that the officers were thereby encouraged in their opposition.

Conway's complaints produced little effect on Congress; and Gates made himself ridiculous by his conduct in a quarrel with his old favorite, Wilkinson. Wilkinson had suggested to Gates that another of his aides, Lieutenant-Colonel Troup, might have innocently mentioned to Hamilton Conway's letter. When Gates discovered that Wilkinson was himself the person through whose indiscretion the letter became known, he spoke with much severity of what Wilkinson had done. Wilkinson challenged his commander, who accepted; but on the morning fixed for the duel Gates sought a private interview, and, if we may believe Wilkinson's account, protested with tears that he would as soon have injured his own child as Wilkinson; and there was a reconciliation. Wilkinson, however, again took offence, and wrote to Congress resigning his position as secretary of the Board of War on account of "acts of treachery and falsehood, in which I have detected Major-General Gates."[1] The letter was returned "as improper to remain on the files of Congress";[2] but Wilkinson had been a protégé of Gates, and the breach must have lowered the opinion in which the latter was held by Congress.

Public opinion was on Washington's side, and the members of the cabal found that their efforts were more likely to injure themselves than Washington. Accordingly they hastened to deny that they had any intentions of driving him out. Gates professed his disbelief in any plot to supersede Washington, and declared that the charge that he was concerned therein was a wicked,

[1] Wilkinson, *Memoirs*, i. 384-389, 409-410.
[2] *Journals of Congress*, iv. 182, March 31, 1778.

false, diabolical calumny of incendiaries.¹ Mifflin is reported to have said publicly that he considered Washington "the best friend he ever had in his life,"² and one of his letters contains a solemn assurance that he neither plotted nor desired the removal of Washington.³ Elbridge Gerry, who was a staunch supporter of Conway, wrote to Knox that Congress was well disposed toward Washington, and that he could discover no evidence of any plan to bring in a new commander-in-chief.⁴

One would not willingly believe that Gates, Mifflin, and Gerry were all lying, and yet it is impossible to doubt that the opposition to Washington was stronger than their words implied. Perhaps the best explanation is that, although there was great dissatisfaction with Washington, yet few members of Congress had any clearly defined intentions of superseding him. Men may have admired Gates and wished to see him in a position of high authority, without meaning to make him commander-in-chief ; they may have even desired an inquiry into Washington's conduct, without acknowledging to themselves any other purpose than to learn the true causes of the American defeats in 1776. Gates probably took no active part. A French officer reported to his government in 1779 that "the Eastern party . . . backs Gates, almost in spite of himself." To use a modern term, the general was in the hands of his friends, or perhaps it would be more appropriate to say in the hands of his enemies; for Lafayette expresses the opinion in his memoirs that the real wish of the plotters was to put General Lee, then a prisoner in New York, in command of the army.⁵

The attack on Washington had failed completely. Congress gave Gates and Mifflin a permission, which was equivalent to a command, to join the army.⁶ Conway found himself stationed at

¹ Letter to a friend, April 4, 1778, Gordon, *History of the American War,* iii. 58–59.
² George Lux to Greene, April, 1778, Greene, *Greene,* ii. 37.
³ Gordon, *History of the American War,* iii. 59–60.
⁴ February 7, 1778, Austin, *Gerry,* i. 241–242.
⁵ Durand, *New Materials,* 23 ; Tower, *La Fayette in the American Revolution,* i. 258, note.
⁶ Gouverneur Morris says that a resolution was passed directing Gates and Mifflin to join the army, but that members immediately recollected that it was

Albany, with no prospect of taking part in the main operations, and unable, as he thought, to protect the country in case of an attack from Canada. He wrote to the president of Congress: "My character must suffer. Therefore, sir, I expect you will make my resignation acceptable to Congress. I am determined not to expose myself to dishonor, to gratify the envy and malice of my enemies, whoever they may be. I have been boxed about in a most indecent manner.... I did not deserve this burlesque disgrace.... It is not becoming to the dignity of Congress to give such usage to an officer of my age and rank."[1]

When this impertinent letter was read, Gouverneur Morris promptly expressed his delight at getting rid of Conway, his friends were reduced to apologies, and of nine States present only one, Virginia, voted against accepting the resignation. Among the few dissentients were Elbridge Gerry and Francis Lightfoot Lee.[2] After the vote had passed, Conway's aide explained to members that his chief did not intend to resign. Conway wrote to the same effect, and then came himself to York, where Congress was sitting, but to no purpose. He wrote to Gates: "I never had a sufficient idea of cabals until I reached this place. My reception, you may imagine, was not a warm one. I must except Mr. Samuel Adams, Colonel Richard Henry Lee, and a few others, who are attached to you, but who cannot oppose the torrent. . . .

"One Mr. Carroll from Maryland, upon whose friendship I depended, is one of the hottest of the cabal. He told me a few days ago almost literally, that anybody who displeased or did not admire the commander-in-chief, ought not to be kept in the army. Mr. Carroll may be a good papist, but I am sure the sentiments he expresses are neither Roman nor Catholic."[3]

not in accordance with etiquette for Congress to issue orders to a subordinate officer, and that therefore a change was made in the phraseology, Gates and Mifflin being permitted to leave the Board on Washington's order. See Morris to Washington, April 18, 1778, Sparks, *Gouverneur Morris*, i. 164; *Journals of Congress*, iv. 223, April 18, 1778.

[1] April 22, 1778, Washington, *Writings* (Sparks), v. 372, note.
[2] *Journals of Congress*, iv. 245, April 28, 1778.
[3] June 7, 1778, Sparks, *Gouverneur Morris*, i. 169.

In July Conway was challenged by General Cadwallader, on account of his abuse of Washington, and was with "almost poetic justice," shot through the mouth. He recovered and returned to France, but for a while he believed himself mortally wounded, and during this time he wrote a letter to the man he had so often abused, which is perhaps the most striking of the many tributes paid to Washington. "I find myself just able to hold the pen during a few minutes," he said, "and take this opportunity of expressing my sincere grief for having done, written, or said anything disagreeable to your Excellency. My career will soon be over; therefore justice and truth prompt me to declare my last sentiments. You are in my eyes the great and good man. May you long enjoy the love, veneration, and esteem of these States, whose liberties you have asserted by your virtues. I am with the greatest respect, &c."[1]

[1] Conway to Washington, July 23, 1778, Washington, *Writings* (Sparks), v. 517.

CHAPTER III.

APPOINTMENT AND PROMOTION.

IN the management of the army, few questions were so troublesome as those of appointment and promotion. There were, indeed, some officers who were high-minded enough to find honor in faithful service, not in rank and place. Lieutenant-Colonel Morris, when disappointed in his hopes of advancement, wrote to his father that he should remain in the army nevertheless. "The officer," he said, "who would resign the service because he did not receive promotion agreeable to his expectations, sacrifices to a false sentiment of honor, the debt he owes to himself and country. I embarked in this cause from principle. I wish to serve my country and rank myself among that number who are instrumental in establishing the liberties of the people and I want no other reward, but the approbation of having done my duty."[1] Congress made Montgomery, who had held a commission in the British army, a brigadier; but appointed Schuyler, who had been only a provincial officer, major-general. Duane, one of the New York delegates, wrote to Montgomery explaining why he received no higher rank. Montgomery replied: "My acknowledgments are due for the attention shown me by the Congress. I submit with great cheerfulness to any regulation they in their prudence shall judge expedient. Laying aside the punctilio of the *soldier*, I shall endeavor to discharge my duty to society, considering myself as the *citizen*, reduced to the melancholy necessity of taking up arms for the public safety."[2]

[1] May, 1778, New York Historical Society, *Collections*, 1875, p. 455.
[2] Lester, *Our First Hundred Years*, 260.

Too many officers were incapable of this ready subordination to civil authority. Greene declared, "For my own part, I would never give any legislative body an opportunity to humiliate me but once;"[1] and Knox's aide, Major Shaw, probably expressed the general sentiment of the officers when he said: "They may make as much noise as they please about patriotism and forbearance, — great virtues indisputably — but of small avail when brought into competition with the delicate sensibility of an honest soldier. Such people ought to know, that the man who suffers the least imputation, expressed or implied, on his own honor can never be a faithful guardian to that of his country."[2]

The whole army was torn with quarrels concerning rank. Washington wrote to the president of Congress: "Not an hour passes without new applications and new complaints about rank. . . . We can scarcely form a court-martial, or parade a detachment in any instance, without a warm discussion on the subject of precedence."[3] Not only did individual officers quarrel with each other, but a feeling grew up between the Continentals and the militia, not unlike that between the regulars and the provincials in the French and Indian War.[4] On one occasion this rivalry caused an unseemly wrangle in the presence of death itself. Colonel Crafts of the militia and Colonel Jackson of the Continental line were to act as pall-bearers at the funeral of a brother officer. Colonel Crafts, who was the older man, claimed the right of walking first; Colonel Jackson replied that, as he was a Continental officer, the privilege belonged to him. Both men were firm, and the dispute ended in Crafts and his friends leaving the house.[5]

[1] Greene to Adams, June 2, 1776, Greene, *Greene*, ii. 423-424. When Greene came to command a separate army and his officers complained about rank, he took a somewhat different view. He then declared: "Rank is not what constitutes the good officer, but good conduct. Substantial services give reputation, not captious disputes. A captain may be more respectable than a general. Rank is nothing unless accompanied with worthy actions." (Greene to Marion, 1782, *Ibid.* iii. 453.)

[2] Shaw to Knox, March 21, 1782, *Knox MSS.* viii. 90.

[3] August 3, 1778, Washington, *Writings* (Ford), vii. 137-138.

[4] Reed to Greene, June 16, 1781, Reed, *Reed*, ii. 355.

[5] Jackson to Knox, August 27, 1777, *Knox MSS.* iv. 46.

With this sensitiveness of the officers on the subject of rank, members of Congress had little sympathy; their jealousy was for the rights of their States. A letter of Adams's shows how widely different were the views of the civilian and the soldier. "This delicate point of honor," he says, "which is really one of the most putrid corruptions of absolute monarchy, I mean the honor of maintaining a rank superior to abler men, I mean the honor of preferring a single step of promotion to the service of the public, must be bridled. It is incompatible with republican principles. I hope, for my own part, that Congress will elect annually all the general officers. If, in consequence of this, some great men should be obliged, at the year's end, to go home and serve their country in some other capacity, not less necessary, and better adapted to their genius, I do not think the public would be ruined. Perhaps it would be no harm. The officers of the army ought to consider that the rank, the dignity, and the rights of whole States are of more importance than this point of honor; more, indeed, than the solid glory of any particular officer. The States insist, with great justice and sound policy, on having a share of the general officers in some proportion to the quotas of troops they are to raise. This principle has occasioned many of our late promotions, and it ought to satisfy gentlemen. But if it does not, they, as well as the public, must abide the consequences of their discontent."[1] Such arguments, however, did not "satisfy gentlemen," and the difference of opinion between Congress and the army concerning the principles by which rank should be determined was a constant source of irritation and even of danger.

In his first official letter to Congress, Washington was obliged to report that the arrangement of the brigadiers had given great offence. General Thomas, a veteran of the French and Indian War, found himself placed below Pomeroy and Heath, although in the State service he ranked above them both. Thomas felt that his just claims had been disregarded, and he determined to resign; but from all sides came earnest remonstrance and entreaty. The Massachusetts legislature interposed, and asked Washington to suspend the delivery of the commissions

[1] Adams to Greene, 1777, John Adams, *Works*, i. 263-264.

until Congress could be consulted and Heath induced to yield his precedence. Fearing serious disorder in the army, Washington complied.[1] Meanwhile, Thomas was begged by the officers under his command, by General Lee, by the Massachusetts House, and by Washington himself, to sacrifice his personal feelings to the good of his country. Before he could reach a final decision, General Pomeroy, who was senior to Heath, left the army; and Congress solved the difficulty by raising Thomas to the vacant place.[2]

Generals Wooster and Spencer of Connecticut were also offended by their treatment. Wooster held the highest post in the State service, and Spencer stood next to him. Putnam, however, had recently made a successful raid on an island in Boston Harbor, and Congress rewarded his energy with a major-general's commission, while Wooster and Spencer received only the rank of brigadier. Wooster was much hurt, but accepted his appointment. He was stationed in Connecticut, and, though outranked by Putnam, would be practically free from his control; but Spencer, at Cambridge, saw himself in danger of being placed under the immediate authority of his former junior, and he hastened home in anger without even waiting to pay his respects to the commander-in-chief. Spencer's officers sent a memorial to their legislature justifying his intention of leaving the service, and expressing grave apprehension concerning the effect of his resignation on the soldiers. The legislature directed Governor Trumbull to write to their delegates in Congress in behalf of both Wooster and Spencer; but Congress, thinking that Connecticut was not entitled to a second major-general, refused to make any change; and Spencer finally returned to Cambridge.[3]

The officers at Cambridge were nearly all from New England.

[1] Washington to President of Congress, July 10, 1775, Washington, *Writings* (Ford), iii. 14-16.

[2] Coffin, *Thomas*, 10-16.

[3] Deming, *Wooster*, 33-36; Webb to Deane, July 11, 1775, Ford, *Correspondence of Samuel B. Webb*, i. 79-81; Connecticut Officers to Connecticut Legislature, July 5, 1775, Force, *American Archives*, 4th series, ii. 1585; Stuart, *Trumbull*, 201-202; Washington to President of Congress, July 10, 1775, Washington, *Writings* (Ford), iii. 15-16.

This caused much dissatisfaction in other sections, and it was expected that a committee of Congress, which was sent to camp in October, 1775, would try to bring about a change. John Adams wrote to a friend in the Massachusetts Council, discussing the matter at some length. He said that Massachusetts could not honorably appoint strangers to the exclusion of capable citizens, for the soldiers would obey less readily, and such appointments would imply that suitable officers could not be obtained at home, though nothing could be farther from the truth. There were many Massachusetts citizens, he said, for whom there was no room in the army, yet who were better acquainted with the theory and practice of war than were any men who could be found in the other colonies.[1] Whatever we may think of the truth of this argument, local feeling was too strong to render a change advisable. Even under the "more perfect union," Massachusetts would have felt insulted if colonels and captains for her regiments in the Spanish War in 1898 had been appointed from the West or the South. The committee, perhaps thinking the subject too delicate to be even mentioned officially, made no reference to it in their report.

The several colonies wished not only to furnish officers for their troops, but also to make appointments for all ranks below that of brigadier-general. The army around Boston was formed before the meeting of Congress; and its officers were necessarily appointed by local authority. When Congress adopted the army, they appointed generals; but made few if any changes in the lower grades. When, however, new forces were raised, it was proposed that Congress exercise greater powers.

Congress recommended, on October 9, 1775, that two battalions be recruited in New Jersey; and Sherman of Connecticut moved that in this and in all similar cases the officers be chosen by the several colonies. The friends of the motion — Dyer, Ward, Deane, and others — urged that colonial appointment was popular, that it was customary, and that Congress had no right to make a change; they also argued with much plausibility that no real change was possible, since members of Congress must,

---

[1] Adams to John Winthrop, October 2, 1775, Massachusetts Historical Society, *Collections*, 5th series, iv. 295.

from lack of personal knowledge of the candidates, depend on the advice of the delegates from the several colonies.

This proposal to continue the previous system of appointment was, however, sharply criticised. Chase of Maryland said: "This is persisting in error. . . . Gentlemen have recommended persons, from personal friendships, who were not suitable; such friendships will have more weight in the colonies." Duane of New York declared that the change suggested would be wise, just, and not without precedent. "Schuyler and Montgomery," he said, "would govern my judgment. I would rather take the opinion of General Washington than of any convention. We can turn out the unworthy, and reward merit; the usage is for it. Governors [that is, representatives of the central authority] used to make officers, except in Connecticut and Rhode Island. But we can't raise an army! We are then in a deplorable condition indeed. We pay! — can't we appoint, with the advice of our generals?" John Jay said: "The Union depends much upon breaking down provincial conventions; the whole army refused to be mustered by your muster-master." Apparently all who spoke against the change were from New England; all who defended it were from other sections.[1]

Two days later, Congress allowed New Jersey to appoint the company officers, but directed that "the appointment of the field-officers be for the present suspended, until the Congress come to a determination on that matter." This produced an immediate remonstrance from the provincial Congress of New Jersey which claimed the privileges allowed other colonies, and said that, if they were permitted to select field-officers at once, it would expedite enlistments. They promised to choose men "generally respected in the province," and explained that under such leaders "captains and subalterns of reputation would offer their services, and the privates enlist more cheerfully." Evidently New England was not alone in selecting her officers on democratic principles.

Congress referred the subject to a committee; and, as a second application from New Jersey obtained only a postponement of the question, the legislature of the colony proceeded to nominate

[1] Debates of Congress, October 10, 1775, John Adams, *Works*, ii. 467-469.

STATE FIELD-OFFICERS. 41

the officers, and after four more postponements Congress elected them.[1] This was a substantial victory for those favoring local appointments, for a precedent was thus set from which it was difficult to depart. Accordingly, a little later, Congress requested the committees of safety of Pennsylvania and Delaware to recommend field-officers;[2] and, in general, Congress appears to have elected field-officers who had already been designated by the colonies.

Even the right of Congress to make promotions out of the ordinary course, or at least the propriety of their doing so, was challenged; but for once Congress clung to their authority. A letter from General Lord Stirling, remonstrating against the appointment of Lieutenant-Colonel Ogden to a New Jersey battalion, was answered by the passage of a resolution declaring that Congress had "reserved and frequently exercised the right of promoting men of distinguished merit."[3] The officers were inclined to consider succession by seniority an absolute right; Washington recommended that this supposed right be denied, or at least that a clear declaration be made, settling the matter one way or the other. Congress thereupon asserted full control over the subject, resolving that "no promotion or succession shall take place upon any vacancy, without the authority of a Continental commission."[4]

This announcement seems to have caused some discontent in camp; and both General Greene and General Parsons wrote to Adams, objecting to such a rule. Greene acknowledged that the principle of special promotion was right in theory; but he said that mistakes in applying it would give great offence, and that Congress should exercise this power in those cases only where the officers themselves would acknowledge the favor shown to be the just reward of exceptional services.[5] Adams replied, defending the action of Congress. He admitted that special

---

[1] Stryker, *Official Register of the Officers and Men of New Jersey*, 12.
[2] *Journals of Congress*, i. 294, December 15, 1775.
[3] *Ibid.* ii. 157, May 3, 1776.
[4] Washington to President of Congress, May 5, 1776, Washington, *Writings* (Ford), iv. 64; *Journals of Congress*, ii. 166, May 10, 1776.
[5] Greene to Adams, June 2, 1776, Greene, *Greene*, ii. 423-424.

promotion was liable to abuse; but he claimed that it was necessary, and that there would be less danger to public liberty in vesting the power in an assembly than in giving it to a general. Moreover in an assembly, he said, various interests would counterbalance each other and furnish a check to partiality, a safeguard which is impossible where authority is intrusted to a single person. He pointed out that the extensive area over which the war was waged rendered absolute succession by seniority impracticable, — that it would not do to leave a vacancy in New Hampshire unfilled until the officer next in rank could be fetched from South Carolina.[1]

Several generals had been recently appointed from the Middle and Southern States and Greene complained that New England was slighted. Adams gave a number of explanations for this seeming partiality, some of which are rather curious. Merit in civil and political affairs, and even family and fortune, were among the causes he assigned for the appointments referred to. He also said that the South was unwarlike, and that it was necessary to awaken her military ardor by a full share of commands. Adams gave as another reason for the treatment of the New England colonels that the most deserving among them were juniors, and that their promotion would have given offence.[2]

But the discrimination, if such existed, was quickly removed. The day after Adams's letter was written, Washington asked Congress to increase the number of generals. Two days later he wrote at more length, admitting the serious embarrassments in making a choice, but urging the need of action.[3] Congress promptly elected four major-generals and six brigadier-generals.[4] All of the former and half of the latter were New England men.

When, in the fall of 1776, arrangements were made for again enlisting an army, the appointment of officers and the filling of

[1] Adams to Greene, and to Parsons, June 22, 1776, John Adams, *Works*, ix. 402–407.

[2] Adams to Greene, August 4, 1776, *Ibid.* i. 251–253.

[3] Washington to President of Congress, August 5 and 7, 1776, Washington, *Writings* (Ford), iv. 320–323.

[4] *Journals of Congress*, ii. 303, August 9, 1776.

vacancies below the rank of general were left to the States.[1] Knox was displeased, and Adams wrote to him: "You complain of the popular plan of raising the new army. But if you make the plan as unpopular as you please, you will not mend the matter." Adams said that the State legislatures were best fitted for the work of selection, that the defects of the American officers were due, not to bad appointments, but to lack of training; and he asked Knox to send him a plan for a military academy.[2] Adams's professed confidence in the legislatures was scarcely justified by the result. Washington wrote to his brother: "The different States, without regard to the qualifications of an officer, [are] quarrelling about the appointments, and nominating such as are not fit to be shoe-blacks, from the local attachments of this or that member of assembly."[3] Gerry wrote to Gates in a similar tone. "If some extra measures are not adopted," he said, "we shall have such a corps of officers as the army have been hitherto encumbered with."[4]

Congress endeavored to remedy these defects by advising the States to consult the generals in making promotions, and hereafter to appoint "men of honor and known abilities, without a particular regard to their having before been in service."[5] Early in November, Congress authorized Washington, after consulting with such of his generals as he could conveniently assemble, to appoint officers himself when the States had not sent commissioners to camp for that purpose.[6]

A little later the serious condition of affairs induced the commander-in-chief to take steps for raising troops without any clear authority to warrant the proceeding. He wrote to Congress, explaining how matters stood, and made numerous requests, one of which was for an increase of power.[7] This

[1] *Journals of Congress*, ii. 358, September 16, 1776.
[2] Adams to Knox, September, 1776, John Adams, *Works*, i. 257.
[3] Washington to John Augustine Washington, November 19, 1776, Washington, *Writings* (Ford), v. 40.
[4] September 27, 1776, Force, *American Archives*, 5th series, ii. 572.
[5] *Journals of Congress*, ii. 403-404, October 8, 1776.
[6] *Ibid.* 443, November 4, 1776.
[7] Washington to President of Congress, December 20, 1776, Washington, *Writings* (Ford), v. 112-122.

letter, together with one from General Greene, testifying to the danger of the country and to the moderation and fidelity of Washington, was read December 26.[1] The reply was the so-called "vote for a dictator." By this vote, Congress declared that " The unjust, but determined purpose of the British court to enslave these free States, obvious through every delusive insinuation to the contrary, having placed things in such a situation that the very existence of civil liberty now depends upon the right execution of military powers, and the vigorous, decisive conduct of these being impossible to distant, numerous, and deliberative bodies :

"This Congress, having maturely considered the present crisis, and having perfect reliance on the wisdom, vigor, and uprightness of General Washington; do hereby

" *Resolve*" that, unless the authority be sooner revoked, he have for six months certain extraordinary powers, including the raising of additional troops, the naming of their officers, and the right " to displace and appoint all officers under the rank of brigadier-general, and to fill up all vacancies in every other department in the American armies."[2] Washington was also requested to fix upon a system of promotion which, in his own opinion and that of his generals, would be satisfactory. Congress suggested that field-officers might rise in State lines,[3] those of lower grades only regimentally.[4] This plan was afterwards recommended to the States, but proved less successful than had been anticipated.[5]

In his letter asking for an increase of power, Washington made a proposition which has an interest quite apart from the special point at issue. " I have labored," he said, " ever since I have been in the service, to discourage all kinds of local attachments and distinctions of country, denominating the whole by

---

[1] Greene to President of Congress, December 21, 1776, Greene, *Greene*, i. 289-291.

[2] *Journals of Congress*, ii. 515, December 27, 1776.

[3] The troops of a State, on the Continental establishment, were called the " line " of that State ; and the infantry regiments in general, as distinct from the cavalry and from the artillery, were sometimes called the " line of the army."

[4] *Journals of Congress*, ii. 514, December 27, 1776.

[5] *Ibid*. iv. 674-675, November 24, 1778.

RULES OF PROMOTION.

the greater name of AMERICAN, but I have found it impossible to overcome prejudices; and, under the new establishment, I conceive it best to stir up an emulation; in order to do which, would it not be better for each State to furnish, though not to appoint, their own brigadiers?"[1]

Military titles were dealt out with a lavish hand. "My blacksmith is a captain," wrote Kalb. Assistant quartermasters and the like were colonels; according to Kalb, it was safe to give the title to every one who addressed you with familiarity.[2] Congress at last woke to the evil of making rank cheap, and resolved that hereafter it should not be conferred upon any one on the civil staff of the army.[3]

In 1780 Washington again brought the matter of promotion before Congress. General Sullivan, who was then a member of that body, had asked him for certain information on that subject. Washington replied: "If in all cases ours was *one* army, or *thirteen* armies allied for the common defence, there would be no difficulty in solving your question; but we are occasionally both, and I should not be much out if I were to say, that we are sometimes *neither*, but a compound of *both*."[4] To the president of Congress Washington now wrote, advising that, as the best means of satisfying the claims of the States, of the Continent, and of individuals, promotions below the rank of brigadier should be by State lines rather than by regiments; under the old system a sergeant in one regiment might be raised over the head of a lieutenant in another. The artillery and cavalry had been treated as separate lines, and Washington advised retaining this arrangement. Some States did not furnish enough men to make a brigade, and their colonels were therefore excluded from promotion. Washington proposed that they be made generals whenever they became the senior colonels of the whole army, and that they be employed on extra service, as in com-

---

[1] Washington to President of Congress, December 20, 1776, Washington, *Writings* (Ford), v. 117–118.
[2] Kalb to Broglie, December 25, 1777, Kapp, *Kalb*, 141.
[3] *Journals of Congress*, iv. 320, May 29, 1778.
[4] Washington to Sullivan, December 17, 1780, Washington, *Writings* (Ford), ix. 63–64.

mand of the light infantry. Rules for the promotion of major-generals were also suggested.[1]

The letter was promptly referred to a committee, which, however, did not report for nearly four months. Congress followed Washington's advice, except in what related to the generals. The country was divided into seven districts, and in these divisions the senior colonels were to rise to brigadiers; thus, for example, a Delaware colonel was not obliged to wait until he ranked all the other colonels in the army. The major-generals were to be drawn according to seniority from the whole army.[2] Washington himself would have recommended such an arrangement had he not feared that it would unduly offend the States, and Congress probably acted wisely in making it.

Congress firmly maintained the right of special promotion, against the excessive regard of the officers for succession by seniority. It is a pity that they could not have been equally resolute when confronted with the claims of the States. Duane struck the true note when he said, "I would rather take the opinion of General Washington than of any convention;" but local feeling was too strong to permit any such plan to be adopted.

[1] Washington to President of Congress, December 20, 1780, Washington, *Writings* (Ford), ix. 68–72.
[2] *Journals of Congress*, vii. 106–107, May 25, 1781.

CHAPTER IV.

FOREIGN OFFICERS.

THE difficulty of officering the army was much increased by numerous and importunate applications of foreigners, first for employment and then for promotion. Silas Deane, our first minister to France, declared that he was "well-nigh harassed to death with applications of officers to go out to America."[1] Franklin wrote to a gentleman who had given him much assistance, but who had also troubled him with many recommendations: "You can have no conception how I am harassed. All my friends are sought out and teased to tease me. Great officers of all ranks, in all departments; ladies, great and small, besides professed solicitors, worry me from morning to night. The noise of every coach now that enters my court terrifies me. I am afraid to accept an invitation to dine abroad, being almost sure of meeting with some officer or officer's friend, who, as soon as I am put in good humor by a glass or two of champagne, begins his attack upon me. Luckily I do not often in my sleep dream of these vexatious situations, or I should be afraid of what are now my only hours of comfort. If, therefore, you have the least remaining kindness for me, if you would not help to drive me out of France, for God's sake, my dear friend, let this, your twenty-third application, be your last."[2]

In America, the president of Congress complained that French officers beset his door like bailiffs watching a debtor.[3] Wash-

---
[1] Deane to Committee of Secret Correspondence, November 28, 1776, Wharton, *Diplomatic Correspondence*, ii. 198.
[2] Franklin to Dr. Dubourg, 1777, Parton, *Franklin*, ii. 233.
[3] Laurens to Livingston, April 19, 1778, Sedgwick, *Livingston*, 270.

ington wrote bitterly of them as men "who have nothing more than a little plausibility, unbounded pride and ambition, and a perseverance in application not to be resisted but by uncommon firmness, to support their pretensions; men who, in the first instance, tell you they wish for nothing more than the honor of serving so glorious a cause as volunteers, the next day solicit rank without pay, the day following want money advanced to them, and in the course of a week want further promotion, and are not satisfied with anything you can do for them."[1]

There was, however, nothing contrary to European customs in requests for employment in a foreign army; the officer of the eighteenth century was "a citizen of the world."[2] Two of the ablest generals of their day, Prince Eugene and Marshal Saxe, served foreign princes. Keith, a Scotchman of high character, an exile for his fidelity to the Stuarts and a man of the strictest integrity, was at different periods an officer of Austria, of Spain, and of Prussia. Frederick the Great had regular agents whose business it was to meet foreign officers passing through his territories, and invite them to enter the service of Prussia.

The majority of foreigners applying for commissions in the American army were Frenchmen. For this there were several reasons. France had been brought into closer relations with America than had any other power except England. Frenchmen consoled themselves for the loss of Canada by the hope that the older English colonies, no longer needing the protection of the mother country, would declare their independence; and in 1764 and 1768 the French prime minister sent secret agents to America to discover whether the people were willing and able to resist England, and whether they would accept the assistance of France, whom they had hitherto regarded as a powerful and deadly enemy.[3] But reports were unfavorable; France was busy with other plans; and when some years afterward the ris-

---

[1] Washington to Gouverneur Morris, July 24, 1778, Washington, *Writings* (Ford), vii. 117.

[2] Greene, *Historical View of the American Revolution*, 288.

[3] One of these agents was "Baron" de Kalb, afterward a major-general in the American army.

ing actually took place, the ministry of that day, though glad to see England embarrassed, were restrained from open war, partly by the conscientious scruples and the monarchical prejudices of Louis XVI., partly by the disorder of the finances.

Many young nobles, however, were eager to assist America. They were weary of the idleness of peace; war would give them excitement and glory, and a chance to take revenge for recent defeats and to restore France to her old place among the nations. Attempts made by the ministry to repress their enthusiasm served only to increase it; the government had lost its moral authority; revolution was in the air. The writings of Voltaire, Montesquieu, and Rousseau attained immense influence; equality was the fashion; the privileged classes, themselves, had much to say in behalf of the rights of man; and their zeal was increased by a belief that their own rights were violated. The nobles were disgusted with a system which condemned them to political insignificance; they recalled the days of the League and of the Fronde, and longed for a position like that of English peers and gentlemen. Men who began by championing the cause of America from personal, or at best from patriotic, motives came to have an earnest, though somewhat vague, love of it for its own sake.

The envoys sent by the new republic were admirably fitted to win the sympathies of these enthusiasts. Their simplicity of manner and of dress formed a pleasing contrast to the artificiality and magnificence of the court. The seeming frankness with which they acknowledged American disasters astonished men accustomed to the evasions of European diplomacy. Here were true successors of Fabricius and of Cato![1]

Several motives of a less idealistic kind speedily led many French officers to enter the army of the United States. Some, who were burdened with debt or disgrace, sought to recover in America the fortunes or the honor they had lost at home.[2] Their desire for a change of service may have been further stimulated by the strict discipline which was then being introduced by a new minister of war.[3] Many came from the love

[1] Segur, *Memoirs*. [2] Wharton, *Diplomatic Correspondence*, i. 397.
[3] Lowell, *Eve of the French Revolution*, 92.

of adventure and glory, and the hope of increased rank and pay; surely, they thought, inexperienced colonists will purchase at a high rate the services of an officer trained in the military schools of Europe.[1]

For a time the strangers were well received, and they were frequently treated so generously that they boasted that they could obtain whatever they desired merely by assuming a high tone and persevering in their demands.[2] Congress was anxious to secure aid and recognition from France, and was therefore unwilling to disoblige men who had friends and patrons at court, especially when, as was often the case, applicants had received encouragement from American agents abroad. Those who came from the French West Indies obtained positions the more easily because of the desire of the Americans to keep on good terms with the governor of Martinique, with which island a very important trade was carried on. Others brought recommendations from French officers of rank, or from the American envoy at Paris.[3] Such testimonials were, however, untrustworthy; those given by French officers had no claim to impartiality, and even those from Deane must have been based largely on the information of interested persons.

It is not surprising that many unfit appointments of foreigners were made. The first comers, those who received commissions before 1777, proved the least valuable; usually ability was lacking, and often character as well. Two officers who were given high rank because of their supposed skill as engineers were found to be of little use.[4] Baron de Woedtke, who had strong recommendations and was appointed brigadier-general, proved a drunken fellow and rendered little service.[5] The danger of the

[1] Hale, *Franklin in France*, i. 78.
[2] Hamilton to Clinton, February 13, 1778, Hamilton, *Works* (Lodge), vii. 537.
[3] Richard Henry Lee to Washington, May 22, 1777, Lee, *Richard Henry Lee*, ii. 17; Washington to President of Congress, June 5, 1777, Washington, *Writings* (Ford), v. 412.
[4] Washington to Deane, August 13, 1777, *Sparks MSS*. lxv. (pt. 1), 174–176; to Richard Henry Lee, May 17, 1777, Washington, *Writings* (Ford), v. 371.
[5] C. F. Adams, *Familiar Letters of John Adams and his Wife*, 144, note.

UNWISE APPOINTMENTS. 51

retreat from Ticonderoga was greatly increased by negligence or disobedience of orders on the part of General Roche de Fermoy.[1] The one illustrious foreign name on the roster of 1776 is that of Thaddeus Kosciusko, the Polish patriot. He remained in the army throughout the contest, was of much service as an engineer at Bemis Heights and West Point, and received a general's brevet at the close of the war.[2]

The liberality of Congress gave great offence at camp. The colonies had never had a standing army or a military caste; and the American officers could not, like those of Europe, forget nationality in a sense of professional brotherhood. Moreover, they had themselves raised and trained the army; their future prospects were staked on the issue of the contest; their emoluments were less than those of European officers; their danger, since England regarded them as rebels, was much greater; and now the principal reward of their services, military rank and command, was lavished on aliens whose motives were selfish, whose abilities were mediocre, and who could not even speak the English language.[3]

In one regiment American officers resorted to dishonorable means to rid themselves of foreigners. Congress had ordered two regiments to be raised in Canada; but the second of these became very much reduced, and it was strengthened by admitting Americans. Many of the officers, however, were Canadians, and, when the army was driven out of Canada, they found themselves exiles, dependent for their support and that of their

[1] *St. Clair Papers*, i. 65.
[2] Washington, *Writings* (Ford), vi. 183-184, note.
[3] Shortly after the rout at Ticonderoga, Washington wrote as follows to General Schuyler:—

" It is out of my power to displace General Fermoy or to get rid of him in any way, his appointment was by Congress, who assigned him to the Northern army. You must endeavor to place some person about him who is master of the French and English languages, and by that means he will be better enabled to receive and give orders to his brigade.

" But if you and the other general officers find him incapable of executing his office, rather than the service should suffer, he must be plainly told of his inability and advised to give up the command at least till he has made himself sufficient master of our language to convey his orders to the officers of his brigade " (July 27, 1777, *Ibid.* v. 518-519, note).

families on the pay which they received from the United States; yet some of their American brothers-in-arms were so lost to all sense of humanity as to try to drive these unfortunates from the service. It is said that Canadian officers were repeatedly court-martialled on false or frivolous charges, and, although honorably acquitted, were accused again and again, until at last they were forced out of the army.

Even if given courteous treatment, the foreign officers often found themselves in very unpleasant situations. It was sometimes difficult for foreign nobles to adapt themselves to American conditions. Inspector-General Steuben wrote: "A considerable number of German barons and French marquises have left the country, and I always feel uneasy when a baron or a marquis is introduced. We are living in a republic, dear friend — here the baron is not a farthing more valued than Master Jacob or Mister John is, and such a state of things is very unpalatable to the taste of a German or French baron."[1] Romand de Lisle, when made a major of artillery, complained that such an appointment was not equal to his deserts, and requested permission to go to camp that he might have an opportunity to give "a specimen of his abilities."[2] Leave was granted, but his "abilities" remain unknown to history. Monsieur de Neuville induced General Parsons to sign a highly laudatory certificate of recommendation written by himself.

Men of this sort were almost sure to feel that they were slighted and that others were unduly favored; and their conduct was sometimes such as to call forth severe rebukes from the much-enduring commander-in-chief. One officer, by his complaints, provoked Washington into replying: "I am sorry that some of the gentlemen promoted by Congress render themselves unhappy, either by forming in their minds the most groundless suspicions of neglect, or torturing themselves by an unwarrantable degree of jealousy at the promotion of others. . . .

"I might add, without any disparagement to your merit, that there are many good officers in the service, who have been in it

---

[1] Steuben to Baron de Frank, July 4, 1779, Kapp, *Steuben*, ii. 657.
[2] *Journals of Congress*, ii. 460, November 15, 1776.

DISSATISFACTION OF THE FOREIGNERS.

from the commencement of the war, that have not received such honorable marks of favor and distinction. If there are foreigners, who came to America when you did, or since, who have been promoted to higher rank without having better pretensions, it has not been through my interest. Though I wish to see every man rewarded according to his deserts, and esteem emulation in officers a laudable quality, yet I cannot but condemn the over-sanguine, unjust, ambitious expectations of those, who think everything should be made to yield to gratify their views."[1] At the same time Washington wrote to another Frenchman: "A perseverance in your mistaken pretensions, after you had seen they could not be complied with, is what I did not expect. . . . Though I wish not to offend or wound, yet justice both to you and myself requires, that I should plainly inform you, that your scruples and difficulties, so often reiterated, and under a variety of shapes, are exceedingly perplexing to me, and that I wish them to cease."[2]

There were, however, many foreigners who had substantial reasons for dissatisfaction. Congress, in haste and ignorance, frequently gave the best places to the least worthy, merely because they were the first to apply. Consequently, a promising young officer with a good reputation at home might find himself only a captain, while a fellow whom every one in France knew to be a failure was already a major. This was not only extremely mortifying to the captain, but it might prevent his rising when he returned to France; for, since the conditions in America were not understood abroad, it would naturally be thought that his low rank was due to his own misconduct or incapacity.

Another circumstance which rendered the American service irksome to foreign officers was the idleness in which they were kept. Their ignorance of English and their lack of influence prevented them from recruiting new regiments, and the jealousy of the Americans kept them out of those already raised; accordingly, many remained idle month after month, the more

[1] Washington to Major Colerus, May 19, 1777, Washington, *Writings* (Ford), v. 366-367, note.
[2] Washington to Malmedy, May 16, 1777, *Ibid.* 365-366.

high-minded chafing at their inability to be of any use to the government which employed them.¹

Sometimes this lack of occupation was due to the nature of the war. M. Garanger, a French captain of bombardiers, arrived in Philadelphia in the latter part of 1778. Six months later the Board of War, with the approval of Congress, sent him to camp with a request that Washington allow him to make experiments in order to ascertain what would be the value of his services. In the fall of 1780 the Board reported that he had proceeded to camp as desired, but that owing to scarcity of powder he had had no opportunity to show his skill, "it being thought best by the commander-in-chief and General Knox to wait for the siege of some fortified place, that the public service and the proof required might be carried on at the same expenditure of ammunition." The Board added that Captain Garanger was now in Philadelphia, in great distress for want of money, and asking assistance to enable him to return to camp.²

The American lack of military training was especially felt in the engineering department. As early as December, 1775, steps were taken to obtain foreign engineers, and in 1777 four were engaged by Deane under special authority from Congress.³ But our friends in France urged that a director of artillery ought also to be sent over, and strongly recommended Tronson du Coudray for the place. Du Coudray held an honorable position in the French artillery, and he had been chosen by the minister of war to visit the royal arsenals and select cannon to be sent to America.⁴ In matters of technical knowledge, therefore, Du Coudray was well fitted for his post; but the choice in other respects was less fortunate, for his

---

[1] Washington to Richard Henry Lee, May 17, 1777, Washington, *Writings* (Ford), v. 369-371; to Deane, August 13, 1777, *Sparks MSS.* lxv. (pt. 1), 174-176.

[2] Board of War to Congress, September 26, 1780, *Board of War Papers*, iv. 567-568.

[3] *Secret Journals of Congress*, ii. 5-6, December 2, 1775. These were the only officers who came over on contracts which bound the United States. They were all able men, and rendered good service. One of them (Duportail) rose to the rank of major-general.

[4] Wharton, *Diplomatic Correspondence*, i. 421-422.

motives were thoroughly selfish, and he was vain, ambitious, and quarrelsome. He had influential friends, however; and, as he was to carry with him a number of cannon,[1] Deane was induced to sign a contract giving him not only the rank of major-general but also the command of the artillery. He thus superseded Knox, who had held that position over a year and who was much esteemed.[2]

In the spring of 1777 Du Coudray landed at Portsmouth. On his way to Philadelphia he stopped at Boston, where he bragged so much that Mrs. Knox, who was at Brookline, heard of him and his expectations, and wrote to her husband: "He says . . . that he is a major-general, and a deal of it. Who knows but I may have my Harry again? This I am sure of, he will never suffer any one to command him in that department. If he does, he has not the soul which I now think him possessed of."[3] Du Coudray spent a night at camp, and Washington, hearing that he might be placed at the head of the artillery, wrote at once to Congress that such an appointment would be followed by the resignation of General Knox, and probably by the disorganization of the whole department. Washington also expressed great doubt whether, as a matter of general policy, so important a position as the command of the artillery should be given to a foreigner.[4] Greene, too, who was always ready to

---

[1] He also took with him some twenty-five commissioned and non-commissioned officers, in spite of the warning of a shrewd Yankee privateer, who bluntly said to him, "Leave some of your officers behind, they don't want 'em over there" (*Journals of Congress*, iv. 70, February 4, 1778; Hale, *Franklin in France*, i. 109).

[2] Deane to Committee of Secret Correspondence, August 18, 1776, Wharton, *Diplomatic Correspondence*, ii. 127.

[3] Brooks, *Knox*, 91. Knox seems to have promptly reassured his wife of his greatness of soul, for on June 19 she wrote to him: "Dearest, best of men, is it possible, is there a dawn of hope, may I expect to be again blessed with him who forms a part of my very soul, whose presence I esteem the greatest good that this world can afford? Yes, it is possible, my Harry says it is. . . . Yet I have another dread, should General De Coudrier [du Coudray] accept of a command foreign to the artillery my fall would be like Phaeton's" (*Knox MSS*. iv. 18).

[4] Washington to President of Congress, May 31, 1777, Washington, *Writings* (Ford), v. 401-403.

offer advice, wrote to Adams that Knox ought not to be displaced; and Adams is said to have replied that the contract would not be ratified.[1]

The Frenchman's claims were very offensive, not only to the American officers, but to his own countrymen as well. Three of the engineers engaged by Congress had just arrived, and they disdained to be commanded by Du Coudray, who was not a member of the Royal Corps of Engineers.[2] Professional feeling was probably intensified by caste pride: Du Coudray's family was engaged in trade, a most inappropriate occupation for relatives of a member of the *noblesse*.[3]

Congress let the matter of Du Coudray's appointment remain undecided for a month. Meanwhile, Greene received a letter from a member, in which he understood his correspondent to say that Du Coudray had been appointed major-general, and that his commission was to be dated August 1, 1776, thereby superseding not only Knox but Sullivan, and Greene himself. The three generals at once sent letters to Congress which were curt almost to insolence. They mentioned the report of Du Coudray's appointment, asked if it were true, and requested leave, in that case, to resign immediately.[4]

Congress, always sensitive to the slightest appearance of military dictation, was very angry at what seemed to be both an insult and a threat. They unanimously ordered their president to send copies of these letters to Washington, "with directions to him to let those officers know that Congress consider the said letters as an attempt to influence their decisions, an invasion of the liberties of the people, and indicating a want of confidence in the justice of Congress; that it is expected by Congress the said officers will make proper acknowledgments for an interference of so dangerous a tendency; but if any of those officers are unwilling to serve their country under the authority of Con-

---

[1] May 28, 1777, Greene, *Greene*, i. 418-420.

[2] Samuel Adams to Richard Henry Lee, June 26 and 29, 1777, Wells, *Samuel Adams*, ii. 471. In European armies the engineers formed a separate corps; but Du Coudray claimed that, by his agreement with Deane, they were to be treated as a part of the artillery and to be under his own command.

[3] Balch, *The French in America*, ii. 106-107.

[4] Greene, *Greene*, i. 420-421; Washington, *Writings* (Sparks), iv. 490, note.

gress, they shall be at liberty to resign their commissions and retire."[1] The generals, however, neither apologized nor resigned. Knox wrote to his wife, "Conscious of the rectitude of my intention and of the contents of my letter, I shall make no acknowledgments whatever. Though my country is too much pressed at present to resign, yet perhaps this campaign will be the last. I am determined to contribute my mite to the defence of the country, in spite of every obstacle."[2] Greene, very characteristically, sent to Congress an elaborate defence of his conduct.[3]

The members of Congress had placed themselves in an awkward position: they must choose between losing men who could ill be spared, or making a mortifying retreat. Wisely and patriotically, they took the latter course. Greene's second letter, though in it he had presumed to justify what Congress had censured, was laid on the table. Du Coudray was told that Deane's contract could not be ratified, but that Congress would cheerfully provide for him in a manner which would not be inconsistent with the honor and safety of the States, and which would not interfere with the great duties that Congress owed to their constituents.[4] A month later he was given the promised rank of major-general, but was appointed "inspector-general of ordnance and military manufactories," an inglorious position which would keep him away from camp most of the time.[5]

Du Coudray soon grew restless, and asked leave to join the army as a volunteer holding the merely nominal rank of captain. Congress gave the desired permission, and Du Coudray promptly set out; but on his way to camp he was drowned in the Schuylkill. His body was recovered, and was buried at the public expense; and Congress passed a resolution lamenting the

[1] *Journals of Congress*, iii. 270, July 7, 1777.
[2] July 13, 1777, Drake, *Knox*, 43.
[3] Greene to President of Congress, July 19, 1777, Greene, *Greene*, i. 422–426.
[4] *Journals of Congress*, iii. 279, July 15, 1777.
[5] *Ibid.* 323, August 11, 1777. The creation of inspectorships was a convenient way of providing for officers whom Congress was unwilling either to dismiss or to introduce into the line. About the same time Congress shelved another French officer, Colonel de la Balme, by making him inspector-general of cavalry (*Ibid.* 271, July 8, 1777).

accident, which they termed most unfortunate.¹ But John Adams probably expressed the true feeling of the members when he wrote in his diary, "This dispensation will save us much altercation." ²

Scarcely was the Du Coudray affair settled, when Congress was embarrassed by the arrival of another group of foreigners, three of whom — the Viscount de Mauroy, the Marquis de Lafayette, and the "Baron" de Kalb³ — had been promised by Deane the rank of major-general. Mauroy is little known; but Lafayette and Kalb have gained honorable places in American history, and may serve as types of the two classes into which the foreign officers may be divided, the idealists and the fortune-hunters. Each, however, is a very favorable representative of the class to which he belongs. Lafayette at the time of his arrival in America was not quite twenty years old, but he was possessed of a considerable fortune, and was connected by marriage with the family of Noailles, one of the most influential houses in France. He was a true Frenchman, brave, warm-hearted, and eager for distinction; and he came to America to win fame for himself and to fight for the cause of "liberty," for which he felt a romantic devotion. Kalb was a prosaic, middle-aged German. He was an officer of fair ability, but no genius, who came to America to advance his own fortunes and to further the interests of his patron, the Comte de Broglie. This nobleman hoped to be appointed commander-in-chief of the American army, with extensive powers, large emoluments, and the promise of a pension after his retirement.⁴ In a letter to the Committee of Secret Correspondence, written the previous December, Deane had suggested such a scheme, and had referred the Committee to Kalb for fuller information.⁵ If Con-

---

¹ *Journals of Congress*, iii. 393–394, 398, September 15 and 17, 1777.

² September 18, 1777, John Adams, *Works*, ii. 438.

³ Kalb was the name of a noble German family; but the "baron" was the son of a peasant, and assumed a title to which he had no right in order to obtain a commission in the French service. See Kapp, *Kalb*, ch. i.

⁴ Broglie to Kalb, December 11, 1776, *Ibid.* 95–97.

⁵ December 6, 1776, Wharton, *Diplomatic Correspondence*, ii. 218. It should be mentioned, in justice to Kalb's good sense, that he quickly discovered that the plan was impracticable.

gress were aware of this preposterous plan, they could scarcely have failed to be prejudiced against Kalb; but whether they suspected his secret purpose or not, they at least knew that here were thirteen more foreigners in quest of employment, and they received them in a way that, to use Lafayette's own words, was "more like a dismissal than a welcome."[1]

One of the newcomers, Chevalier du Buysson, describes how they were kept waiting a long time at the door of Congress, and how at last a member came and talked with them in the street, "where he left us, after having treated us, in excellent French, like a set of adventurers." According to Du Buysson, the member closed the interview thus: "It seems that French officers have a great fancy to enter our service without being invited. It is true we were in need of officers last year, but now we have experienced men and plenty of them." The applicants were astounded. "It would be impossible," says Du Buysson, "for any one to be more stupefied than we were." In a second conference they were treated more politely, but at first Lafayette alone was taken into the American service.[2] The reasons for this partiality were frankly set forth in the resolution granting him a commission:—

"Whereas," it ran, "the Marquis de Lafayette, out of his great zeal to the cause of liberty, in which the United States are engaged, has left his family and connections, and at his own expense come over to offer his service to the United States without pension or particular allowance, and is anxious to risk his life in our cause:

"*Resolved*, That his service be accepted, and that in consideration of his zeal, illustrious family and connections he have the rank and commission of major-general in the army of the United States."[3]

Lafayette had many of the virtues of his countrymen, but he had some of their defects as well. He was by no means backward in asking favors.[4] Although the resolution appointing

---

[1] Tower, *La Fayette in the American Revolution*, i. 182–183.
[2] *Ibid.* 179–180, 183–184.   [3] *Journals of Congress*, iii. 303, July 31, 1777.
[4] Writing to Congress to thank them for the promotion of one friend and to ask a similar favor for another, he refers to the "freedom I have ever been

him a major-general gave him no command, he soon became very pressing in his efforts to obtain one; but to his credit be it said, he also did his best to deserve it. He fought bravely at Brandywine, where he was wounded; and he showed marked zeal and ability in an expedition to New Jersey. He endeavored to soothe the discontent of French officers who were sent home, and he quickly acquired a knowledge of the English language. Pleased by his good conduct, and mindful of the ill effects which might be produced if he should become dissatisfied and return to France, Washington twice wrote to Congress asking what was their pleasure in the matter. Congress replied that it would be highly agreeable to them that the marquis should have a division, and he was assigned to that made vacant by the dismissal of General Stephen.[1]

Lafayette's conduct at Barren Hill, at Monmouth, and in Virginia justified his appointment; but his greatest service was in bringing France and America together. The Americans had been accustomed to look on France as the enemy of their country and their religion. They hated her and they feared her. They believed that her accursed priests were stirring up the Indians to ravage the frontiers, and that her crafty governors were drawing a chain of posts down the Mississippi Valley to confine the English to the Atlantic seaboard. The French themselves they despised as an inferior race. "That one Englishman could whip three Frenchmen was as fundamental an article of colonial as of English belief. In French politeness indulged with," and says, "I beg thousand pardons to Congress for coming again upon an old ground, but I thought I did owe it to friendship." He was about to sail for Europe, and fearing capture by the enemy's cruisers, asked Congress for a written promise that, if he should fall into the hands of the English, they would give one of the generals taken at Saratoga in exchange for him. He said that with this certificate he would, if allowed freedom to travel, go to London and "oblige their king to release me." After the signing of the treaty of peace, Lafayette, although a foreigner, asked to be appointed special envoy to carry the ratifications to London. See Lafayette to President of Congress, November 29, 1778, *Sparks MSS.* lii. (pt. 3), 172-173; to Hamilton, February 5, 1783, Wharton, *Diplomatic Correspondence*, vi. 241.

[1] Washington to President of Congress, November 1 and 26, 1777, Washington, *Writings* (Ford), vi. 161-162, 223-225, and note.

they saw nothing but heartless vanity. In French society nothing but sensuality and corruption. The perfidious French government was still seeking to outwit the honest, unsuspecting government of England."[1]

Much of this old prejudice still remained, and the vanity and ambition shown by many of the French officers were not likely to diminish it. But Lafayette conducted himself in a very different manner. Though accustomed to the luxurious life of a wealthy French noble, he cheerfully adapted himself to American conditions and lived as barely and rigorously as any. His generosity and loyal devotion to the cause made friends for him on every side. The glory which he won in America increased the enthusiasm of the French *noblesse;* and after the alliance was concluded Lafayette returned to France for a time, and urged the government to give efficient support, in both men and money, to the United States. When Rochambeau's army was sent over, Lafayette's influential position, both in France and in America, enabled him to do much to secure a harmonious coöperation.

Kalb was much displeased by his treatment at Philadelphia, and by the preference shown to Lafayette; and he wrote to Congress, demanding either the rank agreed on or a sum of money sufficient to pay the expenses of his return home. He threatened, if the latter demand were refused, to sue Deane in the French courts, an action which would injure not only the reputation and influence of the minister, but that of the United States.[2] Congress finally voted that Mauroy, Kalb, and their companions be thanked, and informed that circumstances would not permit of their being employed, but that the expenses of their journey to America and of their return should be paid them.[3] Most of them accordingly went back to France, but Kalb was recalled before he had quitted Pennsylvania. He was an experienced officer, and could speak English well. He had also strong recommendations, and Congress reconsidered their decision and appointed him a major-general. A few weeks later

---
[1] Greene, *Historical View of the American Revolution*, 308.
[2] Kalb to President of Congress, August 1, 1777, Kapp, *Kalb*, 114-116.
[3] *Journals of Congress*, iii. 378, 393, September 8 and 14, 1777.

they voted that his commission bear the same date as that of Lafayette.[1]

Lafayette was without doubt the chief of the idealists; but Kalb, though a brave and valuable officer, does not occupy the first place among the fortune-seekers. That distinction belongs to Baron Steuben. Unlike Kalb, Steuben was a real baron, for he was a member of a noble Prussian house; but, as Kalb gained his position in the French army by assuming a title to which he had no claim, so Steuben, in order to obtain high rank in the American army, pretended to be a lieutenant-general of the Margrave of Baden, a minor German prince, whose highest officer bore the title of colonel. Steuben had served in the Prussian army throughout the Seven Years' War, but had left it after the peace. In 1777 he was induced to go to the United States by the French minister of war, who knew that his experience would be useful in organizing the departments of the American army and in disciplining the troops. Steuben was not

---

[1] Kapp, *Kalb*, 118-119. Kalb had made equal rank with Lafayette a condition of entering the American army. His letter pointed out what is sometimes forgotten, that Lafayette was not the only foreigner with claims to consideration. "Though I ardently desired to serve America," Kalb said, "I did not mean to do so in spending part of my own and my children's fortune — for what is deemed generosity in the Marquis de Lafayette would be downright madness to me, who does not possess one of the first-rate fortunes. If I were in his circumstances, I should perhaps have acted like he did. I am very glad that you granted his wishes; he is a worthy young man, and no one will outdo him in enthusiasm in your cause of liberty and independence. My wishes will always be that his successes as general-major will equal his zeal and your expectation. But I must confess, sir, that this distinction between him and myself is painful and very displeasing to me. We came on the same errand, with the same promises, and as military men and for military purposes, I flatter myself that if there was to be any preference it would be due to me. 34 years of constant attendance on military service, and my station and rank in that way, may well be laid in the scale with his disinterestedness, and be at least of the same weight and value; this distinction is very unaccountable in an infant state of a commonwealth, but this is none of my business. I only want to know whether Congress will appoint me as general-major, and with the seniority I have a right to expect this (for I cannot stay here in a lesser capacity). It would seem very odd and ridiculous to the French ministry and all experienced military men to see me placed under the command of the Marquis de Lafayette." (Kalb to President of Congress, August 1, 1777, Kapp, *Kalb*, 115.)

actuated primarily either by enthusiasm for liberty or by hope of pecuniary reward; "military distinction and active employment were the chief objects of his ambition, the immediate motives of his conduct." He expected, however, a suitable compensation, and hoped that, if America proved ungrateful, France would provide for him.[1]

Steuben was cordially received by Congress, and was sent to camp as an unattached officer with the rank of major-general. At Washington's request he undertook the duties of inspector-general, and soon after obtained a regular appointment from Congress. The authority which he claimed gave much offence to the other generals, and in order to quiet them his powers, which were intended to be only temporary, were curtailed the sooner; but Steuben's good sense and ability won their esteem in the end. Although a major-general and a baron, he would seize a musket and go through a piece of drill himself; no martinet or pedant, he changed the usual order of instruction to meet the special needs of an army unused to European methods. Officers who had thought it beneath their dignity to play the part of sergeants, now gave much personal attention to the training of their commands; the men responded to these efforts, and a few months wrought a great change in the troops. It is said that when Lafayette and his corps of observation were nearly cut off at Barren Hill, the whole army was put in line to support him within fifteen minutes. At Monmouth the retreating soldiers formed under fire with a precision and coolness which was a revelation to men who were ignorant of what persistent drill can do. The value of Steuben's services was also proved by a great saving of material. Under his management the loss of muskets, which had formerly amounted to from five to eight thousand a year, was reduced to almost nothing.[2]

Other foreign officers appointed in 1777 were Brigadier-Generals De Borre and Count Pulaski; Colonel Armand, Marquis de la Rouerie; and Captains Fleury and Plessis. The generals, though brave and experienced men, were not well fitted to command American troops. De Borre quarrelled with an officer, and attempted to dismiss him without trial. He executed a

---

[1] Kapp, *Steuben*, chs. i.–iii. [2] *Ibid.* chs. v.–vii.

civilian for an offence not cognizable by martial law, although he had no authority to inflict capital punishment even on a soldier. He was accused of blundering in an expedition to Staten Island, and he is said to have disobeyed orders at the battle of Brandywine for the purpose of obtaining the post of honor on the right. In the engagement his men were the first to give way. Congress ordered an inquiry, and De Borre, declaring that it was not his fault if the American troops would not fight, tendered his resignation, which was accepted. Like Conway, he does not seem to have realized what he had done, for he soon wrote to Congress, asking to be appointed a major-general.[1]

Pulaski was at first put in command of the cavalry, but resigned because of friction with his officers. Instead of going back to Europe in disgust, however, he raised an independent corps,[2] and fell while leading them in an assault on Savannah. His gallant death secured his fame; he has been commemorated in prose and verse, and the principal fort on the Savannah River was named after him.

Armand was a French nobleman who came to America on account of a disappointment in love. An opera singer had very sensibly refused his hand on account of their difference in social position; whereupon Armand fought a duel with a supposed rival, and then took refuge from worldly sorrows, or from the anger of his family, in the silent monastery of La Trappe. But the Paris gallant soon wearied of his religious retreat and resolved to try America. Here he raised a partisan corps, and so bore himself as to gain high praise from Washington.[3]

Fleury and Plessis were both very gallant officers, and were soon promoted. Fleury distinguished himself at Brandywine, Germantown, and Monmouth; he showed remarkable bravery and skill at the defence of Fort Mifflin; at the storming of

---

[1] Washington to De Borre, August 3, 1777, Washington, *Writings* (Sparks), v. 12–13, 60, note; Muhlenberg, *Muhlenberg*, 340, note 30; *Journals of Congress*, iii. 391, 406, September 13, October 4, 1777.

[2] Washington to President of Congress, March 14, 1778, Washington, *Writings* (Ford), vi. 422–425.

[3] Wharton, *Diplomatic Correspondence*, i. 399–400.

Stony Point he was the first to mount the wall, and he captured the English flag. He was twice wounded, had a horse killed under him at Brandywine and another at Germantown. For his conduct at Fort Mifflin he received the thanks of Congress, and for his gallantry at Stony Point was rewarded with a medal attached to a piece of the flag he had taken.[1] Plessis won special notice by his conduct at Germantown, Red Bank, and Monmouth, and was recommended to Congress by Washington for possessing "a degree of modesty not always found in men who have performed brilliant actions."[2]

In February, 1778, Gates, who was now at the head of the Board of War, wrote to Congress asking their intentions concerning the employment of foreigners.

"It has," he said, "long since been found that the French officers in general, though possessed of all the requisites of military talents, are of much less utility in the American armies than was once supposed and could be wished . . . because they, for the most part, are unacquainted with our language, and because the number of our own officers is all too great for the men they have to command.

"These officers seem to have been appointed for some time past merely from habit or some latent political principle with which the Board are unacquainted, and, therefore, they will not give a refusal until they know what rules have been established for the receiving or the rejecting of foreign officers.

"If no such rule has been fixed, the Board beg leave to suggest the propriety of doing it, as, at present, they can see no way to employ these officers. There must be something very peculiar in the case of a foreign officer to induce the Board to recommend his appointment, and, therefore, if agreeable to Congress, they will report each man's credentials specially and let Congress judge whether they will appoint him. But if some general plan was established, agreeably to which alone, foreigners should be received into the American service, much trouble could be saved, both to Congress and the subordinate department, less complaint would arise from individuals, and,

---

[1] Balch, *The French in America*, ii. 125-128.
[2] Heitman, *Historical Register*, 330-331.

as our measures in this particular would not seem to flow from fluctuating opinion, our ranks would be held in higher estimation, and our national dignity in the eyes of foreigners would be much less called into question." [1]

As the Board had several applications before them, Gates begged for an answer as soon as possible; Congress at once directed that foreigners of special merit, or of rank and eminence in their own country, should be reported, and that others be dismissed by the Board with thanks.[2] This resolution tended to check the further influx of foreigners, but it did not affect those already in the army; and in July Washington wrote to the president of Congress that the frequent promotion of foreigners had given great offence. He said that there were many deserving officers who willingly acquiesced in such appointments when made on account of military merit or public policy, but that these same officers were deeply hurt by the favor shown to men who had neither ability nor influence. "The truth is," said Washington, "we have been very unhappy in a variety of appointments, and our own officers much injured. Their feelings, from this cause, have become extremely sensitive, and the most delicate touch gives them pain."

One of the most serious difficulties arose from the desire of Inspector-General Steuben to obtain a command in the line. During an absence of many generals at the court-martial of General Lee, Steuben had been selected to conduct one wing of the army on a march. The order assigning him to that duty expressly stated that the command was only temporary; but, although the appointment was, in Washington's opinion, of "evident necessity," it caused much uneasiness and complaint among the brigadiers. To make matters worse, Steuben was unwilling to give up his position, and insisted on obtaining a regular command. Thereupon Washington wrote to Congress, speaking of Steuben himself in high terms, but declaring that the appointment he desired would cause such dissatisfaction in the army that it would be better to allow him to leave

---

[1] Gates to President of Congress, February 10, 1778, *Board of War Papers*, i. 573.

[2] *Journals of Congress*, iv. 91, February 12, 1778.

the service than to give him a command.¹ In a confidential letter to Gouverneur Morris, Washington went so far as to say, "In a word, although I think the baron an excellent officer, I do most devoutly wish, that we had not a single foreigner among us, except the Marquis de Lafayette, who acts upon very different principles from those which govern the rest."²

Washington was hardly just to Steuben, and he might be considered more than just to Lafayette. The work which Steuben did as inspector-general was of great importance; and Lafayette, as well as other foreign officers, was by no means inclined to hide his light under a bushel. Great credit is due to Lafayette; but it should be remembered that he was the richest man in the army, and that probably his yearly income was greater than the whole property of most of his brother officers. He was, therefore, free from the anxieties concerning money which preyed upon so many of his companions.

Nor did he, like other foreigners, have to beg for employment and opportunities for distinction; to him they were readily and generously granted. A mere boy, not twenty years old, who had never seen a shot fired in anger, he was given the rank of major-general, and a few months later he was placed at the head of a division. This success was due in part to his own merits, but in part also to the fact that it was not wise to disoblige a nobleman of his position and connections. He was twice assigned to independent commands; his services were repeatedly and warmly acknowledged; and when, through no fault of his own, he missed opportunities of distinguishing himself, Congress soothed his feelings by passing complimentary resolutions.³

No American should wish to cavil at Lafayette. Personally he was brave almost to rashness, while, as a general, his quickness of thought and action, and his prudent daring did him great honor. He was a generous and loyal friend of our

---

[1] Washington to Laurens, President of Congress, July 24 and 26, 1778, Washington, *Writings* (Ford), vii. 121-123, 124-125.
[2] July 24, 1778, *Ibid.* 118.
[3] *Secret Journals of Congress*, i. 61, March 2, 1778; *Journals of Congress*, iv. 527, September 9, 1778.

country and of liberty. His motives were purer, his services perhaps greater, than those of Steuben; but it is justice to Steuben to remember that, although he grumbled, yet he met with hardship and disappointment, and that Lafayette obtained what he sought easily and in full measure. Steuben was finally persuaded to consent to resume his inspectorship, and later was given a command in Virginia.

In 1781 another difficulty arose, not unlike that caused by the claims of Steuben for a command in the line. A detachment from the troops at West Point had been sent to the South under Lafayette; and two French officers, Major Galvan and Lieutenant-Colonel Gimat had been given commands in it. Seven field-officers of Massachusetts regiments, from which a part of the detachment had been drawn, presented a formal complaint, stating that they were deeply hurt at being left in idleness while their own men were sent to the field. General Heath forwarded their memorial to Washington, with a hint that he felt injured by the favor shown to Lafayette. "As the affair is laid open," he said, "I cannot smother my own feelings, which have been exceedingly wounded under some considerations on this occasion. I never will admit an idea to enter my breast, that it is possible for any officer, especially a foreigner, to have the interest or honor of my country more at heart than I have; and if the conduct of my general in any instance should discover, that he placed less confidence in me, it cannot fail to make a painful impression." [1]

Washington replied in a very interesting letter, which well illustrates his wish to be just, his high sense of the prerogatives of his office, and his willingness to sacrifice individuals for the good of the cause. He explained that the few Massachusetts field-officers who were with the regiments were needed to discipline new recruits, who were expected to arrive in camp at any moment.

"These, and these only," he said, "were the reasons, why no more than one field-officer was taken from the line of Massachusetts, and not, as I have said before, from a want of

---

[1] Heath to Washington, March 2, 1781, Washington, *Writings* (Sparks) vii. 455–456, note.

confidence in them, or because I preferred those that did go. This much justice has dictated and I insert, to remove the idea which these gentlemen seem to have imbibed of an intended slight, but they must excuse me for adding, that I conceive it to be a right inherent in command to appoint particular officers for special purposes.

"That part of your letter, which seems to respect yourself personally, needs explanation; for I never can suppose that you deem it a slight, not to have been taken from the command of the most important post in America [West Point] with four thousand men, to head a detachment from that post of only eight hundred.[1] If this is not your allusion, I am ignorant of your meaning; but I shall take this occasion to observe once for all, that I am not conscious of exercising a partiality in favor of one line, one corps, or one man, more than another; that where appearances have been otherwise, in the eyes of those who were unacquainted with all the circumstances, I could easily have explained them; and that I never did and never will hurt intentionally the feelings of any deserving officer, unless I can be justified upon general principles, and good is to result from it. But, if officers will not see into the political motives by which I am sometimes governed in my appointments, and which the good of the common cause renders indispensably necessary, it is unfortunate; but it cannot, because it ought not, divert me from the practice of a duty, which I think promotive of the interest of the United States, and consistent with the views of that power under which I act.

"I have been thus particular, because it is my wish to convince every officer, over whom I have the honor to be placed, of the sincerity of my disposition to make him as happy, as the times and our circumstances will admit, and as can be done consistently with the observance of that steady line of conduct I ever have pursued."[2]

Yet, in spite of the firm stand taken in his letter, Washington

---

[1] This is hardly fair. There were greater opportunities of distinction in Virginia than at West Point.

[2] Washington to Heath, March 21, 1781, Washington, *Writings* (Sparks), vii. 454–455.

was so troubled by the discontent of the officers that he was only prevented from recalling and reorganizing the detachment by the need of its immediate presence in Virginia; and he wrote to Lafayette that, if dissatisfaction again appeared, he should recall Gimat and Galvan.[1]

In their relations with foreign officers Congress made many blunders, and were guilty of reprehensible vacillation and carelessness. They gave high rank to worthless adventurers, thereby incurring unnecessary expense and disgusting the American officers. It must be remembered, however, that they were anxious to oblige influential persons at the French court, and that they lacked the means of judging of the merits of applicants. In spite of these disadvantages, they obtained some good men, who proved brave and enterprising field-officers, such as Armand, Fleury, and Plessis; valuable engineers, like Kosciusko and Duportail; and a courageous and experienced general, Kalb. More important than all, and outweighing the mischief of all the unlucky foreign appointments, Congress accepted the services of Steuben and of Lafayette, one of whom trained the army, and the other cemented the French alliance.

[1] April 6, 1781, Washington, *Writings* (Sparks), vii. 469-471.

CHAPTER V.

PAY AND HALF-PAY.

THE favor shown to foreigners caused much discontent at camp, but the question which most disturbed Congress and the people was that of a special provision for officers and soldiers in addition to their pay. By a resolve of July 29, 1775, Congress allowed the privates six and two-thirds dollars a month, but almost immediately a cry went up for a bounty. Congress were amazed, for they considered the present pay "greater than ever soldiers had."[1] Certainly it was more than that given abroad; but the soldiers of New England were not, as in Europe, the wanderers of the city streets, or peasants scarcely able, perhaps, to eke out a bare subsistence. They were frequently landowners or the sons of landowners, who lived in a sort of rude comfort, and put by something at the end of the year. Such men considered bad bread, bad beef, and six and two-thirds dollars a month a poor recompense for the dangers and hardships of the camp.

On the other hand, Congress, alarmed by the expenses of the war, would gladly have reduced the pay. New England, moreover, was unpopular, because, in Washington's words, "none but their people have the least chance of getting into office [in the army]."[2] To members from the Middle and Southern States it seemed as if New England regarded the support of the army as a common burden, but its officering as a local privilege. Under these circumstances the "Southern bashaws," as John Adams called them, could not see why they and their con-

---

[1] Washington to Governor Cooke, December 5, 1775, Washington, *Writings* (Ford), iii. 266.
[2] Washington to Richard Henry Lee, August 29, 1775, *Ibid.* 97.

stituents should be subjected to further burdens for the benefit of the pampered privates of New England. Indeed, the demand for a bounty created such indignation that Adams wrote to a friend that he should shudder at the thought of proposing one.[1] Washington became convinced of the wisdom of offering extraordinary inducements for a war enlistment, but Congress was very reluctant to consent.[2]

At last, in June, 1776, Congress promised a bounty of ten dollars for a three years' enlistment,[3] but it was too late: the first fervor of patriotism had passed; the prices of necessaries had greatly increased; and a man could get twenty to thirty dollars by enrolling himself for a few months in the militia.[4] Washington told Congress that at the beginning of the contest men would have enlisted for the war without a bounty; that somewhat later they would have done so for twenty dollars, but that now they must be offered a good money bounty, one hundred to one hundred and fifty acres of land, a suit of clothes, and a blanket.[5] Knox wrote to Adams that it would be as easy to create an army as to raise one by offering so small a bounty as ten dollars.[6]

Adams, however, scarcely knew whether he wanted any considerable permanent army or not. He said that he was less eager to give a bounty to raise one, because, although the cost of the war and the risk of losing some battles might be greater without it, the militia would be improved, and there would be less danger from the corruption and violence of a standing army.[7] Washington, however, worked steadily to induce Congress to make a better offer. Reliance on the militia would, he felt, prove the ruin of the army. Their waste was enormous; and they were reluctant to submit to discipline, thus producing

---

[1] Adams to Hawley, November 25, 1775, John Adams, *Works*, ix. 367.

[2] Washington to Reed, February 1, 1776, Washington, *Writings* (Ford), iii. 400.

[3] *Journals of Congress*, ii. 233, June 26, 1776.

[4] The term of service for militia was usually from two to six months.

[5] Washington to President of Congress, September 24, 1776, Washington, *Writings* (Ford), iv. 441–442.

[6] August 21, 1776, *Knox MSS.* iii. 23.

[7] Adams to Parsons, August 19, 1776, John Adams, *Works*, ix. 431–432.

jealousy and insubordination in the regular troops. Unaccustomed to the hardships of camp life, many became sick and others deserted; after the defeat at Long Island they went home almost by companies and regiments. The frequent calls for the services of the militia made them tardy in responding; in the retreat through New York and New Jersey, Washington was obliged to abandon defensible positions because he could not get a sufficient number of men to guard the numerous fords. When the army was composed chiefly of militia it was necessary to discharge the troops just as they were beginning to understand their duties, for it was almost impossible to induce them to remain after their term of service had expired. Short enlistments made it necessary to recruit an army in the face of the enemy, and seriously interfered with military operations. Washington's army was dangerously reduced by the necessity of reënlistments at the close of 1775; and General Montgomery was hurried to his fatal assault on Quebec by the knowledge that some of his men were resolved to leave him on the first of January.[1]

In September, 1776, Congress yielded to the force of circumstances, and voted to give men enlisting for the war a larger bounty. All were to receive land in proportion to their rank: generals and colonels were allowed five hundred acres; lieutenant-colonels, four hundred and fifty; majors, four hundred; captains, three hundred; lieutenants, two hundred; ensigns, one hundred and fifty. Non-commissioned officers and soldiers were promised one hundred acres, and twenty dollars in money payable on enlisting; after considerable debate, Congress added to the latter offer a suit of clothes every year, or twenty dollars if a soldier furnished it himself. The "suit" included "two pair of overalls, a leathern or woollen waistcoat with sleeves, one pair of breeches, a hat or leathern cap, two shirts, two pair of hose, and two pair of shoes."[2]

---

[1] Washington to Governor Cooke, December 5, 1775, and to President of Congress, February 9, September 2, 24, and December 5, 1776, Washington, *Writings* (Ford), iii. 264–266, 406–411; iv. 378–381, 443–446; v. 66–69.

[2] *Journals of Congress*, ii. 357–358, 361, 404, September 16 and 18, and October 8, 1776; Washington to Trumbull, November 10, 1776, Washington, *Writings* (Ford), v. 19.

The grants of land alarmed the Maryland legislature. They feared that Congress would recognize the claims of Virginia and other States to the "back country" west of the mountains, and that Maryland would be taxed to help buy bounty land from her overgrown neighbors. Accordingly, the legislature voted to buy off the claims of the Maryland privates by a payment of ten dollars to each man. Congress thereupon declared that the soldiers of other States might refuse to reënlist unless the Continent made a similar offer, a measure which would make the bounty excessive. Congress asserted that a single State could not, by satisfying the claims of its own citizens, release itself from the joint obligation to provide for the Continental troops; and they requested Maryland to reconsider. The legislature so far yielded as to direct their agents at camp to say nothing about the ten dollars, but forbade them to mention the land. The right of Congress to bind the States was neither admitted nor denied. On this point the Maryland convention resolved that they had "a strong disinclination to go into any discussion of the powers with which the Congress is invested, being fully sensible that the general interest will not be promoted by either the Congress affirming, or this convention denying, the existence of a fulness of power in that honorable body; the best and only proper exercise of which can be in adopting the wisest measures for equally securing the rights and liberties of each of the United States, which was the principle of their union."[1]

This theory, that the obligation of obedience was moral rather than legal, is worthy of careful consideration by students of our constitutional history. There is very strong reason to believe that the States, having united to win their freedom, allowed Congress a temporary and indefinite authority for the purposes of the war, and left their permanent relations to be determined by future agreement.

Not only was the amount of the soldiers' wages unsatisfactory, but the sum allowed was paid irregularly, and in paper instead of specie. The neglect to pay the troops could not, in the early part of the war, be excused by the difficulty of collect-

[1] Scharf, *Maryland*, ii. 273-277.

ing taxes. At that time Congress relied entirely upon the printing-press for procuring revenue; when they wanted money, they had only to order it struck off; but the officers whose duty it was to sign the Continental bills were either too few or too lazy.[1] This particular fault was soon remedied, but the scarcity continued.

The frightful depreciation of the money made it, when it did come, of little use. The soldiers, however, were slow to understand the true cause of its fall in value. They saw that it took a great deal of money to buy anything; but, accustomed to handle only Continental bills, they did not appreciate the difference in purchasing power between paper and specie. Therefore, when, in 1778, some members of Congress proposed to give half the twenty-dollar bounty in coin, Washington earnestly remonstrated. He feared, he said, that after such an object-lesson the soldiers would insist on specie payments, and Congress deferred to his opinion.[2]

Another source of dissatisfaction was a difference in the monthly wages of the troops. For some time the privates from the Middle States received less than those from New England; but it was impossible to maintain such a distinction, for, however anxious a State might be to keep down the soldiers' pay, she would hardly permit her own citizens to fare worse than their neighbors. Moreover, the inequality made it more difficult for her to raise her quota, since men enlisted in the lines of other States where they could obtain larger pay. On June 7, 1776, the New York convention wrote to Congress as follows: —

"Persuaded that the pay allowed the Eastern army during the last campaign was unreasonably high, this convention received great satisfaction from the measures taken by the Congress (as they supposed) with a view to reduce it. The inferior allowance of pay given to the troops raised in this colony . . . was considered as a precedent which would soon become general, and it was expected that the patriotism and laudable pride

---

[1] Washington to Richard Henry Lee, November 27, 1775, Washington, *Writings* (Ford), iii. 238; Orderly Book, December 29, 1775, *Ibid.* 305, note.

[2] Washington to Gouverneur Morris, September 5, and to Richard Henry Lee, September 23, 1778, Washington, *Writings* (Ford), vii. 179-181, notes.

of the other colonies would not long permit them to accept higher wages than their neighbors for fighting in the same glorious cause and for the attainment of the same great and valuable object.

"This convention are most sensibly affected by the continuance of that discrimination; and though ready to consent to a still greater reduction of pay, provided it be general, yet a due regard to the honor of this colony will no longer permit them, by a silent acquiescence in so odious a discrimination, to give posterity reason to conclude that it was established on just and proper principles."[1]

Congress responded to this protest by a resolution that the pay of the soldiers of the Middle States should be the same as that of the Eastern.[2]

Washington regarded a difference in the pay of the troops with special anxiety, and he was quick to notice and to remonstrate against any distinction. For instance, in the fall of 1775 the question arose whether a "month" meant a calendar or a lunar month; the matter was left to Congress, the proper authority, and they decided in favor of the calendar month. Washington was indifferent as to the rule adopted, provided that it were uniform; but a report that Massachusetts was to pay by lunar months the militia sent to act with the Continentals caused him to send a strong remonstrance to the legislature. "It aims," he wrote, "the most fatal stab to the peace of this army that ever was given, and . . . Lord North himself could not have devised a more effectual blow to the recruiting service."[3]

About a year later, Connecticut proposed to increase the pay of her soldiers twenty shillings a month. Washington at once wrote to Governor Trumbull that he seldom interfered with the acts of any public body, but that in the present case, affecting as it did the whole continent, he must take the liberty to say

[1] Force, *American Archives*, 4th series, vi. 793.
[2] *Journals of Congress*, ii. 205, June 10, 1776.
[3] Washington to President of Congress, September 21, and to President of the Council of Massachusetts Bay, December 6, 1775, Washington, *Writings* (Ford), iii. 140-141, 265, note.

that, in his opinion and in that of all the generals he had consulted, the increase would have the worst effect upon recruiting in other States; and that, even if men could be raised without hearing of the Connecticut bounty, when the army was formed they must discover that it had been given. "When it is certain," said he, "that . . . the moment they come to act with troops, who receive a higher pay, jealousy, impatience, and mutiny will immediately take place, and occasion desertions, if not a total dissolution of the army, — it must be viewed as injurious and fatal. . . . That troops will never act together, in the same cause and for different pay, must be obvious to every one. Experience has already proved it in this army."[1]

So sensitive was Washington to any inequality of pay that he even disapproved of a gratuity of a month's extra pay, which, in December, 1777, Congress voted to the officers and privates in acknowledgment of their "patience, fidelity, and zeal." Washington said that, while it was best to exclude only those absent without leave, yet the circumstances of the soldiers were so different that the sharing of men who were more fortunately situated than their companions — as, for example, those who had had special opportunities of seeing their families — would create disgust; and that he wished the grant had not been made.[2]

The officers as well as the soldiers were discontented. There was comparatively little difference between the pay of the lower officers and that of the privates. Shortly after Congress assumed control of the army the subalterns united in a petition for an increase, and Washington forwarded it to Congress with a favorable recommendation. He said that the inadequate allowance was one source of the unbecoming familiarity between the officers and privates, and that many of the officers declared that they would leave the service at the expiration of their terms.[3] In October, 1775, Congress sent a committee to camp to obtain information on this and other subjects; delegates from

---

[1] Washington to Trumbull, November 10, 1776, Washington, *Writings* (Ford), v. 18.

[2] Washington to President of Congress, January 9, 1778, *Ibid.* vi. 284-286.

[3] Washington to President of Congress, September 21, 1775, *Ibid.* iii. 141-142.

the New England colonies came to headquarters, and a conference was held between the committee, the delegates, and the commander-in-chief. A majority voted that to raise the officers' pay would be "inconvenient and improper"; but Congress so far departed from this recommendation as to raise the pay of the company officers about one-third.[1]

This change greatly disturbed the good people of the town of Harvard, Massachusetts; and they presented a petition to the General Court begging that body to use their influence to obtain a reduction. They professed themselves ready to devote their fortunes to the cause of liberty, but said that they were grieved by anything which might disturb the unanimity on which success depended. The excessive stipends granted to officers and others, except soldiers, had already in their opinion "much chilled the spirits of the commonalty"; that the "distresses of America should prove a harvest to some, and a famine to others, this," they said, "we deprecate."[2] The petition was referred to a committee, but nothing seems to have been done to warm the chilled spirits of the commonalty.

In 1776 the officers again demanded an increase of pay, and this time the clamors were not confined to officers of the lower grades. Necessaries were high, yet an American captain received only five shillings a day; a British captain was paid twice as much, and could purchase everything he desired at moderate rates.[3] Knox wrote to Adams: "They [the officers] are not vastly riveted to the honor of starving their families for the sake of being in the army. I wish you to consult Marshal Saxe on the matter of paying the troops. I am not speaking for myself, but I am speaking in the behalf of a great number of worthy men who wish to do the country every service in their power at a less price than the ruin of themselves and families."[4]

---

[1] Force, *American Archives*, 4th series, iii. 1155-1157; Washington, *Writings* (Ford), iii. 173-174, note; *Journals of Congress*, i. 232-233, November 4, 1775.

[2] December 27, 1775, Force, *American Archives*, 4th series, iv. 1245.

[3] Washington to President of Congress, September 24, 1776, Washington, *Writings* (Ford), iv. 441.

[4] August 21, 1776, *Knox MSS.* iii. 23.

Congress consented to raise the pay of the officers, except the generals, about one-half;[1] but this increase and the grants of land did not satisfy the officers, and in about a year they put forth new claims. Great Britain gave her retired officers half-pay for life; and they thought that America might do as much. Washington, however, at first looked coldly on any such project as expensive and contrary to the spirit of the country.[2] It was also extremely unpopular in Congress. On January 13, 1778, Elbridge Gerry, who professed himself well inclined to the plan, wrote to Washington that a proposition for giving half-pay to the officers for a term of years would probably fail. He said that the principal objections to the measure were: "the infant state of the country, its aversion to placemen and pensioners, whereby Great Britain is likely to lose her liberty, the equality of the officers and soldiers of some States, before the war, and the bad effect that such provision would have on the minds of the latter."[3]

After further reflection, Washington himself became convinced that half-pay must be granted. He told a committee of Congress, then in camp, that the very existence of the army depended on making a proper provision for the officers. Self-interest, he said, was the basis of human action, and all institutions, if they were to stand, must be based on the recognition of this "presumptive truth." He admitted that the officers had enlisted from patriotic motives; but said that, when they found that their pay would not support them, and that the war would last much longer than they at first supposed, their zeal cooled. Many, he said, had resigned, and more would do so; it was therefore necessary to encourage them by the offer of half-pay for life, thus securing the future comfort of them and their families. He assured the committee that, although giving half-pay might appear to be very costly, it would really save expense; for it would increase the efficiency of the army and so shorten the war. Anything that tends to lengthen the contest, said he,

---

[1] *Journals of Congress*, ii. 402–403, October 7, 1776.

[2] Washington on Bland's paper, November, 1777, Washington, *Writings* (Ford), vi. 384–385, note.

[3] Sparks, *Correspondence of the Revolution*, ii. 67–68.

"though dictated by a well-intended frugality, will, I fear, in the end prove erroneous economy." He also said that not only policy, but justice, required that the officers should receive a special reward for the great sacrifices which they had made.[1]

Some members of Congress were fully alive to the exigencies of the situation, but the attendance was small and the opposition to the proposal strong. After a long discussion, Congress postponed the question by an almost unanimous vote.[2] On April 10 Washington wrote a letter to Congress, in which, among other important subjects, he discussed that of half-pay, saying, "I am ready to declare, that I do most religiously believe the salvation of the cause depends upon it." Commissions, he wrote, had lost their value, and nearly every day was marked by two or three resignations. Reports came that officers on furlough had no intention of returning, while those remaining with the army were often extremely negligent.[3]

The friends of half-pay moved that extracts from Washington's letter be entered on the journals; but the motion failed to pass. Encouraged by this success, its opponents then introduced a resolution declaring that "Congress, however desirous of giving every reasonable encouragement to officers of the army who bravely hazard their lives in defence of their country, and however anxious to make an honorable provision for them after the close of the war, being apprehensive of the consequence of a military establishment, especially without knowing the sense of their constituents on a subject of such high importance," — postpone the question, and desire the States seriously to consider and give their opinion on the question of making a provision for the officers, and to say whether it should be for a term of years or for life; and of doing the same for widows of officers dying in captivity or in the service; also to say whether there ought not to be some further provision or reward for privates continuing in the army until the close of the war.

[1] Washington to Committee of Congress, January 28, 1778, Washington, *Writings* (Ford), vi. 301–304.
[2] *Journals of Congress*, iv. 186, April 2, 1778.
[3] Washington to President of Congress, April 10, 1778, Washington, *Writings* (Ford), vi. 465–468.

But this attempt to postpone failed. Congress manifested a commendable desire to meet the issue fairly, and even held a Sunday session in order to hasten the decision.[1]

Laurens, the president of Congress, wrote to Governor Livingston of New Jersey: "Sir, we have, within a month past, improved many whole days, and some tedious nights, by hammering upon a plan for a half-pay establishment for officers who shall continue in the army to the end of the present war. A most momentous engagement, in which all our labor has not yet matured one single clause, nor even determined the leading questions, to be or not to be. The combatants have agreed to meet to-morrow *vis à vis*, and by the point of reason, and by some things proxies for reason, put an end to the contest. I'll be hanged [if] they do."[2]

Laurens was right in his forecast: the differences were too great to permit of an agreement. New Hampshire was absent; Connecticut, Rhode Island, New Jersey, and South Carolina were opposed to any provision; Pennsylvania changed from day to day according to the attendance of her representatives; the other States were willing to do something for the officers, but Massachusetts and New York were not ready to go so far as Delaware, Maryland, Virginia, North Carolina, and Georgia.

The opponents of half-pay fought the proposal most bitterly. President Laurens said that he was willing to make provision for all who were in need, even for "some of the brave, whose expenses have been princely in extravagance, while they complained of insufficiency of pay;" but he declared that the loss of half his estate would not have caused him the concern which the introduction of this "untoward project" into Congress had done. He told Washington that the number of resignations was due to a changeableness which was characteristic of men south of the thirty-eighth parallel of latitude, and that he wished that more officers had followed the example of the commander-in-chief and served without pay.[3]

---

[1] *Journals of Congress*, iv. 217–219, 221–222, 228–229, 239–243, April 16, 17, 21, 25, 26, 1778.

[2] April 19, 1778, Sedgwick, *Livingston*, 272.

[3] Perhaps more would have done so had they possessed as large fortunes.

Laurens indignantly denied that the officers were unanimous in desiring half-pay. "How superior are many, . . ." he said, "to the acceptance of a half-pay, contributed to by widows and orphans of soldiers who had bled and died by their sides!—shackled with a condition of being excluded from the privilege of serving in offices, in common with their fellow-citizens;[1] voted in every House of Assembly as the drones and incumbrances of society, pointed at by boys and girls,—there goes a man, who every year robs me of part of my pittance. I think, sir, I do not overstrain. This will be the language of republicans; how pungent, when applied to gentlemen who shall have stepped from the army into a good remaining estate; how much deeper to some, who, in idleness and by speculation, have amassed estates in the war!"

To Governor Livingston, Laurens said that the demand of the officers was "unjust, because inconsistent with the original compact. Officers were not compelled, but eagerly solicited commissions, knowing the terms of service; loss of estate, neglect of family, sacrifice of domestic happiness, exorbitancy of prices of every species of goods for the necessities or comforts of life, are [applicable] to every citizen in the Union, and to thousands who are not officers, with greater force and propriety."

Laurens even went so far as to threaten repudiation. "If we cannot make justice one of the pillars," he said to Washington, "necessity may be submitted to at present; but republicans will, at a proper time, withdraw a grant which will appear to have been extorted." In the same letter Laurens asserted, "I have ever detested, and never practised, parliamentary jockeyings for procrastinating an unpalatable business."[2] It is to be hoped that he did not seriously contemplate breaking faith with the officers, a much worse measure than filibustering.

The feeling against making the officers a favored class was very strong. A member from New Jersey wrote to Stirling:

---

[1] It was proposed that the holding of any State or national office should operate as a disqualification for receiving half-pay.

[2] Laurens to Livingston, April 19, 1778, Sedgwick, *Livingston*, 272-274; to Washington, May 5, 1778, Sparks, *Correspondence of the Revolution*, ii. 119-121.

"It is said many good officers are weary of the service, and wish to resign unless they are placed upon a permanent establishment; that they are weary and wish for ease, I don't wonder, but who are there engaged either in civil or military departments but are weary and wish for retirement if the service they are engaged in would admit? The service in every part is severe — the militia in some parts are half their time out, the legislatures spend much of their time and substance, Congress sit day and night taking little rest. Must we all therefore resign? This is no time to talk of ease and retirement. Let us first establish our liberties, our desires of ease will then be obtained — I do not mention this as applicable to your Lordship. I never heard of your desire to turn your back upon a service the most noble and glorious. Some, however, do it. We all engaged, I hope, upon patriotic principles — may the same, separate from every lucrative and ambitious view, carry us through this contest."[1]

To such arguments, the friends of half-pay probably replied that the officers had peculiar claims: that it was true that the people were burdened with taxes, but the property of the officers paid with the rest; that the militia had no special reason for complaint, since they served only a part of the time and received high pay; that not only were the soldiers paid more liberally than privates ever were before, but many also received State bounties; furthermore, that it was not a question of abstract justice, but of what was best for the country, and, if the army was to be properly officered, half-pay must be given.

Congress reluctantly accepted this view. They voted down a proposition for the payment of a definite sum at the close of the war, to be distributed according to rank; and also one to give half-pay estimated on the pay of 1775. They even consented to make a grant for life; but this resolve was reconsidered, and all the States agreed that present or future officers serving till the close of the war and not holding offices under the United States or any State should receive half-pay for seven years, if they lived so long. The generals were given only half the pay of a colonel; and every officer who availed himself of the provision was required to take an oath of allegiance to the United

[1] Clark to Stirling, January 15, 1778, *Sparks MSS.* xxxix. 115-116.

States and to reside in them. The non-commissioned officers and soldiers serving throughout the war were at its close to receive a bounty of eighty dollars, which was equivalent to one year's pay of a private.[1]

After so fierce a contest, it seems strange to see an almost unbroken list of ayes appended to the resolution in the journals. Only two delegates, Lovell of Massachusetts and Wolcott of Connecticut, voted in the negative. This agreement was probably due in part to a desire for harmony and in part to the fact that the measure was a compromise. The grant did not satisfy either the public or the officers. Many citizens objected to creating a privileged class; and Washington said that, although the resolution exceeded his hopes, it fell short of his desires, for the officers considered seven years too short a time.[2]

At the beginning of 1779 there was prospect of an inactive season, with ample opportunity to brood over grievances. On January 20 Washington reported the condition of affairs to a committee of Congress, and, after suggesting palliatives, urged that the half-pay be given for life; this, he said, would be much more satisfactory to the officers, and would not greatly increase the expense. For fear of the bad effect of failure, however, he advised that no attempt be made unless there were every prospect of success.[3]

In May he wrote in more alarming terms. The officers, he said, were unable to support themselves, and were either resigning or, what was worse, "spreading discontent, and possibly the seeds of sedition."[4] Congress voted half-pay for life; and then receded, and merely recommended the States to make "adequate compensation" to the officers for their many dangers, losses, and hardships, either by giving half-pay for life or in such other manner as might appear most expedient.[5]

---

[1] *Journals of Congress*, iv. 240, 242–243, 288–289, April 25 and 26, and May 15, 1778.

[2] Washington to Gouverneur Morris, May 18, 1778, Washington, *Writings* (Ford), vii. 16.

[3] Washington to Committee of Congress, January 20, 1779, *Ibid.* 328–335.

[4] Washington to Armstrong, May 18, 1779, *Ibid.* 456.

[5] *Journals of Congress*, v. 312–313, 316–317, August 11 and 17, 1779.

By 1780 a change of feeling toward the army took place in Congress. Congress, in response to a memorial of the general officers, made their half-pay proportioned to their pay and not to that of a colonel. Congress also gave half-pay for seven years to the widows, or children when there were no widows, of officers dying in service.[1] Sullivan wrote to Washington, " Jealousy of the army, which has long obstructed salutary measures, dare not appear in public."[2] Some of the States had either given half-pay for life or were expecting to do so, and they were therefore anxious that the Continent should assume their burdens.

A letter from Washington urging Congress to grant half-pay for life now met with a very favorable reception; and on October 21, 1780, it was voted to give officers who should serve throughout the war half-pay for life.[3] It was argued, indeed, that the United States were not concerned with the rewards paid by the several States, provided their troops were suitably officered; and that the grant of half-pay would cause disgust, and would diminish the exertions of the States that were opposed to it. "But no reason," wrote Clark, "could prevail upon men fixed and determined."[4] There had been one hundred and sixty resignations since January;[5] and Congress may have thought it safer to run the risk of offending the States than to permit this fearful discontent among the officers to continue.

Congress had at last made generous provision for the officers; but it remained to be seen whether the States would provide the funds necessary for the fulfilment of the promise.

---

[1] *Journals of Congress*, vi. 172–173, August 24 and 25, 1780.
[2] November 12, 1780, Sparks, *Correspondence of the Revolution*, iii. 145.
[3] Washington to President of Congress, October 11, 1780, Washington, *Writings* (Ford), viii. 481–493; *Journals of Congress*, vi. 219–220, October 21, 1780.
[4] Clark to Hornblower, October 31, 1780, *Sparks MSS*. xxxvi. 326–327.
[5] Circular letter to the States, October 18, 1780, Washington, *Writings* (Ford), viii. 507.

CHAPTER VI.

SUPPLYING THE ARMY.

IF the troops were to be kept in a state of efficiency, there was need of a well-organized system of procuring supplies. An attempt to live off the country near the camp was certain to fail unless the army moved from district to district, a course which strategic considerations must often prevent. Moreover, the people were unused to military exactions, and a system of foraging would alienate them from the American cause. Accordingly, when Congress took control of the army, they provided for a quartermaster-general to superintend transportation and a commissary-general to purchase provisions.[1] Later a clothier-general was added. In the British army, though the soldiers purchased their own clothing, the government furnished many of the articles and deducted the price from the soldiers' wages. Some such arrangement quickly became necessary in the American army. In the fall of 1775 Congress ordered a committee to purchase a large quantity of clothing, and directed the quartermasters to resell it to the soldiers at prime cost and charges, plus a five per cent commission to themselves for their trouble.[2]

In 1776 Congress promised to give each man enlisted for the war, a suit of clothes every year.[3] The States also endeavored to purchase clothing for their troops, but they often found great difficulty in obtaining it. Assistant-Inspector Fleury, who was sent to drill Smallwood's Marylanders, informed Steuben: "Most of the recruits are unprovided with shirts, and

[1] *Journals of Congress*, i. 121, June 16, 1775.
[2] *Ibid.* i. 205, September 23, 1775.   [3] *Ibid.* ii. 404, October 8, 1776.

the only garment they possess is a blanket elegantly twined about them. You may judge, sir, how much this apparel graces their appearance on parade."[1] On the other hand, Connecticut held her towns responsible for the equipment of their quotas;[2] and at Valley Forge, when at least two thousand soldiers were unfit for duty because of lack of clothing, there was not a single Connecticut man disabled on this account. Washington wrote to Governor Trumbull: "Among the troops returned unfit for duty for want of clothing, none of your State are included. The care of your legislature in providing clothing and necessaries of all kinds for their men is highly laudable, and reflects the greatest honor upon their patriotism and humanity."[3]

Congress early took measures to supply deficiencies, but nevertheless there was considerable difficulty in obtaining clothing. America was not a manufacturing country, and prices rose enormously. Congress thereupon recommended the States to purchase clothing at prices fixed by their own authority. Congress also resolved that: "Whereas certain persons, devoid of and in repugnance to every principle of public virtue and humanity, instigated by the lust of avarice, are, in each State, assiduously endeavoring, by every means of oppression, sharping and extortion, to accumulate enormous gain to themselves, to the great distress of private families in general and especially of the poorer and more dependent part of the community, as well as to the great injury of the public service: . . . it is most seriously recommended to the several legislatures aforesaid, forthwith to enact laws, limiting the number of retailers of goods, wares and merchandise in their several counties, towns and districts, and obliging them to take license and enter into bonds for the observance of all laws made for their regulation."[4]

Congress tried importing on their own account, but found that this method involved much delay and danger. They had to bring the goods over three thousand miles of ocean, and run the

---

[1] May 13, 1778, Scharf, *Maryland*, ii. 345, note 2.
[2] Stuart, *Trumbull*, 369.
[3] March 31, 1778, Washington, *Writings* (Ford), vi. 457.
[4] *Journals of Congress*, iii. 587, December 20, 1777.

risk of capture by English cruisers. Nor did the difficulties of
transportation cease when at last the supplies were landed in the
United States. They might be brought to Portsmouth when the
army was on the Delaware, and, as the presence of the British
fleet rendered long coasting voyages dangerous, wagons must be
procured to drag the goods slowly along for hundreds of miles.
Congress was embarrassed by the competition of the States,
which not only hastened to buy up private cargoes, but even
managed to get hold of those belonging to the Continent; and
Congress were at length obliged to direct their agents to give
out no clothing to State officers without a special order from
the department of the clothier-general.[1]

During the first year of the Revolution the troops were reasonably well fed. The war began in eastern Massachusetts, a
thickly settled, agricultural district inhabited by zealous Whigs,
who were willing to supply the army, although they were likely
to charge good prices for doing so. There were, however, many
complaints in regard to the quality of the rations. The bread
was said to be sour and unwholesome; and in 1775, as in 1898,
considerable dissatisfaction was expressed with army beef. General Greene convened a court of inquiry made up of butchers,
who found that much of the "beef" examined by them was horse-flesh.[2] Furthermore, it was difficult to cook the food properly.
Congress generously furnished kettles, but there was little fuel;
Washington wrote that regiments were ready to cut each other's
throats for the possession of a few trees, and that, unless fuel
were furnished, even houses would be attacked.[3]

In the spring of 1777 Congress reorganized the system of
supplying the army. They created the office of "superintendent
of bakers and director of baking in the main army," and appointed
Christopher Ludwig of Philadelphia to the post. They proposed
that Ludwig furnish a hundred pounds of bread for every hundred and thirty-five pounds of flour delivered to him. Ludwig
replied that he had money enough, and did not wish to get rich;

[1] *Journals of Congress*, iii. 239-240, June 17, 1777.
[2] Greene to Cooke, July 14, 1775, Greene, *Greene*, i. 97-98.
[3] Washington to General Court of Massachusetts, November 2, 1775, Washington, *Writings* (Ford), iii. 195-196.

for every hundred pounds of flour he would furnish a hundred pounds of bread. Ludwig was not only an unselfish and patriotic man, but a skilful baker, and there was no more bad bread after he took office.[1]

The commissary department was also remodelled. Under the new arrangement there was a commissary of purchases with four deputies, and a commissary of issues with three; each deputy commissary of purchases was allowed to appoint such assistants as he might need, and to each deputy and assistant was assigned a particular district, beyond which he was not to act without special order. The purchasers had often, from lack of integrity or skill, bid against each other; under the new arrangement every purchaser was sworn to buy at the lowest price that he honestly could.[2] Unfortunately Congress, who were always anxious to retain power in their own hands, appointed the deputy commissaries themselves; and it was therefore impossible for the head of the department to exercise an efficient control. Commissary-General Trumbull, who had shown himself a valuable officer, resigned;[3] and his successor, William Buchanan, either from incapacity or from lack of power over his subordinates, proved unequal to his duties.[4]

For a while the army was reasonably well supplied with bread and meat; but Washington wrote to Congress on July 19, 1777, that, during the greater part of the last campaign and during all the present, the soldiers had scarcely tasted vegetables, that they were very inadequately supplied with beer, cider, and rum, and that the allowance of soap was much too small.[5] Congress did their best to remedy these defects. They directed the Board of War to make contracts for soap, vegetables, spirits, etc., and authorized Washington to increase the allowance of soap at his discretion. On September 12 they ordered that thirty hogsheads

---

[1] *Journals of Congress*, iii. 167, May 3, 1777; Scharf and Westcott, *Philadelphia*, i. 335, note.

[2] *Journals of Congress*, iii. 138, 221–229, April 14 and June 10, 1777.

[3] Stuart, *Trumbull*, 423–424.

[4] Scammell to Pickering, February 7, and Pickering to Scammell, February 17, 1778, Pickering, *Pickering*, i. 204, 206.

[5] Washington to President of Congress, July 19, 1777, Washington, *Writings* (Ford), v. 495–496.

of rum be distributed among the soldiers in compliment for their gallant behavior at the battle of Brandywine.¹

Notwithstanding all the efforts of Congress, however, the condition of the army grew worse instead of better. The country in the vicinity of the camp was exhausted, the enemy were close at hand, and, either from disaffection or from the hope of better prices from the British, the farmers refused to thresh and the millers to grind. Congress, on April 19, and again on September 17, 1777, had directed Washington to remove, from the districts threatened with invasion, provisions and other articles which might be useful to the enemy;² but Washington refrained from using to the full extent the power given him. On December 10, 1777, Congress passed a resolution declaring that they had observed with deep concern that at great expense the army had been irregularly and insufficiently supplied from a distance, though there were large quantities of provisions and cattle in the country near by, which might soon fall into the hands of the enemy. The resolution went on to say that "Congress, firmly persuaded of General Washington's zeal and attachment to the interest of these States, can only impute his forbearance in exercising the powers vested in him . . . to a delicacy in exerting military authority on the citizens of these States — a delicacy which, though highly laudable in general, may on critical exigencies prove destructive to the army and prejudicial to the general liberties of America." Washington was informed that Congress expected him to draw subsistence for his troops from the exposed districts; he was explicitly ordered to require the farmers within seventy miles of the camp to thresh their wheat on penalty of its being seized and paid for as straw; and in general to carry off or destroy everything in the route of the enemy which might be useful to them and was not absolutely necessary to the owners.³

Washington replied that he had drawn much more from the country near Philadelphia (which was then held by the British) than Congress supposed, and that no exertions should be want-

¹ *Journals of Congress*, iii. 295, 390, July 25 and September 12, 1777.
² *Ibid.* iii. 148, 399, April 19 and September 17, 1777.
³ *Ibid.* 567–569, December 10, 1777.

ing to furnish his own troops with supplies and to prevent the enemy from obtaining them. He admitted that an "ill-placed humanity" might have restrained him unduly; but this, he said, was not the only reason for his forbearance. "I have been well aware," he wrote, "of the prevalent jealousy of military power, and that this has been considered as an evil, much to be apprehended, even by the best and most sensible among us. Under this idea, I have been cautious, and wished to avoid as much as possible any act that might increase it. . . . The people at large are governed much by custom. To acts of legislation or civil authority they have ever been taught to yield a willing obedience, without reasoning about their propriety; on those of military power, whether immediate or derived originally from another source, they have ever looked with a jealous and suspicious eye."[1]

Washington did not mistake the feelings of the people. When, a little later, absolute necessity compelled him to make some small seizures of clothes and provisions, he reported that his action "excited the greatest alarm and uneasiness even among our best and warmest friends."[2] This strange readiness of the civil power to go beyond the military in desire for exaction at the point of the bayonet, may be explained partly by Washington's own caution and moderation, and partly by the impatience of Congress, who, irritated by Howe's successes, were ready to mistake violence for strength. It must be remembered, too, that this was the period of the Conway Cabal.

Congress appointed December 18, 1777, as a day of thanksgiving, "particularly in that He hath been pleased in so great a measure to prosper the means used for the support of our troops and to crown our arms with most signal success."[3] When this resolution was passed, the condition of the army may have been moderately comfortable; but if, on December 18, the poor soldiers reckoned the success in supplying them a special cause for gratitude, they must have shared the pious meekness of

---

[1] Washington to President of Congress, December 15, 1777, Washington, *Writings* (Ford), vi. 248–249.

[2] January 5, 1778, *Ibid.* 281.

[3] *Journals of Congress*, iii. 468, November 1, 1777.

the Pilgrim Brewster, who is said to have thanked the Lord, over water and clams, for giving "the fulness of the sea and the treasures hid in the sands." There was a lack of spiritual nourishment as well as of material. Lieutenant Wild wrote in his journal, "We had no chaplain in our brigade, and we had but a poor Thanksgiving, — nothing but fresh beef and flour to eat, without any salt, and but very scant of that."[1] But for General Sullivan, Major Dearborn would not have fared much better than Wild. Dearborn wrote: "This is Thanksgiving Day through the whole continent of America, but God knows we have very little to keep it with this being the third day we have been without flour or bread — and are living on a high uncultivated hill, in huts and tents. Laying on the cold ground, upon the whole I think all we have to be thankful for is that we are alive and not in the grave with many of our friends — we had for Thanksgiving breakfast some exceeding poor beef which has been boiled and now warmed in an old short-handled frying-pan in which we were obliged to eat it having no other platter — I dined and supped at General Sullivan's today and so ended Thanksgiving."[2]

On the following day, December 19, 1777, the army marched to Valley Forge, where it went into winter quarters. The sufferings of the troops during this winter were more severe than at any other period of the war, with the possible exception of the winter of 1779-1780. Three times the soldiers were left without provisions, and once for six days they had no meat.[3] It was suggested that the English race was unduly addicted to meat, and there was talk of possible substitutes. Pickering proposed soup thickened with bread; Greene, a mixture of wheat and sugar.[4]

The army suffered the extremes of cold as well as of hunger.

[1] December 18, 1777, Massachusetts Historical Society, *Proceedings*, 1890-1891, p. 105.
[2] December 18, 1777, Henry Dearborn, *Journals*, 13.
[3] Washington to Cadwallader, March 20, 1778, Washington, *Writings* (Ford), vi. 436.
[4] Pickering to Scammell, February 17, 1778, Pickering, *Pickering*, i. 205; Greene to Washington, February 15, 1778, Greene, *Greene*, i. 554.

Washington wrote to Congress that men were obliged to sit by fires all night on account of the lack of blankets. "The soap, vinegar, and other articles allowed by Congress," he said, "we see none of, nor have we seen them, I believe, since the battle of Brandywine. The first, indeed, we have now little occasion for; few men having more than one shirt, many only the moiety of one, and some none at all."[1] Lafayette says in his memoirs, "The unfortunate soldiers were in want of everything; they had neither coats, nor hats, nor shirts, nor shoes; their feet and legs froze till they grew black, and it was often necessary to amputate them."[2] The men slept on the frozen ground; and a committee of Congress early in 1778 reported that sick soldiers had died in their huts for lack of straw on which to lie. Straw could have been obtained in the neighborhood, but there were no wagons to fetch it. "Almost every species of camp transportation," said the committee, "is now performed by men who, without a murmur, patiently yoke themselves to little carriages of their own making, or load their wood and provisions on their backs."[3]

On December 23 there were 2898 men unfit for duty on account of lack of shoes and clothing; on February 5 the number had risen to 3989, an increase of more than a thousand in less than two months.[4] Washington wrote in disgust: "Perhaps by mid-summer, he [the soldier] may receive thick stockings, shoes, and blankets, which he will contrive to get rid of in the most expeditious manner. In this way, by an eternal round of the most stupid management, the public treasure is expended to no kind of purpose, while the men have been left to perish by inches with cold and nakedness!"[5]

The officers suffered less than the soldiers, but they too were

---

[1] Washington to President of Congress, December 23, 1777, Washington, *Writings* (Ford), vi. 260.

[2] Lafayette, *Mémoires*, i. 36, quoted in Tower, *La Fayette in the American Revolution*, i. 255.

[3] Committee to President of Congress, February 12, 1778, Reed, *Reed*, i. 362.

[4] Washington to Executives of the Eastern States, December 29, 1777, Washington, *Writings* (Ford), vii. 267; Marshall, *Washington*, iii. 375.

[5] Tomes, *Battles of America*, ii. 87.

very ill supplied. On December 21 and 22 Surgeon Waldo wrote in his diary: "What have you for our dinners, boys? 'Nothing but fire cake and water, sir.' At night — 'Gentlemen, the supper is ready.' What is your supper, lads? 'Fire cake and water, sir.' . . . What have you got for breakfast, lads? 'Fire cake and water, sir.' The Lord send that our commissary of purchases may live on fire cake and water. . . . I am ashamed to say it, but I am tempted to steal fowls if I could find them — or even a whole hog — for I feel as if I could eat one." Then, recalling his philosophy, "But why do I talk of hunger and hard usage, when so many in the world have not even fire cake and water to eat?"[1]

Baron Steuben's aides gave an officers' supper, to which no one who possessed a whole suit was admitted; and there was no difficulty in obtaining guests. The baron himself said, "I saw officers, at a grand parade at Valley Forge, mounting guard in a sort of dressing-gown, made of an old blanket or woollen bed-cover."[2]

The family of a private often received assistance from the town, but no relief was given to that of an officer. Coming to his hut from work in cold and snow, he might find a letter from his wife saying that she did not see how she and her children could live through the winter, and begging him to consider "that charity begins at home, and not suffer his family to perish with want, in the midst of plenty."[3] Naturally, the feelings of the officers were very much embittered. Brooks of Massachusetts blamed the commissary, and "the cursed Quakers and other inhabitants," but congratulated himself that supplies were coming from New England.[4] The Virginians, and in fact the whole army, were loud in blame of Congress. Major Clark wrote in his diary that even colonels "spoke of them with the greatest contempt and detestation; indeed every body of men who were intrusted with supplies for the army shared largely in the profusion of curses and ill will of the camp." And Clark,

---

[1] *Historical Magazine*, v. 132–133.   [2] Kapp, *Steuben*, i. 118–120.
[3] December 28, 1777, Waldo, "Diary," in *Historical Magazine*, v. 169.
[4] Letter of Brooks, January 5, 1778, Massachusetts Historical Society, *Proceedings*, 1873–1875, p. 244.

who was well disposed toward Congress and ready to make excuses for them, added, "I plainly saw that those whom the cry of Liberty had called into the field, could now (when the same cause ceased to be a novelty) be held in it by no other tie than that of interest." [1]

This is certainly a severe judgment. Men might be true patriots, and yet be thoroughly indignant at a state of affairs which forced the army to encounter "every species of hardship, that cold, wet, and hunger, and want of clothes, were capable of producing." [2] But some officers did worse than grumble; they shirked their duties, took up quarters in houses at a distance from the camp, or went on furlough. Such conduct was but too common in the American army. Steuben says: "The captains and colonels did not consider their companies and regiments as corps confided to them by the United States for the care of the men as well as the preservation of order and discipline. . . . The idea they had of their duty was, that the officers had only to mount guard and put themselves at the head of their regiment or company when they were going into action." [3]

The privates on the whole behaved admirably. "See the poor soldier," says Surgeon Waldo in his diary, "when in health — with what cheerfulness he meets his foes and encounters every hardship — if barefoot — he labors through the mud and cold with a song in his mouth extolling War and Washington — if his food be bad — he eats it notwithstanding with seeming content — blesses God for a good stomach — and whistles it into digestion." [4] Sickness, indeed, affected their spirits. Waldo thus describes the sick soldier: "He comes, and cries with an air of wretchedness and despair — 'I am sick — my feet lame — my legs are sore — my body covered with this tormenting itch — my clothes are worn out — my constitution is broken — my former activity is exhausted by fatigue — hunger and cold — I fail

---

[1] January, 1778, Joseph Clark, "Diary," in New Jersey Historical Society, *Proceedings*, 1st series, vii. 104.
[2] Washington to Cadwallader, March 20, 1778, Washington, *Writings* (Ford), vi. 435.
[3] Kapp, *Steuben*, i. 118–119.
[4] December 14, 1777, *Historical Magazine*, v. 131.

fast, I shall soon be no more! and all the reward I shall get will be — "Poor Will is dead."'"[1]

As was to be expected considering the extreme sufferings to which the men were exposed, desertions were more numerous than ever before; and the soldiers who remained, sometimes forgot military subordination and discipline. Once they made the camp ring with cries of "No meat! No meat!" and with callings and hootings like those of crows and owls.[2] At other times they would pop their heads out of their huts and call "No bread, no soldier!"[3] On two or three occasions there was almost a mutiny. Early in 1778 the lack of provisions produced an outbreak which the officers found difficulty in suppressing.[4] It is said that once the soldiers were without bread for a week. "The seventh day they came before their superior officers and told their sufferings in as respectful terms as if they had been humble petitioners for special favors; they added that it would be impossible to continue in camp any longer without support." Parties had already been sent out to forage, however, and supplies arrived in sufficient quantities to keep the army together.[5] Washington tried to calm the men by praising their fortitude, and by telling them that all troops must suffer occasionally, and that on the whole the army had been unusually well supplied with provisions; American soldiers engaged in such a cause should, he said, rise above little accidents. But, within a week, in writing to President Wharton of Pennsylvania, he said of the troops, "With unparalleled patience they have gone through a severe and inclement winter, unprovided with any of those conveniences and comforts, which are usually the soldier's lot after the duties of the field are over."[6]

Much of the suffering at Valley Forge was due to mismanagement and negligence. Mifflin, the quartermaster-general, had

---

[1] December 14, 1777, *Historical Magazine*, v. 131–132.
[2] *Ibid.* 132.   [3] Kapp, *Steuben*, i. 120.
[4] Washington to President of Congress, December 23, 1777, and to Wharton, March 7, 1778, Washington, *Writings* (Ford), vi. 258, 394–396.
[5] Greene to Knox, February 26, 1778, Greene, *Greene*, i. 563.
[6] March 7, 1778, Washington, *Writings* (Ford), vi. 395; Orderly Book, March 1, 1778, *Ibid.* 393, note.

in the early part of the war faithfully discharged his duties; but in the summer of 1777 he went home on the plea of ill health, and remained there over two months. Finally, on October 10, he tendered his resignation. Congress waited a month and then accepted it; but, instead of promptly choosing a new quartermaster-general, they left the position unfilled for over three months.[1] Many subordinate offices in the department were also allowed to remain vacant. The commissary-general was detained in Philadelphia when he should have been with the troops; and, finally, the military rank conferred on the wagon-master and his deputies had so filled them with a sense of their own importance that they considered it beneath their dignity as officers to do the work which their positions required.[2] As spring advanced, affairs improved. The melting of the snow made it easier to bring supplies to camp; and Congress at last reorganized the quartermaster and commissary departments and appointed competent heads.

A committee had been sent by Congress to examine and report on the condition of the army, and they asked General Greene to accept the position of quartermaster-general. Greene hesitated: it was a well-paid office, and he was far from wealthy; but, on the other hand, no one, as he afterwards complained, ever heard of a quartermaster in history,[3] and Greene had an unconquerable desire for glory. He offered to take the position for a year, without additional pay; but, this plan proving unsatisfactory, he finally consented to accept a permanent appointment on condition that he should be allowed as assistants Messrs. Cox and Pettit. Cox was a Philadelphia merchant, Pettit was secretary of New Jersey, and both were well fitted for their positions.[4] Congress complied with Greene's request, and also voted that the heads of the department should be allowed one per cent of the money expended, to be divided among them as they should agree.[5] The quartermaster had formerly

[1] *Journals of Congress*, iii. 426, 481, October 10 and November 7, 1777.
[2] Washington to Committee of Congress, January 28, 1778, Washington, *Writings* (Ford), vi. 335.
[3] Greene to Washington, August 24, 1779, Greene, *Greene*, ii. 466.
[4] *Ibid.* 48, 50.   [5] *Journals of Congress*, iv. 125, March 2, 1778.

received a definite salary; but a commission was now substituted; for Congress, though satisfied that higher pay should be given, dared not make the change openly lest other officers demand a similar increase.

Under the new arrangements for the commissary department, there were purchasing commissaries, who were allowed two per cent of the money which was disbursed by them; there were also deputy commissaries, who acted as superintendents and were given one-half of one per cent of the money they paid out; and a commissary-general, who was paid at the same rate,[1] and who was permitted to appoint and remove all his subordinates, thus avoiding the error which had driven Trumbull from office. The new commissary-general was Jeremiah Wadsworth, a former deputy.[2]

The reorganized departments proved very expensive, but the condition of the soldiers greatly improved. Washington wrote to Congress that the public was much indebted to General Greene, for he had brought order out of confusion, and had enabled the army to leave Valley Forge and promptly pursue the British when, in the spring of 1778, they evacuated Philadelphia. He also told Congress that since Wadsworth's appointment the troops had been plentifully supplied with provisions. There was, indeed, no complaint of lack of food from the early summer of 1778 to November, 1779.[3] This was partly due to the mildness of the winter of 1778, but the personal ability of Wadsworth and of Greene probably counted for much.

Though the army was comparatively well off for provisions, the supplies of clothing were still scanty. Late in June, 1778, a quantity imported on Continental account reached New Hampshire. The Board of War ordered it sent directly to camp.

[1] The language of the resolutions is "monies . . . received and expended," or "received and paid," by the commissaries in the discharge of their duty. This might be construed as giving a double commission; but probably Congress meant to estimate the per cent on the amount paid from the funds intrusted to the commissary department.

[2] *Journals of Congress*, iv. 150–152, 204, March 13 and April 9, 1778.

[3] Washington to President of Congress, August 3, 1778, and November 24, 1779, Washington, *Writings* (Ford), vii. 141, viii. 124.

By August 5, loads were ready for nearly one hundred teams, but an expedition to Rhode Island rendered it impossible to procure them at that time. Two months later the Board informed Congress that a part of the clothing was still at Portsmouth, and that none had got farther than Springfield.[1] The chief hope of relief seemed to be an expected attack on New England; in that case, wrote Wayne, "we shall like Mahomet and the mountain, go to the clothing if the clothing won't come to us."[2]

Attempts were also made to obtain clothing at home, but sometimes with poor success. Three hundred hats proved so small that they had to be resold. Blankets thought to be large enough for two men were found too small for one. Agents sent by the Board of War to Virginia to buy a cargo of cloth discovered that it had already been purchased by that State. The governor promised that a portion should go to the Continent, but a request for the greatest possible quantity of coarse linen proved unavailing; since, however, Virginia sent liberal supplies to her troops, the cloth may nevertheless have reached the army. A second application for linen for thirteen thousand shirts and fifteen thousand overalls was answered by a promise of thirty thousand yards. Some three months after the request thirteen hundred yards arrived, but it proved so poor that it was all rejected. Fortunately, a moderate quantity of linen and other necessaries was obtained in Philadelphia.

Late in November, 1778, Washington was able to report that the soldiers were now well clad; and in March, 1779, he wrote to Lafayette that the army was better clothed than ever before.[3] But the papers of the Board of War show that at least some of the officers did not share this general good fortune. In 1778 Congress temporarily put upon the Board the responsibility of clothing the army, and then neglected to relieve them of their

[1] Board of War to Congress, October 5, 1778, *Board of War Papers*, ii. 305.
[2] Wayne to Morris, October 5, 1778, New York Historical Society, *Collections*, 1878, p. 439.
[3] Washington to President of Congress, November 27, 1778, and to Lafayette, March 8, 1779, Washington, *Writings* (Ford), vii. 280, 360.

extra duties. In February, and again in March, 1779, the Board informed Congress that the officers were in a destitute condition; they said that supplies of clothing had arrived, but that there was no authority to purchase. The Board added that they, being busy with other matters, could not attend to details, and that they feared their characters would suffer; and they begged for relief.[1]

On March 23 Congress took into consideration the report of a committee which had conferred with Washington; and the clothing department was organized anew. A clothier-general was placed at the head; and there was a clothier for each State, appointed by the State but removable by the commander-in-chief. The duties of the State clothiers were to reside near the troops of their several States; to receive all clothing purchased at Continental expense in their own States, and a due proportion of that imported on Continental account; and to issue the same to the paymasters of the regiments, who were to act as regimental clothiers. If there was a deficiency, the State executive was to be informed at once; if there was a surplus, it was to be delivered to some other State agent on the order of the clothier-general. When possible, material was to be bought instead of ready-made clothing, both for the sake of economy and that the clothes might fit better.[2]

In July the Board of War, which still retained a supervision of the clothing of the troops, once more called the attention of Congress to the wants of the army. They said that the officers had applied for the poorest grade of cloth issued to the common soldiers, and had been refused because there was not enough for the latter. They reported that the cargoes of some vessels lately arrived might be bought to good advantage if speedy orders were given; and they submitted a long list of articles of clothing which should be purchased abroad. They acknowledged that their demand was large, but said that allowance had been made for probable captures by the enemy, and that, should there be a surplus, it could be used for the succeeding year. The

---

[1] Board of War to Congress, February 18 and March 2, 1779, *Board of War Papers*, iii. 71, 109; *Journals of Congress*, iv. 315, May 28, 1778.

[2] *Ibid.* v. 109–112, March 23, 1779.

recommendations were very detailed: the beaver hats should be plain, but should have smart cockades; the coats should not slope away so much as to lessen protection in cold or rainy weather, "whatever be the fashion of Europe"; they should be made up, but in such a manner as to be capable of being altered if found too small. The Board advised that care be taken to obtain shoes which were durable; they said that some of those imported from France had been worn out by one day's march, although they ought to have lasted three months. The list was very comprehensive: mention was made of buttons for shirts, collars, hats, and caps; of stocks; of velvet and cambric to be made into stocks; of garters; of combs, and combs with fine teeth; of needles and thread, hooks and eyes; and of shoemakers' tools.[1]

Importation, however, was a slow and uncertain process. The clothing did not arrive, and the condition of the army grew worse and worse. The articles most needed were hats, hose, shirts, blankets, and shoes. On September 18, 1779, Congress recommended the several States to provide clothing for their own troops in addition to that furnished by the Continent, and later voted that a "suit"[2] of clothes should be sold annually to the officers at an advance of fifty per cent over the prices before the beginning of hostilities.[3]

Late in the fall clothing arrived from France; but there was not enough of it; it was badly assorted and of varying quality. Many clothiers were absent, and the distribution was slow and difficult.[4] General Glover wrote to Hancock: "The whole of the army has gone into winter cantonments excepting General Nixon's and my brigades, who are now in the field (eight hundred of my men without shoe or stocking) enjoying the sweets of a winter campaign, while the worthy and virtuous citizens of

---

[1] Board of War to Congress, June 11, 1779, *Board of War Papers*, iii. 418-443.

[2] A "suit" was defined as one hat, one watch coat, one body coat, four vests, four pairs of breeches, four shirts, four stocks, six pairs of stockings (three worsted and three thread), and four pairs of shoes.

[3] *Journals of Congress*, v. 340-341, 427-428, September 10 and 25, 1779.

[4] Washington to President of Congress, November 24, 1779, Washington, *Writings* (Ford), viii. 122-123.

America are enduring the hardships, toils, and fatigues incident to parlors, with good fires, and sleeping on beds of down. Who, that loves his ease, and wishes to enjoy a good constitution, and at the same time make his fortune, would not be a soldier!"[1]

The regiment of artificers was exposed to peculiar hardships, and the Board of War made its situation the subject of a special report to Congress. The privates, the Board said, drew "grating comparisons" between their scanty pay and the large wages obtained by hired artificers. Most of them had families to support; for "their situation," the Board explained, "being stationary, induces them to enter into matrimonial engagements, more than the men in the marching regiments." The officers of the artificers were also in great distress; one of them, having run into debt until he was ashamed to borrow more, sold his bed-curtains. The Board said that it was important to retain these men in service, since, from habit and attachment to the cause, they were willing to accept much less than they could obtain by resigning and working on their own account, or than must be paid to new men, "who, having for some time past attended only to their private affairs, have contracted more avaricious inclinations."[2]

The discontent of the army was much increased by a belief that civilians were unduly favored. They were probably more regularly paid, but they had their trials also. Prices rose much faster than salaries: shoes cost $100 per pair, flour $90 to $100 per hundredweight, beef 22s. 6d. per pound, pork 25s. to 30s., salt £75 per bushel, sugar £150 to £200 per hundredweight, Indian corn £12 to £15 per bushel.[3] A member of Congress wrote that he wished that his pay, when it came, would keep him alive. He said that he owed his tailor, shoemaker, and others; also "one hundred and forty-seven dollars for board and some little borrowed of my landlady. . . . I own no horse, or I might ride away from these great debts and ask charity on the

---

[1] November 25, 1779, Essex Institute, *Historical Collections*, v. 160.

[2] Board of War to Congress, May 1 and June 4, 1779, *Board of War Papers*, iii. 365-371, 385-386.

[3] Pickering to his brother, December 13, 1779, Pickering, *Pickering*, i. 245, note.

road for a delegate from —— to enable him to reach home."[1] On November 22, 1779, Pickering wrote to Congress that during the past year he had paid fourteen thousand dollars for the support of himself and his family, and that he would not have escaped so easily had he not begun the year with a considerable stock of articles.[2]

That food as well as clothing did not fail was probably due to Greene and Wadsworth; yet by 1779 they had become unpopular. The arrangements made by them caused disgust and resignations among the old staff, while the expense, and the reports of fraud in both the quartermaster and the commissary departments made an unfavorable impression on Congress and the people. Greene, on his side, was much displeased by the blame laid upon his department, and by what he considered a lack of support from Congress; in April, 1779, he offered his resignation. It was thought that General Lincoln might retire from the command of the Southern army, and Greene wrote to Washington that he would like the post. Referring to the attacks on the quartermaster department, he said: "I will not sacrifice my reputation for any consideration whatever. I am willing to serve the public; but I think I have a right to choose that way of performing the service which will be most honorable to myself."[3] But Lincoln was given only a leave of absence, and Greene remained quartermaster-general. On June 1, 1779, Congress unanimously passed a resolution expressing full confidence in the quartermaster and the commissary. They added that, although they suspected that some of the inferior officers had committed abuses, they were persuaded that many of them deserved well of their country; and they promised a speedy investigation which would do justice to all. Wadsworth, who had also tendered his resignation, was informed that a change at the opening of the campaign would be inexpedient, and that Congress expected that his deputies would manifest their ability and public spirit by exerting their utmost efforts to procure supplies for the army. At the close of 1779, however, Wadsworth was

---

[1] Austin, *Gerry*, i. 332.   [2] Pickering, *Pickering*, i. 243–245.
[3] Greene to Washington, April 24 and 26, 1779, Sparks, *Correspondence of the Revolution*, ii. 271–275, 279–281.

allowed to resign, and his place was taken by one of his deputies, Ephraim Blane.[1]

At this time the army was again suffering from want of food. Congress had promised not to emit more than two hundred million dollars in paper, and that amount had now been issued. The commissaries were without money, no one would give them credit, and for five or six weeks the troops were on half rations. In December, Washington wrote to the governors of the Middle States that the magazines were empty, and that, even if the army were put on one-third the daily ration of bread, the supply would be exhausted in three days.[2]

The deficiency of provisions may have been increased by the confusion and relaxation incident to a change of system. Being almost without money or credit, Congress threw the burden of feeding the army on the States: the Continent ceased to purchase, and the different States were called upon for "specific" supplies, — so much beef on the hoof or salted, so many barrels of flour, etc. As might have been foreseen, the plan proved an utter failure from the first; it was both inefficient and expensive.[3] The States frequently obtained their quotas by taxes in kind, and under this arrangement the supplies were very irregular. Sometimes the soldiers starved; at other times fresh beef spoiled before it could be eaten. The system was burdensome to the States, and yet of little use to the army. Washington declared, "A great proportion of the specific articles have been wasted after the people have furnished them, and . . . the transportation alone, of what has reached the army, has, in

---

[1] *Journals of Congress*, v. 244, 444, June 7 and December 4, 1779.

[2] Washington to Executives of Pennsylvania, New Jersey, New York, Maryland, and Delaware, December 16, 1779, Washington, *Writings* (Ford), viii. 160-161, note.

[3] Clark, a delegate from New Jersey, had the sense to see that it was bad business to buy provisions in all the States, instead of at those places where they could be obtained with most convenience and economy, but he stood by an extreme doctrine of responsibility to his constituency. "I am assured," he wrote to the speaker of the New Jersey House, "the plan is agreeable to the wishes of our legislature, by whose opinion I shall always be governed" (Clark to Camp, February 17, 1780, *Sparks MSS*. xxxvi. 324-326).

numberless instances, cost more than the value of the articles themselves.[1]

Congress failed to apportion the State quotas before the beginning of 1780; and though they had taken measures for supplying the army, the plan proved totally ineffectual. The troops, both officers and men, were "almost perishing for want," and Washington prepared to forage on the country. He wrote an urgent letter to the magistrates of New Jersey, setting forth the sufferings of the troops, calling on them to exert themselves in procuring supplies, and intimating that, if compliance were refused, force would be resorted to. Certain officers were ordered to apply to the magistrates of the neighboring counties, and to seize provisions by their own authority if there was any delay in furnishing them. The value of the goods taken was to be estimated by a commissary and two magistrates; and certificates were to be given for the present price, or for that at the time of payment, as the owners chose. Milch cows and subsistence necessary for families were to be spared.[2]

Fortunately it was not necessary to resort to extreme measures, for officials and people responded zealously and a fair amount of supplies was obtained. Meanwhile a heavy frost improved the roads. The frost, indeed, was not an unmixed blessing, for it stopped the mills; yet, if wheat and Indian corn could no longer be ground, they might be issued in the sheaf or the ear, to be beaten out and boiled by the soldiers themselves.[3]

The relief, however, was not permanent; in March, 1780, there was another failure of supplies, and the army was on the

---

[1] Circular letter to the States, January 22, 1782, Washington, *Writings* (Ford), ix. 435.

[2] January 8, 1780, Washington, *Writings* (Ford), viii. 155–158, and note. At this very time, when extraordinary exertions were necessary to save the army from starving, a number of cattle belonging to the Continent, "kept and I suppose ill kept" at a great expense, were detained at Princeton for lack of orders to bring them forward (Witherspoon to Washington, January 14, 1780, *Sparks MSS.* xlix. (pt. 3), p. 141) — an excellent illustration of the slipshod methods of management which too often prevailed in the armies of the Revolution.

[3] Washington to Heath, February 1, 1780, Massachusetts Historical Society, *Collections*, 5th series, iv. 153.

verge of dissolution. No help could be expected from New Jersey, which was already exhausted; and the Board of War wrote in great haste to the governors of Delaware and Maryland, begging them to forward as much flour as possible. This scarcity of food was partly due to the inability of the commissary of purchases to hire assistants: men would not work for Continental money. The Board of War suggested payment in specie, or, as this was difficult to come by, in wheat, which was, at least, more stable than paper.[1]

In May, 1780, the distress of the army became acute. Officers gave up their rations, and lived on bread and water, rather than take any of the scanty allowance from the men. On several days there was no meat, and for some time the troops had been kept on one-half, one-quarter, and even one-eighth of the regular allowance. On the evening of May 25 two Connecticut regiments turned out under arms. In addition to their other grievances, their pay was five months in arrears, and, as the Continental money was worth less than two cents on the dollar, even when received it was of little value. When reminded of the promises of Congress, their own past good conduct, and the cause in which they were engaged, the soldiers answered that their sufferings were too great, that they must have present relief and some substantial recompense. At last, after a little violence, their officers, aided by others in the Pennsylvania line, induced them to return to their huts; a few came out again, but were arrested.

It was a narrow escape; the rising might easily have spread through the army, which was ripe for mischief. The officers themselves were very discontented. They had no baggage for the same reason that the soldiers had no tents, — the camp was isolated; and the allowance for the use of teams was so small that the farmers hid their horses and harnesses, and even broke up their wagons, for fear that they would be seized.

The summer brought little relief. There were alternate failures of bread and meat, with an occasional dearth of both; and

[1] Board of War to Congress, March 23, 1780, *Board of War Papers*, iv. 267, 269.

a deficiency of clothing and blankets. The trouble was due largely to the slowness of the officials at Philadelphia and to the lack of a directing mind.[1] The Board of Treasury required every detail to be explained. For example, on June 21 Assistant-Quartermaster Pettit, then at the capital, sent in an application for money; ten days later he received an answer, and on July 13 obtained one-fifth of the sum desired. This, he said, was a favorable specimen of the way in which business was done.[2] Congress usually left matters to the States, and when they took action themselves showed less care for the effectiveness of resolutions than for the proper expression and punctuation of them.[3]

Congress did, however, remodel the quartermaster department, hoping, probably, to obtain equal efficiency with a less elaborate and expensive organization. But Greene vigorously opposed the change; he thought it unwise in itself, and believed that it was part of a scheme to ruin him and to embarrass Washington, especially when he saw Mifflin active in its support.[4]

Congress, in the spring of 1780, sent a committee to camp; and Greene warned Schuyler, who was one of the members, that if the changes made were such as to prevent competent men from seeking positions in the department, he would immediately resign, let the consequences be what they might.[5] When Greene received a copy of the new plan, he at once declared that it made demands which were physically impossible of execution. He complained that places had not been provided for Cox and Pettit, and announced that he would give no further order, except to acquaint his deputies with what had been resolved upon and to direct them to close their accounts.

---

[1] Irvine to Reed, May 26, 1780, Reed, *Reed*, ii. 201–202; Washington to President of Congress, May 27, and to Reed, May 28, 1780, Washington, *Writings* (Ford), viii. 288–293; Reed to Washington, June 22, Greene to Reed, June 29, and Wayne to Reed, September 17, 1780, Reed, *Reed*, ii. 215–218, 286.

[2] Pettit to Greene, July 13, 1780, Greene, *Greene*, ii. 313–314, note.

[3] Cornell to Greene, July 21, 1780, *Ibid.* 300.

[4] Greene to Washington, March 31, 1780, *Ibid.* 257–258.

[5] Greene to Schuyler, June 14, 1780, *Sparks MSS.* lxv. (pt. 3), 108–110.

"Systems without agents," he wrote to Congress in July, 1780, "are useless things, and the probability of getting the one should be taken into consideration in framing the other. Administration seems to think it far less important to the public interest to have this department well filled and properly arranged than it really is, and as they will find it by future experience.

"My best endeavors have not been wanting to give success to the business committed to my care, and I leave the merit of my services to be determined hereafter by the future management of it under the direction of another hand.

"My rank is high in the line of the army, and the sacrifices I have made on this account, together with the fatigue and anxiety I have undergone, far overbalance all the emoluments I have derived from the appointment. Nor would double the consideration induce me to tread the same path over again, unless I saw it necessary to preserve my country from utter ruin and a disgraceful servitude."[1]

So frank, not to say so insolent, a letter naturally gave great offence. Greene's claims were considered exorbitant; the reference to "administration" was regarded as a direct reflection upon Congress; and Greene's resignation in the midst of a campaign seemed like an attempt to force his own plans upon the government. Congress felt that they were being censured and bullied by their own servant. Some members suggested that Greene be immediately dismissed from the service; "others, more moderate, though not at bottom more friendly," says one of Greene's friends, proposed that he be suspended from command until his accounts as quartermaster were settled.[2] A letter written in Greene's behalf by the committee of Congress at camp gave further offence; and the committee to whom Greene's letter was referred brought in a resolution "that General Greene be acquainted that Congress have no further service for him." The report of the committee was debated for a week and then postponed, and Greene was allowed quietly to resume his command in the line.[3]

[1] Greene to President of Congress, July 26, 1780, Greene, *Greene*, ii. 314–316.
[2] Cox to Greene, August 7, 1780, *Ibid.* 324.   [3] *Ibid.* 322–323.

The moderation of Congress was probably due in part to the influence of Washington. One of the members who had assisted in preparing the new regulations for the quartermaster department was Joseph Jones of Virginia. Jones and Washington corresponded freely on public affairs, the delegate giving information of the feelings and intentions of Congress, and the general indirectly advising the government in a way which might have been imprudent in an official letter. Jones, on August 7, 1780, wrote to Washington that, if Greene had pointed out any defects in the new system, Congress would doubtless have remedied them; but he declared that Greene demanded freedom from all control but Washington's,[1] and said that it was doubtful if the matter would end merely in the acceptance of Greene's resignation.[2] Washington understood Jones's letter to refer to the suspension of Greene from command, and he promptly wrote to Jones begging him, if he possibly could, to prevent Congress from taking so unwise and dangerous a step; pointing out that the suspension of Schuyler and St. Clair, though these generals were much blamed by the public on account of the loss of Ticonderoga, had given dissatisfaction to many discerning men, and that the suspension of Greene would be generally condemned in the army.[3]

"My sole aim at present," he said, "is to advertise you of what I think would be the consequences of suspending him from his command in the line . . . without a proper trial. A procedure of this kind must touch the feelings of every officer. It will show in a conspicuous point of view the uncertain tenure by which they hold their commissions. In a word, it will exhibit such a specimen of power, that I question much if there is an officer in the whole line, that will hold a commission beyond the end of the campaign, if he does till then. Such an act in the most despotic government would be attended at least with loud complaints.

[1] In this particular, Jones may have been unjust to Greene. A letter of the quartermaster's to the committee at the camp was probably misunderstood.
[2] Jones to Washington, August 7, 1780, Greene, *Greene*, ii. 327–328.
[3] Washington to Jones, August 13, 1780, Washington, *Writings* (Sparks), vii. 151–152; Greene, *Greene*, iii. 329–330.

"It does not require with you, I am sure, at this time of day, arguments to prove, that there is no set of men in the United States, considered as a body, that have made the same sacrifices of their interest in support of the common cause, as the officers of the American army; that nothing but a love of their country, of honor, and a desire of seeing their labors crowned with success, could possibly induce them to continue one moment in service; that no officer can live upon his pay; that hundreds, having spent their little all in addition to their scanty public allowance, have resigned, because they could no longer support themselves as officers; that numbers are at this moment rendered unfit for duty for want of clothing, while the rest are wasting their property, and some of them verging fast to the gulf of poverty and distress."

"Can it be supposed, that men under these circumstances, who can derive at best, if the contest ends happily, only the advantages which accrue in equal proportion to others, will sit patient under such a precedent? Surely they will not; for the measure, not the man, will be the subject of consideration, and each will ask himself this question: If Congress by its mere fiat, without inquiry and without trial, will suspend an officer to-day, and an officer of such high rank, may it not be my turn to-morrow, and ought I to put it in the power of any man or any body of men to sport with my commission and character, and lay me under the necessity of tamely acquiescing, or, by an appeal to the public, exposing matters, which must be injurious to its interests?"

Greene's stubbornness in this affair was due to personal feeling, as well as to disapproval of the regulations for his department. He was much offended by the treatment of Cox and Pettit at the hands of Congress; by some rules concerning financial responsibility he might have been made liable for losses for which he was not to blame; and he concluded that there was a plot to force him out of the service by requiring him to perform impossibilities. Pettit, however, thought that the new plan was not so difficult of execution as Greene believed, and Greene's friends at Philadelphia disapproved of his resigning in the midst of a campaign. Greene's sensitive nature had led him to commit an error which might have resulted seriously both to himself and to the country.[1] Greene was induced to retain his office until a new quartermaster-general was appointed, managing the department, not under the new system, but under orders received from Washington.[2] On September 30, 1780, he retired with a certificate of good service from Washington, and was succeeded by Timothy Pickering, the chairman of the Board of War. Pickering was a more careful and frugal manager than Greene; and at the cost of considerable unpopularity he effected certain economies. But the new system did not improve the condition of the army; it is doubtful, indeed, if any reform would have been of much service in this respect so long as the soldiers had to rely upon State supplies. In October, 1780, the army was obliged to live on the country. In November, Washington wrote to General Sullivan, now a member of Congress, that ten months' pay was due, and that there was not credit enough to send a single express. He called for better organization, and advised that more business be confided to small boards or to individuals.

"For I am very well convinced," he said, "that, for want of system in the execution of business, and a proper timing of things, that our public expenditures are inconceivably greater than they ought to be.

"Many instances might be given in proof, but I will confine myself to the article of clothing, as we are *feelingly* reminded of it. This, instead of being ready in the fall for delivery, is then to be provided, or to be drawn from the Lord knows whither; and, after forcing many soldiers from the field for want of it, is eked out at different periods, as it can be had through the winter, till spring, and in such a piecemeal way, that the soldier deriving little comfort from it, is hurt both in appearance and pride, while the recruiting service is greatly injured by it. Were this the result of necessity, not a word would be said; but it is the effect of a divided attention, or

[1] Cornell to Greene, July 29, and Greene to Reed, August, 1780, Greene, *Greene*, ii. 320-321, 335-337.
[2] Greene to Schuyler and Peabody, of date July 28, 1780, *Ibid.* 319-320.

overmuch business; for, at the periods of the extreme suffering of the army, we can hear of clothing in different places falling a prey to moths, and canker worms of a worse kind; and I am much mistaken, too, if the clothing system (if ours can be called a system) does not afford a fruitful field for stock-jobbing, etc." Later he wrote, "I am well convinced that the public is charged with double what it receives, and what is received is doubly charged."[1]

The soldiers were on half-rations nearly half the time. On December 10, 1780, Surgeon Thacher wrote in his journal that it was the third day without sufficient food to appease the appetite.[2] On the same day Washington informed Gouverneur Morris that there was neither money nor credit to purchase boards for doors to the log huts; and shortly before, he had given directions to General Heath to discharge a portion of the troops whose service would soon expire, because there were not enough provisions to feed them.[3]

By January, 1781, supplies arrived and the cabins were finished, but money was still scarce.[4] Quartermaster Pickering issued orders to a subordinate to sell a part of the State supplies and use the proceeds to bring the rest to camp. Washington interposed saying that such a measure was liable to great abuse, and giving Pickering authority to impress wagons. The Board of War were anxious to make some purchases in Philadelphia; but Congress had failed to comply with their contracts, and the merchants refused further credit. "It is in vain," said the Board, "to press for new credit while old engagements remain unsatisfied, and particularly such as were, in an especial manner, notwithstanding public embarrassments, agreed to be paid."[5]

[1] Washington to Sullivan, November 20, and to Duane, December 26, 1780, Washington, *Writings* (Ford), ix. 33-34, 76.

[2] Thacher, *Journal*, 236.

[3] Washington to Morris, December 10, 1780, Washington, *Writings* (Ford), ix. 46; to Heath, November 28, 1780, Massachusetts Historical Society, *Collections*, 5th series, iv. 178-179.

[4] Thacher, *Journal*, 240.

[5] Pickering to Hughes, Washington to Pickering, April 17 and 25, 1781, Historical Index to Pickering Papers in Massachusetts Historical Society,

In the summer of 1781 the condition of the army began to improve. The executive power was centralized: the Board of Treasury was replaced by a superintendent of finance, commonly called the financier; the States were relieved of all responsibility for clothing the army; and the whole business was intrusted to a clothier-general, who was to select his own agents, first obtaining the approval of the financier. The system of specific supplies was abolished,[1] and the financier was allowed to make such arrangements for feeding the army as he should deem best.

The person to whom this extensive power was given was Robert Morris. Morris was a prosperous Philadelphia merchant, a man of great ability and business experience, with an excellent commercial credit — a circumstance of which the army quickly felt the benefit. Scarcely had Morris accepted his appointment when he learned that the troops were suffering greatly from lack of bread. He at once took measures for purchasing a considerable quantity of flour, giving his personal guarantee to secure his agents from loss. Writing to Washington to inform him of what he had done, he said: "I shall make it a point to procure the money, being determined never to make an engagement that cannot be fulfilled; for if by any means I should fail in this respect, I will quit my office as useless from that moment."[2]

Congress permitted the financier to make his own arrangements for supplying the army. Continental and State management had both failed; Morris therefore determined to try the system established in Europe, and to feed the army by contract. On December 6, 1781, he signed an agreement with Mr. Comfort Sands and others, by which they promised that, during the ensuing year, they would deliver, at certain specified places, as many rations as should be called for. Disputes as to quality or quantity were to be referred to three arbitrators, one to be

---

Collections, 6th series, viii. 225, 518; Board of War to Congress, February 22, 1781, *Board of War Papers*, vi. 177-179.

[1] *Journals of Congress*, vii. 29, 38, 118, 127-131, February 7 and 20, June 4 and 18, 1781.

[2] May 29, 1781, Washington, *Writings* (Sparks), viii. 67, note.

appointed by the Continent, one by the contractors, and a third by the other two. If deficient rations were not immediately replaced, the Continent was to be at liberty to buy equivalents at any price for which they could be obtained, and to charge the same to the contractors.[1]

The plan was a good one, but Sands was not well fitted for a position which required both tact and liberality. Washington described him as "extremely plausible — extremely narrow-minded — disingenuous" and unaccommodating, "yielding nothing himself, requiring everything of others, and failing in the most essential parts of his contract." Washington reported that West Point was so ill supplied with provisions that, should the enemy besiege it, the fort could not hold out three days. The army was frequently without food; it was said that, when salt meat rose, Sands left the troops unsupplied, waiting for a fall in price. He also arranged that his droves of cattle should not arrive until they were needed, and so saved the expense of maintaining them at camp; if there was any delay on the road, the army might suffer, but the profits of the contractors were secure.

Another cause of complaint was Sands's strictness in regard to the extra rations. Officers were sometimes away from camp, and sometimes they wished to entertain their friends or some visiting foreign officer; and they thought they should be permitted to draw their rations at such times as suited their convenience. Sands, however, insisted that the officers should regularly draw their exact rations, or forfeit whatever was left undrawn. Washington did his best to calm the officers, though in private he made strong representations to Morris.[2] The financier seemed inclined to support Sands, but he was himself soon involved in a difficulty with the contractors. The United States were paying for supplies in notes which were below par; and Sands wrote to Morris that the sub-contractors were calling on him to make good the difference between the real and the nominal value of these notes, and that it was impossible for him

---

[1] *Knox MSS.* viii. 7–13.

[2] Washington to Morris, May 17 and June 16, 1782, Washington, *Writings* (Ford), x. 15–21, 31–35.

to fulfil his agreement unless he were supplied with money to satisfy these demands. Morris was unable to advance the money, and the matter ended in Sands's being released from his bargain. For a while it seemed as if the army must starve, but Morris found some persons who were ready to feed the troops and wait three months for their pay. They stipulated, however, for a considerably higher rate per ration than Sands had charged.[1]

The winter of 1782–1783 opened inauspiciously. A heavy fall of snow blocked the roads, and the farmers could not or would not get their wagons to camp. Washington was inclined to blame the quartermaster-general for the scarcity. He wrote him an angry letter declaring that the horses had been without feed "long or short" for fourteen days; that General Gates had lost two fine horses; that his own had been without forage for four days, and that he had obtained some only by paying for it out of his own pocket. He said that the mails must stop on account of the weakness of the horses; that some generals had sent theirs into the country; and that others had notified him that they could not come to headquarters because it was too far to walk, and that they could not ride because their horses were not strong enough to bear them. Pickering, on his part, claimed that he had foreseen the difficulty and had attempted to lay up supplies in reserve, but that he could not get money to purchase them.[2] The scarcity, whatever its causes, was only temporary; as the roads grew better, forage came into camp.

During the last year of the war the army was, on the whole, well fed. There was, however, some complaint about the meat. Knox wrote to one of the principal contractors: "The beef contractors go on from bad to worse. There are now forty cattle killed, so infamously poor that the troops absolutely refuse it although their provisions were out last night — come here as early as possible to-morrow morning and decide for yourself.

---

[1] Sumner, *Financier and the Finances of the Revolution*, ii. 61–63. Washington to McHenry, October 17, 1782, Washington, *Writings* (Ford), x. 96.

[2] Washington to Pickering, December 25, 1782, and Pickering to Hodgdon, January 12, 1783, Pickering, *Pickering*, i. 390–393.

Some remedy must be instantly provided, as there is no salt beef in the garrison."[1]

In general the contractors seem to have given satisfaction. Early in 1783 Washington wrote: " I have no doubt of a perfect agreement between the army and the present contractors; nor of the advantages which will flow from the consequent harmony. Sure I am, the army will ask no more of the contractors than their indubitable rights ; and I am persuaded there is too much liberality and good sense in the latter to descend to the *low dirty* tricks which were practised in the time of Comfort Sands, whose want of liberality — I will go further, and say lack of common honesty — defeated his favorite scheme of making money, which appears to be the only object he had in view."[2]

The condition of the army in regard to clothing during the last period of the war is difficult to determine. Sands had a contract for supplying the officers with clothes; and February 28, 1782, Washington wrote to Heath saying that Sands's prices had been found satisfactory, and that he hoped the States would put the army on as good footing in regard to pay as they now were in the matter of provisions and clothing.[3]

On the very same day, however, Colonel Jackson wrote to Knox, complaining most bitterly of neglect in providing the army with clothing. "From the general down to the common soldier," he said, "not one dollar to be found, and many of their best officers ragged and shabby not able to do the necessary duties of camp, not a friend or a farthing to help themselves, a uniform coat and a cockade are sufficient reasons with the inhabitants why they will not assist or relieve their distresses — From morn to night, and from night to morn you will hear some of the best officers and soldiers (that any nation could ever boast of) execrating the very country they are risking their lives, limbs, and health to support for their inattention and neglect of them — they may talk of arrangements and rearrange-

---

[1] Knox to Duer (or Parker), February 21, 1783, *Knox MSS.* xi. 147.

[2] Washington to Morris, January 8, 1783, Washington, *Writings* (Ford), x. 128.

[3] Massachusetts Historical Society, *Collections*, 5th series, iv. 243-244.

ments and inspectors till the words are worn out and time is no more, unless they feed, clothe and pay the army, they are names without a meaning and will have no more effect on the discipline of the army than so many blank pieces of paper — I never knew the troops half so ragged and destitute of clothing as they have been this winter, it's true about six weeks ago they drew, one shirt, one pair hose and one pair overalls per man, when they received them they were naked and that clothing has been on their backs ever since without being able to shift them and there is but very few men in the army but is eat up with the itch — we have received a proportion of cloth for coats and vests which are to be made by the regimental tailors and such country workmen as will engage — by the time this clothing is done, the overalls etc. will be completely worn out, but the coats and vests as they are exceeding good, will answer the purpose to keep the heat out in summer and everybody knows their feet and legs are proof against any season." [1]

If either Jackson's or Washington's letter stood alone, it would rightly be regarded as trustworthy evidence of the condition of the troops; but, to reconcile both letters, is impossible. The commander-in-chief, however, had better opportunities of learning the condition of the army as a whole than did Colonel Jackson; and his testimony is therefore more convincing.

In February, 1783, Washington wrote to Heath: "Without amusement or avocation, I am spending another winter (I hope it will be the last that I shall be kept from returning to domestic life) amongst these rugged and dreary mountains. I have, however, the satisfaction of seeing the troops better covered, better clothed, and better fed than they have ever been in any former winter-quarters; and this circumstance alone would make any situation tolerable to me." [2]

Hitherto, attention has been confined to the main army, but a few words at least should be said concerning the condition of the troops in the South. Because of the greater mildness of the climate, the Southern army suffered less perhaps than the

---

[1] Jackson to Knox, February 28, 1782, *Knox MSS.* viii. 80.
[2] February 5, 1783, Massachusetts Historical Society, *Collections*, 5th series, iv. 280.

Northern. It was, however, exposed to great hardships, partly on account of defeats and long marches, and partly because it was obliged to rely on specific supplies. Greene, who succeeded Gates in December, 1780,[1] after the latter's defeat at Camden, found that all the wagons had been lost, that the soldiers were literally naked and living from hand to mouth, and that there was not a single dollar in hard money in the military chest.[2] In the pursuit of Cornwallis after the battle of Guilford Court-House, the troops were so ill supplied that many fainted from lack of food; at the battle of Eutaw a number of the soldiers were totally destitute of clothing, and fought with nothing but pieces of moss tied on shoulder and flank to keep the musket and the cartridge-box from galling. Many fell sick with Southern fevers, and they and the wounded suffered severely, for hospital stores on their way from Virginia had been captured by the enemy's raiders. On October 25, 1781, Greene wrote to the president of Congress: "Numbers of brave fellows who have bled in the cause of their country, have been eat up with maggots, and perished in that miserable situation. Hospital stores and medicine have been exceeding scarce; not an ounce of bark have we in the department at this time."[3]

A little later, indeed, there came a delightful change: the army was moved nearer to Charleston, to a district hardly touched by war, and remarkably fertile. Here the men obtained, not only necessaries, but luxuries. Lieutenant-Colonel Morris wrote to his father: "The enemy [at Charleston] are still apprehensive of a siege, and are making every preparation to defend themselves. We are enjoying our ease and fattening upon the luxury of the rice plantations. The riches and natural resources of this country surpass my expectations. During the whole course of my service I never lived so well. The best of poultry, all kinds of wild game and vegetables in abundance; wine, porter and punch — fine girls, the patriotic fair of the country — as much to be applauded for their firmness as their virtue. I envy everything I see, except the poor unhappy blacks, who, to the disgrace of human nature, are subject to every species of

---

[1] Greene, *Greene*, iii. 33.   [2] *Ibid.* 71–72.   [3] *Ibid.* 407.

oppression while we are contending for the rights and liberties of mankind."[1]

But the troops could not remain here forever, nor, indeed, could even this district satisfy all their needs; and for the remainder of the war the army alternated between serious want and comparative comfort. Though the system of specific supplies had been abolished for the main army, it was continued in the South. After Yorktown, Virginia refused to furnish her quota; she confined herself to attempting to provide by contract for her own officers and soldiers,—and of the latter there were very few in Greene's army. North Carolina failed to raise money to transport her supplies to camp; the quartermaster was also without money, and consequently little assistance was given by that State. Georgia was exhausted and helpless. South Carolina earnestly endeavored to answer Greene's calls, but the attempt was only partially successful. For this, Greene put the blame on State Quartermaster Hort. April 1, 1782, Greene wrote to the governor: "We are from day to day kept uneasy for want of regular supplies of provision. One day we are without beef, the next without rice, and some days without either. . . . I am not acquainted with Mr. Hort, but I am afraid he has more method than despatch. To fill the place he is in, activity is no less requisite than method and integrity. . . . Our troops were never without provisions so much during all last campaign as they have been since Mr. Hort has undertaken the business and the provisions not more than twenty or thirty miles off." The want of clothing was as serious as that of provisions; more than a thousand men were kept from duty on this account.[2]

For some months these conditions continued, and then there was a slight relief. In July, Greene declared that the people began to think the army could live on air and that the troops had been without provisions more than a third of the time. A little later, however, he was able to report an improvement. "For upward of two months," he wrote on August 13, "more than one-third of our men were entirely naked, with nothing but

[1] Lewis Morris, Jr., to Jacob Morris, December 10, 1781, New York Historical Society, *Collections*, 1875, p. 496.
[2] Greene, *Greene*, iii. 445-449.

a breech cloth about them, and never came out of their tents; and the rest were as ragged as wolves. Our condition was little better in the article of provision. Our beef was perfect carrion; and even bad as it was, we were frequently without any. An army thus clothed and thus fed may be considered in a desperate situation. However, we have struggled through it. Our supplies of provision are better, but scanty and uncertain. Some clothing is arrived, and added to what the governor procured, renders the troops pretty comfortable; and the army very contented and easy, especially as we have it now in our power to issue rum eight times a month."[1]

In October, 1782, a merchant, John Banks, offered to clothe the army for partial payment in hard money, and bills on the financier for the remainder. An officer of the Treasury Department was in camp, with secret instructions to dole out money to Greene when absolutely necessary.[2] This gentleman was induced to advance the thirty-five hundred dollars which Banks asked for; and the latter fulfilled his contract so well that General Wayne declared that he had never seen an American army clothed as this one was. Later, Banks offered to feed the army; and, after much hesitating and bargaining on the part of Greene, an agreement was made. Banks, however, was a speculator; his affairs became involved, his creditors pressed, and he was unable to meet his obligations. The army would have been again thrown on its own resources, had not Greene stepped forward and given his personal guarantee for the payment of Banks's debts, taking for his own protection an assignment of certain securities, which proved to have been already disposed of. The arrangement secured supplies for the army, but it was a source of trouble and loss for Greene.[3]

In 1781, the army in Virginia suffered greatly. Specific supplies came in slowly; one county refused to furnish its quota on the ground that it had already been taxed enough. There

---

[1] Greene to Barnwell, July 31, 1782, Johnson, *Greene*, ii. 351; Gordon, *History of the American War*, iv. 292-293.

[2] Morris did not dare to let Greene know that his agent had authority to do this, lest Greene should rely too much on the depleted treasury.

[3] Greene, *Greene*, iii. 412, 459-466.

was some embezzlement, and great mismanagement and waste. Public property was in one case bought by the man in charge of it, doubtless to his own great profit. Grain and flour were carelessly left to be eaten up by weevils, or were thrown out of doors by angry millers who wished to make room for their own stores. During the siege of Yorktown the sick and wounded suffered terribly for lack of stimulants. About that time a French brig was driven ashore, and the authorities went so far as to seize twenty barrels of rum from her cargo; but the rum was taken to a storehouse and left untouched till the next summer.[1]

The difficulties of supplying the army were greatly increased by the desperate financial condition of Virginia. Paper money was of little use, and the State had neither gold, silver, nor credit. Grain could not be moved, cloth could not be made up, for lack of money to pay the workmen. Steuben had called on State Quartermaster Claiborne for wagons, camp equipage, and accoutrements for five hundred men. Claiborne replied that he was unable to give any assistance, that he had not a farthing of money, and that there was not a person who would trust the government two days. "My representations to the quartermaster-general and the government of this State," he said, "have been early and frequent; but little or no aid is given to me. I have received only five hundred thousand pounds of paper money since I have been in this department, which, at one hundred and forty for one, went but a small way. . . . To hire [horses] is impossible, as no one will take the price to which we are limited, when they can get three times as much from private individuals. . . . In short, sir, I have no money, no materials, no credit, and beg, while this is my situation, you will place no dependence on anything to come from the department."[2]

The story of the sufferings of the Revolutionary army has usually been regarded as a glorious proof of endurance and patriotism, and this it is; but it is also a proof of weakness and folly on the part of Congress and the country. Undoubt-

---

[1] Sumner, *Financier and Finances of the Revolution*, i. 240-245.
[2] Claiborne to Steuben, April 4, 1781, Kapp, *Steuben*, ii. 395-396.

edly, liberal allowance should be made in judging a young, ill-organized people, who were inexperienced in great affairs, and whose circumstances were peculiarly unfavorable to executive efficiency. Yet the fact remains that the army starved, not because the country could not furnish food, but because the people were unwilling to endure taxation, and because Congress themselves did not understand the importance of administrative centralization. Some of the hardships that the army endured were, indeed, unavoidable; but the greater part of them were caused by incompetent or negligent officials, bad management, and an excess of paper money.

During the first years of the war, Commissary-General Trumbull and Quartermaster-General Mifflin did their duties faithfully and well; sufficient powers were allowed them, and the Continental currency was freely taken. But in 1777 there came a change. Congress always wished to be an administrative as well as a legislative body; and when obliged to delegate power to others, they sought security in multiplication of agents and in elaborate systems, which, whether they checked dishonesty or not, were pretty certain to prevent rapid and efficient action.

They began with depriving the commissary-general of the power to appoint and remove his deputies. Trumbull thereupon resigned; and Congress put a weaker man in his place, and moreover kept him at Philadelphia instead of sending him to camp. Mifflin, too, who had begun to neglect his duties, was allowed to hang about the capital, intriguing against Washington; and when he at last resigned, the office was left vacant for months. As was to be expected under such conditions, the army starved. Clark was not wholly wrong when he said, "We may talk of the enemy's cruelty as we will, but we have no greater cruelty to complain of than the management of the army."[1] He should not have blamed Washington, however, but Congress themselves, who crippled one of the great supply departments and left the other without a head. When, in the spring of 1778, they chose able men as quartermaster-general and commissary-general, and allowed them to appoint their

[1] See above, pp. 25–26.

own deputies and manage their departments themselves, complaints ceased; and the army was well fed for a year and a half.

By this time Congress had become terrified at the enormous quantity of paper money. They dared not issue more; they could not levy taxes; and so they resorted to the system of specific supplies, and bade the several States care for the army. Instead of one central authority, whose sole business was to feed the troops, and who could buy in the best places and at the best times, and deal with a few responsible persons, there were now thirteen separate governments, which were expected, in addition to their many other duties, to furnish the army with regular supplies. The States saw fit to rely, not on contracts, but on taxes in kind, and to stake the subsistence of the troops on the ability and honesty of local tax-collectors. The worthlessness of the paper currency made it extremely difficult to procure transportation; and there was confusion and suffering, until, in 1781, Morris became financier, established a new system of contract, and did his best to put the country on a basis of specie payments. This produced a great improvement; and, though the officers had to endure the mortification of feasting their friends on "stinking whiskey and beef without vegetables," yet there was little physical suffering.

For the lack of clothing in the army there was more excuse than for the deficiency in food; yet here also much of the suffering of the troops was due to mismanagement. James Mease, clothier-general during the winter at Valley Forge, seems to have been unfit for his post.[1] When he left office, his duties were transferred to the Board of War, which had neither the leisure nor the authority to conduct the business properly; and, when the department was again reorganized, too much authority was given to the States. But among the great centralizing measures of 1781 was the appointment of a clothier-general, with suitable powers and with entire control over the clothing of the troops; and in the last period of the war the soldiers are said to have been better clad than ever before.

[1] Washington to Mease, April 17, and to President of Congress, August 3, 1778, Washington, *Writings* (Ford), vi. 469-470, note, vii. 142; Scharf and Westcott, *Philadelphia*, i. 390, note.

CHAPTER VII.

MUTINIES OF 1781.

PREVIOUS to 1781 there were few mutinies, and none of them were serious. The only one which resulted in bloodshed was a revolt of a New England brigade in November, 1777. These troops had taken part in the capture of Burgoyne, and both officers and men felt that they had done their share of the work and deserved repose; several regiments had received no pay for six or eight months, and all were in want of necessaries. When, therefore, they received orders to leave the Hudson and join the main army in Pennsylvania, the troops, unwilling to make so long a march, refused to go. A captain killed one of the mutineers, and was himself shot by the man's comrade. The efforts of the brigade commanders, however, and the activity of Governor Clinton of New York, who borrowed some money to pay the troops, soon induced the men to set out for the Delaware.[1]

In 1780, the year when the army began to depend on specific supplies, the situation became very serious. In May there was a mutiny of Connecticut troops;[2] and in December Wayne, who was temporarily commanding the Pennsylvania division, then stationed at some distance from the main army, wrote to a friend that he wished the Ides of January were past.[3] The event justified his fears: on the first of January, 1781, his division,

---

[1] Hamilton to Washington, November 10 and 12, 1777, Sparks, *Correspondence of the Revolution*, ii. 32–38.

[2] See page 106.

[3] Wayne to Johnston, December 16, 1780, Stillé, *Wayne*, 240.

amounting to between fifteen hundred and two thousand men, threw off the authority of their officers and left the camp.¹

Besides the grievances which the Pennsylvanians shared with the whole army, — want of pay, provisions, and clothing, — several special reasons have been given for this revolt. One is the number of deserters and foreigners in the division. Some historians say that many of the soldiers were Irish; and this has been thought to explain both the courage which the Pennsylvanians had shown in action and their impatience under long-continued hardships. The British had thought it worth while to make a special appeal to Irish feeling; a paper urging Washington's soldiers to desert contained this sentence, "I am happy in acquainting the old countrymen [a name given to the Irish], that the affairs of Ireland are fully settled, and that Great Britain and Ireland are firmly united, as well from interest as from affection." ² There is, however, no evidence to show that foreigners were responsible for the mutiny; besides, though nearly all the Pennsylvanians were of non-English descent, many, perhaps a majority of them, were born in the country, while very few were recent immigrants. Furthermore, it is probable that there were not over three hundred real Celts in the whole line; the rest of the so-called "Irish" were emigrants, or the children of emigrants, from Ulster, and were of Scotch descent.³

The soldiers themselves had much to say of the oppressions of their officers. They alleged that the officers had, by intimidation and trickery, induced men who were enlisted for a definite time to accept gifts of money which bound them to serve during the war. They also accused the officers of roughly treating men who claimed their discharge, of inflicting severe punishment without adequate investigation, and of obtaining an undue proportion of the State supplies.

These complaints were probably not without foundation. The

---

¹ For general references to the Pennsylvania mutiny, see Hazard, *Register of Pennsylvania*, ii. 137-138, 158-160, 164-168, 188-190, 204-206, 218-219; Reed, *Reed*, ii. ch. xiv; *Pennsylvania Archives*, 2d series, xi. 631-674.

² Washington, *Writings* (Ford), viii. 292, note.

³ Stillé, *Wayne*, 248-250.

action of the mutineers corresponded with their words. They had such a respect for Congress that it was thought unwise for a committee of that body to confer with them, lest they should be unduly encouraged by so great an honor. They treated the president of Pennsylvania with a respect which showed that they had by no means lost their reverence for the government of the State; but when their officers came among them at the close of the mutiny, they received them with insults.

Perhaps the insubordination, as well as the harshness, of the officers should be reckoned among the causes of the mutiny. Many of them had twice united to oppose an appointment which they claimed infringed their rights, and in one case at least, had threatened to resign. This would naturally have an effect upon the soldiers. Moreover, as privates were employed as servants, the complaints of the officers may have reached ears for which they were not intended, and so have stirred up the men to redress their own wrongs.[1]

The most important special cause of the mutiny was an ambiguity in the terms of enlistment. At the close of 1776 Congress had allowed the States to enlist men for three years or for the duration of the war. Most of the recruiting agents kept separate rolls, one for three-year men and another for war men; but some from Pennsylvania put all under the head of "three years, or during the war." The soldiers interpreted this as meaning three years if the war should last so long; the government, as three years at least, and longer if the war should continue beyond that time.

In 1779 this misunderstanding threatened serious consequences. In February of that year, General St. Clair wrote to President Reed of Pennsylvania that the soldiers had become discontented because of the exposition given to the disputed phrase by the government; that the officers agreed with the men, and that he himself believed they were right. In June Washington called the attention of the Board of War to the matter, and announced his purpose of making a careful investigation; but he added that he must not be understood as admit-

---

[1] Stillé, *Wayne*, 229-233; Thacher, *Journal*, 240-241; *St. Clair Papers*, i. 464-465, note, 533, note.

ting the claim of the soldiers. The Board replied that, from such information as they had been able to collect, it appeared that some of the officers, more from expediency than from mature consideration, had given the "wider interpretation," — that is, that the enlistment was for the war. The Board said that much uneasiness had arisen, and that for political reasons they had discouraged the interpretation of the men, but that justice and policy required that something should be done to ease their minds. The Board proposed that a gratuity be offered to soldiers who had early enlisted for the war; they hoped that all the soldiers would accept it and thus set the question of enlistment at rest. Congress adopted the suggestion, and voted a bounty of one hundred dollars to all who had engaged to serve during the war before January 23, 1779, on which date Congress had authorized Washington to give a bounty of not over two hundred dollars to men reënlisting for the war.[1] St. Clair's opinion and the tone of the Board's letter indicate that three years at most was the true meaning of the disputed phrase; and this seems the more reasonable view, for so strong was the prejudice against a standing army that it was unlikely that either Congress or Pennsylvania would wish to keep up any considerable force after the end of the war, while enlistments might be made more easily by a promise to the soldiers that they would not, under any circumstances, be detained beyond a definite period. But, though the interpretation of the soldiers was probably correct, comparatively few seem to have suffered any injury by the opposite construction; after the mutiny was over the original enlistment rolls were collected, and it was found that a large majority of the mutineers were explicitly engaged for the war.[2]

The immediate occasion of the mutiny was the arrival in camp, on the 1st of January, 1781, of Pennsylvania recruiting agents, who paid twenty-five dollars apiece in coin to six months' troops

---

[1] Marshall, *Washington*, iv. 393; St. Clair to Reed, February 21, 1779, *St. Clair Papers*, i. 461; Washington to Board of War, June 9, and Board of War to Washington, June 17, 1779, *Board of War Papers*, 461-463; *Journals of Congress*, ii. 473-474, v. 34-35, 263, November 12, 1776, January 23 and June 22, 1779.

[2] Marshall, *Washington*, iv. 403.

who had enlisted for the war.[1] The government owed the old soldiers many months' pay;[2] the bounty voted by Congress the preceding summer had been discharged in worthless paper; and the sight of these new men receiving a handsome sum in hard cash was more than the veterans could bear. To make matters worse, an extra amount of spirits had been served out in honor of New Year's Day, and the soldiers contrived to buy more.

Until evening, however, the camp was unusually quiet; but about nine o'clock, the men came out of their huts and began to huzza. A number of the officers went to the spot to calm them, supposing that they had merely to deal with a little excitement due to liquor; and they had almost succeeded in securing quiet when firing began on the right and quickly ran through the line. The officers drove their horses among the mutineers, and used their swords freely. The soldiers retaliated with stones and bayonets, and discharged their muskets. They rushed to the cannon and dragged them into the road with much shouting and firing. A captain was shot through the body and soon died; and others on both sides were seriously injured.[3] The mutineers then compelled, at the point of the bayonet, those of their comrades who hesitated, to take an active part. They forced the artillerymen to join, and trained the guns on the Fifth and Ninth regiments, which had stood aloof. After several shots had been fired over their heads, these left their post, and the greater part went over to the mutineers. The men rifled the magazine, and also broke into General Wayne's stable and took his horses to draw the guns.

Wayne did his best to suppress the mutiny. He had formerly quelled one at Ticonderoga, by clapping a pistol to the breast of the leader; but now, as he approached with pistols cocked, the soldiers met him with fixed bayonets and threatened death if he fired. Yet even with their violence they mingled expressions of

---

[1] Shaw to Eliot, January 6, 1781, Quincy, *Shaw*, 85.

[2] Wayne said that he had not been paid a dollar for over a year; and Major Church declared that his regiment had not received any money for over fourteen months. See Stillé, *Wayne*, 240.

[3] *Pennsylvania Archives*, 2d series, xi. 631.

THE OUTBREAK. 129

respect and affection. They protested that they loved him and that they were loyal to the American cause, declaring that, should the enemy appear, they would fight under his orders; but now, they said, they were resolved to march to Philadelphia and obtain redress from Congress.[1] Wayne and some of his officers were swept along to the fork of a road, one branch of which led toward the sea-coast, the other inland. Here they made a stand, as if at all costs to bar the way to New York. But their courage, or prudence, was not put to the test; the mutineers made no attempt to pass them, but streamed off to the Delaware.

Wayne promptly wrote two letters to Washington, January 2, 1781, giving an account of the mutiny, and announced his own intention of following the troops, accompanied by his brigade commanders, Colonels Stewart and Butler. He ordered the New Jersey brigade to Chatham, to meet any attack from New York; and with Butler and Stewart set out after the soldiers.[2] By great exertions on the part of the officers, about half the line had been induced to stay in camp; but the mutineers halted some four miles off, and sent back messengers who won over all but about a hundred. Elias Boudinot, afterward president of Congress when that body fled to Princeton during the mutiny in 1783, watched the second exodus and talked with one of the soldiers. The man said that if the British came out, the Pennsylvanians would fight them with greater spirit than ever, but that now they were going to Congress.[3]

On January 3 the mutineers reached Princeton. The citizens were much alarmed, and were desirous of getting their unwelcome guests over the Delaware as soon as possible, both for public reasons and because they thought that the mutineers' "own State ought to be exposed to the inconveniences" which they might occasion, rather than New Jersey.[4] It was found that the troops were in no haste to move. Their first plan

---

[1] Stillé, *Wayne*, 243.
[2] Wayne to Washington, January 2, 1781, 4.30 A.M., *Ibid.* 242; and 9 A.M., Washington, *Writings* (Ford), ix. 90, note.
[3] Boudinot to Washington, January 2, 1781, Boudinot, *Boudinot*, i. 207-208.
[4] Smith to Livingston, January 3, 1781, *Sparks MSS*. xlix. (pt. 3), 155-156.

K

had been to go to Philadelphia and lay their grievances before Congress; but, once in Pennsylvania, many might slip off to their homes; accordingly they remained in Princeton, with headquarters at the college. The men were fully organized. They elected a certain Williams commander with the title of major-general, and other officers whom they called brigadiers and colonels. There was also a board of war to superintend the police of the camp; and a "committee of sergeants," to which was given the general direction of affairs. Care was taken that there should be no tampering with individuals and no unauthorized negotiations. Wayne, Butler, and Stewart, who had gone into Princeton with the troops, had guards assigned them, nominally out of respect, but really to prevent communication with any one without the permission of the committee of sergeants. The chief justice of New Jersey and some members of the legislature came to Princeton, but they were not allowed to address the soldiers. Generals Lafayette and St. Clair, who had hurried from Philadelphia to try their influence with the men, were peremptorily ordered out of town. Discipline was well maintained, and men were sent to Philadelphia to contradict reports that the country had been plundered.[1]

The news of the revolt caused much anxiety at headquarters. Washington's first impulse was to leave the army and hasten to Philadelphia to confront the mutineers; but it seemed unwise for the commander-in-chief to put himself in a situation where he could not enforce his orders, and it was not possible to detach at once a sufficient escort. His own army, too, was very discontented, and a mutiny might break out in his absence. Furthermore, circumstances favored an attack from New York: the Hudson, near which the army was encamped, was free from ice and open to the British fleet; and Arnold could furnish the enemy with full information concerning the defences of West Point. Further, it was probable that by the time Washington could reach the capital, Congress would have taken matters into their own hands. Washington, therefore, determined to remain at head-

[1] Scammell to Weare, January 18, 1781, *Sparks MSS.* xxxv. 157–165, St. Clair to Reed, January 4, and to Washington, January 7, 1781, *St. Clair Papers*, i. 532–534.

quarters for the present. He had already written to Wayne, giving his advice in this emergency. Force, he said, should not be used; it would be better to get the men over the Delaware, and then to halt them at Bristol or Germantown, if possible. Congress, he thought, should not leave Philadelphia; to fly would be undignified, and the troops in their anger might injure the city.[1]

Two Pennsylvania gentlemen who were at Morristown when the mutiny broke out rode post-haste to Philadelphia with the news, and Congress met at once in special session and appointed a committee to confer with the Council of the State.[2] The Council read a letter from Wayne, and other communications relating to the mutiny; and, say the records, " It appearing to be of great importance to put a stop as soon as possible to so dangerous a measure, the Council are unanimously of opinion that it is expedient for the president [Joseph Reed] and General Potter immediately to set out for New Jersey, and to use their endeavors to quiet the minds of the said people, and if nothing less will satisfy them, to discharge the whole of them." [3]

Meanwhile Wayne had already opened negotiations on his own responsibility. At his suggestion the mutineers chose certain sergeants to represent them, and before the troops reached Princeton he held a conference with these delegates, who accepted his terms; but the men refused to ratify their action. At Princeton another attempt was made to come to an agreement. The soldiers demanded the pay that was due, a supply of clothing, and very liberal concessions in the matter of enlistments; they were then to return to duty, and no aspersions were to be cast upon them. Wayne offered a full pardon, an immediate supply of good, warm clothing, prompt settlement of arrears, and a reference of questions concerning enlistments to a committee consisting of the colonels and a delegate from each regi-

---

[1] Washington to Wayne, January 3, and to President of Congress, January 6, 1781, Washington, *Writings* (Ford), ix. 87–91, 94.

[2] *Journals of Congress*, vii. 6, January 3, 1781. The constitution of Pennsylvania did not provide for a governor or other chief magistrate, but vested administrative authority in an Executive Council, with president and vice-president.

[3] *Pennsylvania Colonial Records*, xii. 593.

ment. He declared that these proposals were founded in justice and honor, and were all that a general could offer consistently with the mutual benefit of the country and "the line which he has so long had the honor of commanding." He said that if the soldiers were determined not to let reason and justice govern on this occasion, he could only lament the situation to which they would reduce themselves and their country. To an inquiry whether the men who had received the twenty-dollar bounty in 1776 and 1777 would be discharged, coupled with an exhortation to "be punctual what you say, and do as we reasonably think our due," Wayne answered that, if the soldiers would not accept the arbitration of the proposed committee, he could not decide so important a matter himself, but that he would send an express to the president and Council.

January 6th, 1781, a letter came from Reed, addressed to Wayne, but intended more for the mutineers than for him. The president stated that he was ready to receive any proposition from the soldiers, and that he would redress any wrongs which they had sustained; but that after the indignities offered by them to Lafayette and St. Clair he could not put himself in their power. The letter became known to the men, and seemed to produce a good effect upon them. They anxiously inquired if President Reed had any unkind feelings toward them; and privates and even sergeants took pains to say quietly to the gentlemen who brought the letter that they disliked the business. The committee of sergeants wrote to Reed that if he came to Princeton he would be treated with perfect respect, and that all would be gratified by a speedy settlement of this "unhappy affair." Wayne and Colonel Stewart went to the place appointed in Reed's letter, and the report which they brought of the conciliatory disposition of the troops, together with the thought of the dreadful consequences which might follow from their desertion, induced the president to risk a visit to Princeton. He wrote to the committee of Congress: "I have but one life, and my country has the first claim for it. I therefore go with the cheerfulness which attends performing a necessary, though not a pleasant, duty."[1]

---

[1] January 7, 1781, *Pennsylvania Archives*, 2d series, xi. 649.

About three in the afternoon of January 7th, Reed rode into Princeton. The guards turned out; the main body was drawn up near the college to receive him; and, as the visitors rode by, the sergeants, standing in the officers' places, saluted, and the president, subordinating inclination to policy, returned the courtesy. The men would have greeted him with a salvo of artillery; but Reed prevented this, lest the country should be alarmed. After the party had dismounted, a number of men came up, nominally to ask when they could have a conference, but really to identify the president; for so suspicious were the mutineers that they feared they might have been tricked.

In the evening the conference was held. Reed found "Major-General" Williams a "very poor creature or very fond of liquor"; but he was much impressed with the ability with which some of the sergeants stated their grievances, and was convinced that the officers had taken an unfair advantage of the men in the matter of enlistments. He offered terms similar to those offered by Wayne, except that questions concerning enlistments were to be referred to a committee appointed by the Executive Council of Pennsylvania. He said, however, that the acceptance of the bounty given in the summer of 1779 was not to be regarded as equivalent to an enlistment for the war, and promised that, if the original muster-rolls were lost, the soldiers' oaths should be decisive.[1] The sergeants wished to secure the release of men who had received the twenty-dollar bounty of 1776 and 1777. They urged that at that time neither Congress nor the people expected so long a war, and that regard should be paid to the spirit rather than to the letter of the contract. Reed, however, refused to nullify a voluntary agreement; and the sergeants admitted that he was right, but frankly said that they did not think they could persuade the men.

Reed feared that he should be obliged to grant discharges on any principle that the soldiers chose to demand, or on no principle whatever. The position of the government was weak; Washington and his army were at a distance, and the citizens

---

[1] Reed justified these great concessions on the ground that officers, in their desire to reënlist the men, had compelled many soldiers to take the bounty against their will.

could not be relied upon. It was said that a general of the New Jersey militia declared that he would not act against the mutineers while they behaved in a loyal and peaceful manner; and that some officers of the Philadelphia militia proposed to send an assurance to Princeton that they would not take arms against the soldiers. The next morning, however, Reed's terms were substantially agreed to, except that the men claimed leave to choose commissioners to sit with those appointed by the State. Reed refused this demand as implying distrust of the justice of the government, and as derogatory to its authority. That afternoon Wayne determined to settle the matter; and at half-past four the officers in Princeton sent word to the sergeants that, if the men did not start for Trenton in the morning, they would be left to act as they pleased and abide the fatal consequences of their own folly. The threat was successful; the sergeants resolved to march, and the troops obeyed them.

By proceeding to Trenton the men showed that they had no intention of seeking aid from New York. Their self-restraint was due to sentiments of honor and patriotism, not to any remissness on the part of Sir Henry Clinton. At the news of the revolt, Sir Henry hurried a large body of troops to Staten Island; but he feared to invade New Jersey before communicating with the mutineers, lest, as he wrote to Lord George Germaine, he should drive them to unite with their oppressors.[1] He therefore sent two agents to Princeton with tempting offers. They carried, concealed in sheet lead, a letter addressed to "The Person appointed by the Pennsylvania Line to lead them in the Present Struggle for their Liberty and Rights." Sir Henry reminded the troops of their sufferings, and of the severe punishments which, he asserted, they must expect from Congress; and he advised the men to move behind South River, where, if they desired, a British force should protect them. Clinton offered to every soldier full payment of arrears, and permission either to enlist under the British flag or to remain neutral, as he chose.

The spies reached Princeton in safety and were taken to Williams, but they had no sooner explained their errand than he

---

[1] *London Gazette*, February 20, 1781, in *Remembrancer*, xi. (pt. 1), 148.

arrested them both. The soldiers expressed great indignation at the thought of "turning Arnolds," and the officers in Princeton did their best to strengthen this feeling; but the troops were unwilling to break openly and irretrievably with the British general, — indeed, it is said that about three hundred of them wished to accept his offer.[1]

During Reed's visit to Princeton, Wayne asked the soldiers to execute the spies themselves, or at least to request him to do so; but Williams and some others seemed to prefer to send them back to New York with a taunting message to Clinton. Seeing the risk of a complete failure, Reed suggested as a compromise that they be kept prisoners. This occasioned a warm debate in the committee of sergeants, for the men knew that their best hold on the government was the apprehension that they might come to an understanding with the enemy. Reed's proposal was finally accepted; but he still feared that the spies might be set free, or at least allowed to escape, "though," he wrote, "we have taken such measures as I trust will hasten their journey to a different place than New York."[2] The soldiers kept the prisoners safe; and at Trenton they were given up and promptly tried and hanged.[3]

Wayne had promised a reward of a hundred guineas to the sergeants who brought him Clinton's letter; and, as he insisted on the speedy fulfilment of his pledge, the Pennsylvania Council sent him the money. It was offered to the two sergeants who brought the spies to Wayne.[4] They refused it, saying that they had merely obeyed the order of the committee of sergeants. It was then tendered to the committee, who declined it in language a little inflated, but highly honorable nevertheless, "As it has not been for the sake, or through any expectation, of receiving a reward, but for the zeal and love

---

[1] Dickinson to Washington, January 12, 1781, Sparks, *Correspondence of the Revolution*, iii. 206. Curiously enough, three hundred is said to have been the number of real Irish in the line.

[2] Reed to Committee of Congress, January 8, 1781, Reed, *Reed*, ii. 328.

[3] Dickinson to Washington, January 12, 1781, Sparks, *Correspondence of the Revolution*, iii. 206.

[4] Apparently it was promised as a reward for bringing the letter, but tendered for surrendering the spies; perhaps the same sergeants brought both.

of our country, that we sent them immediately to General Wayne, we therefore do not consider ourselves entitled to any other reward but the love of our country, and do jointly agree that we shall accept of no other."[1] The refusal shows a delicacy of feeling truly remarkable, when we consider what twenty-five or thirty dollars each must have meant to these men.

Whether the concessions made to the mutineers were wise or not is hard to say. Reed justified them on the ground of the unwillingness of the people to act, and the good behavior and the sufferings of the soldiers; but after the first alarm had passed away he was severely criticised for his liberality, and in the summer, at his request, the Pennsylvania Assembly appointed a committee of investigation, which reported that President Reed and General Potter "did render on that occasion every service to their country that circumstances and the nature of the transaction would admit of."[2]

During the mutiny the sentiment at Philadelphia had been divided: some thought that the mutineers should be compelled to submit; others (and these were probably the more numerous) wished to treat with the men. Sullivan, formerly major-general in the Continental army, now a member of Congress, wrote to Washington, "Constitutionally, no concession has been granted them, that the critical situation of our affairs did not warrant, and justice dictate."[3] But some of the officers in the army took a different view. Major Shaw thought that the compromise would reflect no honor on those who made it.[4] Colonel Alexander Scammel believed that force should have been used.[5] Washington himself had advised conciliatory measures; but he was keenly alive to the effect that the success of the Pennsylvanians might have on the rest of the army, and perhaps would not have gone so far as Reed. There was one

---

[1] Hazard, *Register of Pennsylvania*, ii. 218. Reed wrote, "By a little address we have saved the 100 guineas, and our credit" (*Ibid.*). It would be interesting to know the nature of the "address." This evasion of a promise reflects no honor on the State.

[2] June 11, 1781, Reed, *Reed*, ii. 337.

[3] January 10, 1781, Sparks, *Correspondence of the Revolution*, iii. 198.

[4] Shaw to Eliot, February 13, 1781, Quincy, *Shaw*, 88–89.

[5] Scammell to Weare, January 18, 1781, *Sparks MSS*. xxxv. 163.

circumstance which might have encouraged the government to take a bold stand. It was known that there were great divisions both among the men and in the committee of sergeants, although every effort was made to conceal the dissensions, for the soldiers understood how important it was that they should appear to be firmly united. Nevertheless, it is not improbable that if force had been used, — for which, let it be remembered, the government was ill prepared, — radicals and moderates would have joined to resist it, and that the mutineers might even have fought their way within reach of Clinton. Considering all the circumstances, Reed was at least excusable in acting as he did.

A revolt in the "patriot army" could hardly fail to wound American pride, for it cast dishonor either on the government or on the soldiers; and a general desire was manifested to put the affair in the best possible light. Sullivan, to prevent the ill effect which the mutiny might have abroad, wrote a letter to Luzerne, the French minister, in which he laid much emphasis on the good behavior of the troops.[1] The *Pennsylvania Packet* censured the mutineers, but praised their loyalty, and pointed out how superior they were to "mercenary troops, who bear arms for pay and subsistence only, uninspired by their country's rights, or the justice of the cause which they have engaged to support."[2] The *New Jersey Gazette* said, "Upon the whole, this affair which at first appeared so alarming, has only served to give a new proof of the inflexible honor of the soldiery, and their inviolable attachment to American liberty; and will teach General Clinton, that though he could bribe such a mean toad-eater as Arnold, it is not in his power to bribe an American soldier."[3] Governor Livingston of New Jersey wrote to Schuyler: "Throughout the whole contest, good has always come out of evil. This reflection has supported me in every difficulty. Even this alarming mutiny has ended to our honor and the confusion of the enemy."[4]

[1] January 13, 1781, Amory, *Sullivan*, 181–183.
[2] Hazard, *Register of Pennsylvania*, ii. 138.
[3] January 17, 1781, Moore, *Diary of the American Revolution*, ii. 374.
[4] January 18, 1781, Sedgwick, *Livingston*, 359.

The loyalty and moderation of the mutineers rendered it easy to publish reassuring accounts of the affair, but it was difficult to prevent a bad effect on the troops of other States. The news of the revolt made such an impression on the New Jersey line that their commander marched a part of them to Chatham, thinking a mutiny less liable to occur there.[1] The legislature also took alarm, and sent commissioners to camp to inquire into the conditions of enlistment; but they arrived too late. A portion of the line was stationed at Pompton, under Colonel Shreve. Part of the money allowed them on account of the depreciation of the Continental currency had recently been paid, and most of them celebrated their good fortune by getting drunk. On the evening of January 20, Colonel Shreve learned that the soldiers were planning a mutiny. He at once ordered them to fall in, meaning to scatter them in small detachments; but only a few obeyed his command. The rest broke into revolt, announced claims similar to those of the Pennsylvanians, and started, as was supposed, for Trenton, but really for the camp of their comrades at Chatham. There they received little encouragement. On the approach of the mutineers, Colonel Dayton, the commander at Chatham, requested his men to scatter, and about two-thirds complied.

The mutineers were followed by the commissioners appointed by the legislature, who promised them a hearing only when they returned to their camp and to duty. The commissioners also refused to discharge any soldier on the evidence of his own oath, even if the original muster-rolls were missing. The men protested, for the Pennsylvania troops had been allowed this privilege; nevertheless, they accepted the terms proposed. Colonel Dayton offered pardon to such as should, "without hesitation . . . return to their duty and conduct themselves in a soldierly manner"; and the men began their march back to Pompton. Dayton, however, was uneasy. He wrote to Washington that he feared that there would be more trouble when the soldiers found that the commissioners would not dis-

---

[1] For general references to the New Jersey mutiny, see Washington, *Writings* (Ford), ix. 117-119, 121-124, and notes; *Writings* (Sparks), vii. Appendix x.

charge them, and he suggested that the militia be called out. He also expressed a wish to make an example of some who had not complied with the conditions of pardon.

This request was quite in accordance with Washington's own feelings. He thought that, unless this fatal spirit of insubordination were stamped out at once, the troops of other States would be infected and the whole army ruined. Although doubtful of the support of the force at West Point, Washington resolved to risk all on one bold stroke. General Heath, the commander at West Point was directed to prepare a detachment of five or six hundred men, composed of the most robust and best-clothed soldiers in the garrison; and these were sent off under Major-General Howe, who was ordered to enforce "unconditional submission" and instantly to execute some of the leaders of the mutiny.[1]

Howe carried out his instructions with diligence and skill. On arriving at Ringwood on the evening of the 26th he learned that the soldiers had returned to Pompton, but that they had behaved in a disorderly, insulting manner, and had merely allowed a few of the more popular officers to exercise an influence which was advice rather than command. Howe, who did not believe in halfway measures in dealing with insubordination, resumed his march at midnight, and at daybreak the mutineers woke to find themselves surrounded.

Colonel Barber was sent to the huts to bid them parade unarmed within five minutes. Though surprised and outnumbered, they hesitated, some calling out that if there were no conditions they might as well die where they were; but at a second and more peremptory summons they formed as directed. Three men, one from each regiment, were selected for execution. Two of these were shot, the firing party being composed of leaders in the mutiny; but the third, the commander, was reprieved at the intercession of the officers, who testified that he had acted under compulsion and had advised submission. The officers now assumed command; and Howe himself addressed each platoon of the mutineers, reprehending their conduct in the severest terms. They received his rebuke very

[1] Washington to Howe, January 22, 1781, Washington, *Writings* (Sparks), vii. 380-381.

penitently, and he felt assured of their future good behavior; nevertheless, Washington thought it prudent to leave a detachment with artillery near them for a time. The affair was closed by a general order, warmly thanking Howe and his men and exhorting the army to patience.[1] The danger which seemed so formidable suddenly disappeared. The timely severity strengthened discipline, and Washington wrote to Steuben that the mutiny was a fortunate event.[2]

The committee appointed, in accordance with the agreement at Princeton, to inquire into the conditions of enlistment, promptly began its duties. The Pennsylvanians at first intended to remain together until the work was completed, but, on being told that this could not be permitted, they consented to go off when discharged. The committee, however, was much alarmed, and it determined to get rid of the men as soon as possible; so great was its haste, indeed, that it did not wait to get the muster-rolls from camp, but set to work at once. Those men who were adjudged to have completed their term of service were discharged, and the others were given short furloughs; if there were no other evidence available, the oath of the soldier as to the duration of his enlistment was accepted as conclusive. When the muster-rolls arrived, it was found that the great majority of those who had sworn themselves off, and also of those whose claims were still unexamined, had enlisted for the war. There was some thought of notifying the perjurers to return on penalty of being considered deserters; but, as such an order would have been difficult to enforce and would have looked like a breach of faith, the matter was dropped.[3] It is said that over one-half the line was dismissed; Wayne wrote to Washington that about thirteen hundred discharges had been given, and estimated the number remaining in service as a little less than eleven hundred and fifty.[4]

---

[1] Washington to Howe, January 29, 1781. Washington, *Writings* (Sparks), vii. 389–390, 565–566.

[2] Gordon, *History of the American War*, iv. 22; Washington to Steuben, February 6, 1781, Washington, *Writings* (Ford), ix. 123–124, note.

[3] St. Clair to Washington, March 2, 1781, *St. Clair Papers*, i. 542.

[4] January 29, 1781, Stillé, *Wayne*, 245, 260.

A detachment of the Pennsylvanians was ordered south in the spring of 1781, but the march was delayed by the slowness of the government in furnishing supplies and settling accounts. The State had promised to make good the depreciation of the Continental currency; but this very depreciation-money was worth less than one-seventh of its nominal value. The inhabitants refused to accept it in trade, and urged the soldiers not to advance farther till their wrongs were redressed. The day before that fixed for the march, a few men on the right of the regiment called out to pay them in "real, not ideal money," saying that they would be trifled with no longer. They were ordered to their tents, peremptorily refused, and were immediately arrested by their officers, who were prepared for an outbreak. A court-martial was at once ordered; and the leaders were tried, sentenced, and shot, all in the face of the discontented troops. "Whether by design or accident," says Wayne, "the particular friends and messmates of the culprits were their executioners, and while the tears rolled down their cheeks in showers, they silently and faithfully obeyed their orders without a moment's hesitation. Thus was this hideous monster crushed in its birth, however to myself and officers a most painful scene."[1]

[1] Letter of Wayne, May 20, 1781, Stillé, *Wayne*, 264-266.

CHAPTER VIII.

NEWBURG ADDRESSES.

WHEN the patience of the soldiers was exhausted, they mutinied; when the officers could no longer restrain themselves, they presented a memorial or threatened to resign. In the last year of the war the army was perhaps more comfortable than at any previous time, but the officers were discontented and irritable. Their condition was like that of a man who, exhausted with carrying a heavy load, has at last been relieved of a part of it: the help comes too late; he still staggers, and the slightest increase in his burden may cause a complete collapse. The long war and the intercourse with the French army had produced their natural results: there was less pride in Spartan simplicity, more sensitiveness at being compelled to live in a manner unbecoming "an officer and a gentleman."

In justice to the American officers it must be admitted that the position in which they were placed was a trying one. The government was in desperate straits for money, and Quartermaster Pickering pinched and pared at every opportunity. Major Shaw wrote that he hoped Pickering would be removed, for the baleful effects of his economy were felt all over the continent.[1] At the same time Sands was refusing the officers the privilege of drawing their extra rations at their own convenience. Washington wrote to the Secretary at War that he was "exceedingly impressed with the necessity of economizing the public monies"; but warned him that "we

[1] Shaw to Knox, December 27, 1781, *Knox MSS.* viii. 24.

must not spin the thread so fine as to break it, nor should the economy seem to bear hardest upon those who have already experienced a double share of all the distresses which have been felt." A few months later he wrote again: "Only conceive, then, the mortification they (even the general officers) must suffer, when they cannot invite a French officer, a visiting friend, or a travelling acquaintance, to a better repast than stinking whiskey (and not always that) and a bit of beef without vegetables will afford them."[1]

The officers might have borne these temporary discomforts with more patience but for their anxiety for the future. Their pay was in arrears, their accounts unsettled, and no provision had been made for discharging the half-pay that had been promised them; the war would probably end soon, and they would then be left, without money, credit, or business connections, to seek support for themselves and their families.

The officers of the Massachusetts line resolved to endeavor to obtain a guarantee for half-pay, or at least a commutation, that is, the payment of a sum in gross instead of an annuity for life. They were uncertain, however, to whom they should apply. The most natural and obvious course was to appeal to Congress, the body which had granted half-pay. Opposition to half-pay was, however, very strong, especially in New England; and, as no tax or appropriation could pass Congress without the assent of nine States, it was doubtful if this could be obtained for measures to discharge so unpopular a debt. Moreover, Congress had no means of compelling the payment of taxes; they could only make "requisitions" for money on the States. By 1782 the States had almost ceased to pay these demands; and it was probable that, even if Congress could be induced to call for money to satisfy the claims of the officers, the States would refuse to furnish it. On the other hand, the officers, knowing the feelings of their several States, could negotiate with them to advantage; and a State would be more willing to be taxed for half-pay if its money went exclusively to its own citizens. It might be hoped, too, that some States would

[1] Washington to Lincoln, May 28, 1782, *Sparks MSS*. lxv. (pt. 3), 263-264; October 2, 1782, Washington, *Writings* (Ford), x. 91.

immediately provide for their officers, and that their example would influence the rest.[1]

Accordingly, the Massachusetts officers decided to seek relief at Boston rather than at Philadelphia. They prepared a petition asking the State to adjust the claims for the depreciation of Continental money in the year 1781, and also those for the retained rations,[2] and to make good the depreciation of the money promised to the soldiers in lieu of clothing; "all of which," said the petition, "form as just a debt as the monthly pay." The officers wished one of their number to be present when their accounts were examined, but they were unable to support a delegate at Boston for the time which would be required to complete so extensive a piece of work; moreover, the papers from which the amounts due might be ascertained were at camp. Accordingly, the officers requested the legislature to send a committee to camp, with authority to make a settlement and give interest-bearing certificates for the amount due. The officers also asked the State itself to assume their half-pay, or to give a lump sum in commutation. Should reasons of policy compel a refusal, they begged that the answer might be definite, and said that they then would apply to Congress.[3]

General Knox and Colonels Rufus Putnam, Brooks, and Hull were chosen a committee to go to Boston to present the memorial. When Washington was asked for leave of absence, he replied that, although he was surprised that it should be requested for so many officers of high rank, yet, as the line desired it, he would allow the colonels to go, but that Knox could not be spared.[4] Knox was therefore obliged to content himself with writing a letter to Governor Hancock, explaining why he did not attend in person, begging Hancock's assistance, and appealing

---

[1] Lincoln to Knox, August 26, 1782, *Knox MSS.* ix. 99.

[2] Extra rations were allowed to officers to keep a table; Congress had withheld them, but promised compensation.

[3] Petition of Massachusetts Officers to the General Court, July, 1782, *Knox MSS.* ix. 67.

[4] Washington to Heath, August 29, 1783, Massachusetts Historical Society, *Collections*, 5th series, iv. 277.

to his well-known vanity by saying that the officers looked up to him as their political head.[1]

On September 9, 1782, the committee reached Boston. They were received very politely by Hancock, who promised them his full support, — a promise which the popularity-hunting governor failed, however, to keep. They also obtained great encouragement from John Adams, who declared that he would favor a liberal commutation. Many members of the legislature appeared cold or even hostile; some of them, however, had an exaggerated idea of the immense amount due as half-pay, and Brooks hoped that they might be frightened into promising a substantial sum to get rid of so dangerous a claim.[2]

It will be remembered that, when the grant of half-pay was discussed in Congress, the proposal was received with more favor by the wealthy and aristocratic Southerners than by the delegates from New England.[3] A somewhat similar division of sentiment now appeared in the Massachusetts legislature: the Senate and the seaport members were ready to gratify the officers, but in the House the friends of half-pay were in a minority of nearly four to one. This branch of the legislature was filled with members from the country districts, where the financial distress was sharpest and where the dogmas of equality were pushed to their furthest extent. The farmers thought that officers whose services were no longer needed should, like the rest of the community, depend upon their own labor for support; and they were much alarmed at the prospect of increased taxation.

The petition of the officers was referred to a joint committee of the legislature; but, while the question was still undecided, a member received a letter from Samuel Osgood, one of the Massachusetts delegates to Congress, in which Mr. Osgood declared that half-pay was unequal and excessive, and stated that Congress would themselves discuss the claims of the officers on the third Wednesday in January. This letter was read in the legislature, and gave an excellent pretext for postponing the consideration of the question of half-pay; while the consideration

---

[1] September 2, 1782, *Knox MSS.* ix. 123.
[2] Brooks to Knox, September 26, 1782, *Ibid.* x. 13.
[3] See above, p. 81.

of the claims for depreciation and retained rations were postponed until further information on those subjects could be obtained from Congress.[1]

Osgood afterward wrote to Knox explaining his action; he said that his letter was not meant for the public eye, and that the gentleman to whom it was written had always been a friend of the army. But Osgood, while disavowing any intention of stirring up feeling against the officers, maintained that Massachusetts ought not to make special provision for her own officers, since it had been asserted on the floor of Congress that such an arrangement would not free a State from the obligation of contributing to the half-pay of officers of other States. He also argued that, in providing for the officers, regard should be paid to length of service. He urged that, while eight years in the army would entirely unfit a man for private business, it was not so, even proportionately, with lesser periods: "I esteem eight to be much more than four times two, in this view of the matter," he said.[2] The argument was a strong one, but it did not touch the crucial point; the faith of Congress was already pledged to grant half-pay to the officers.

The legislatures of the State and of the nation had sought refuge from their perplexities in a policy of delay; to them it brought at least temporary relief, but to the officers it meant humiliation for the present and uncertainty for the future. Then, too, the fact that civil officers were regularly paid, while those of the army were unprovided for, was an additional source of irritation. The officers were also much excited by reports that members of Congress had said that the solemn promises of half-pay were only intended to answer certain purposes for the time being. Major Shaw wrote home, "If our enlightened countrymen considered common honesty as a moral duty, I should have it in my power to spend a little money in Boston, and enjoy the company of my friends in that quarter."[3]

[1] Brooks to Knox, October 17, 1783, *Knox MSS*. x. 60. Lowell to Lincoln, November 28, 1782, Massachusetts Historical Society, *Proceedings*, 1873-1875, p. 127.
[2] Osgood to Knox, December 4, 1782, *Knox MSS*. x. 130.
[3] Shaw to his brother, November 14, 1782, Quincy, *Shaw*, 98.

PREPARATION OF A MEMORIAL, 1782.

Washington was much alarmed, and remained in camp instead of going to Mount Vernon for the winter, as he would have done had the outlook been more favorable. The precaution was a wise one, for the discontent became so serious that a kind of cumulative strike was proposed: some officers were to resign on a fixed day; if redress were not given by a certain time, others were to send in their commissions; and successive resignations were to continue until Congress should yield. By some skill and management, however, the officers were induced to adopt the more patriotic measure of a joint address to Congress.[1]

The first steps were taken by the Massachusetts officers. On November 16, 1782, three representatives from each infantry regiment of the line (except the Second), three from the light infantry, two from the artillery, and one from the hospital department met in conference and invited the different regiments to draw up a list of grievances to be presented to a general committee, which was to prepare an address to Congress. Within two days the lists began to come in, including one from the Second Regiment. All referred to the delay in paying the troops; in many of them was a demand for a definite sum of money, usually three months' pay. Occasionally a date was fixed — the 1st of January, or February, or March — and a similar instalment was requested for the 1st of July. Massachusetts had given her troops interest-bearing certificates of indebtedness, to make good the loss caused by the depreciation of the Continental money; but these certificates had themselves depreciated, and on some the State had refused to pay the interest unless the time for which the notes ran were extended. One regiment complained that, although the securities of the State were worth only one-third or one-fourth of their face, Massachusetts had obtained credit from Congress for the full par value of her depreciation-certificates. "By this means," they said, "the distresses of the army have been withheld from that august body." Another regiment expressed a similar belief that the members were not aware of the condition of the troops.

[1] Washington to McHenry, October 17, and to Joseph Jones, December 14, 1782, Washington, *Writings* (Ford), x. 97, 117–119.

The officers were seriously alarmed lest they should be deprived of their half-pay, but they were not agreed as to the best means of securing it. Some thought that Congress should obtain the necessary funds; others considered this impossible, and merely asked that Congress recommend the several States to provide for their own officers. The money allowed in lieu of extra rations was inadequate, and this was felt to be a great grievance. Much was said about the condition of the "deranged officers"— that is, officers who had been compelled to leave the army by the merging of several small regiments into one. It was asserted that they had been obliged to pay their debts by selling their clothes, and to beg for support on their way home; and yet that they were treated by their neighbors as idlers living on the public bounty, and were pointed at as "half-pay officers." The generosity of Congress had proved absolutely harmful, and the officers remaining in the army feared a like fate for themselves.

Considerable attention was given to the claims of the soldiers, especially to those of men who had enlisted early in the war on small bounties. Two regiments asked for a settlement of accounts. Complaint was also made that the army was obliged to build its own quarters without receiving any extra pay, or rations, or even the thanks of Congress.

On the way in which the petition ought to be presented to Congress, opinion was divided. Some officers favored sending a committee to Philadelphia, others suggested methods more in accordance with military discipline,— as, that the address be laid before Congress by the commander-in-chief or by the Secretary at War. The tone of the memorial was variously requested to be "free and spirited," "very spirited," "humble but spirited." The officers of some regiments, either directly or by implication, threatened to resign unless relief were afforded. The phrases used ran from a mild request that those whose circumstances would not permit them to remain in the army might have leave to retire, to keen complaints of the treatment which compelled such a course; and the artillery officers added to their remonstrance a mutual pledge of honor to lay down their commissions unless redress were given.

The sharpest paper came from the officers of the Sixth Regiment. "We believe," they said, "that we engaged to serve the public, not as slaves at discretion for life, but as freemen upon contract for a definite period; that in order to make any contract binding on one party, the stipulations must be fulfilled by the other, or at least endeavors manifested by the other for their fulfilment. We flatter ourselves that no endeavors, or actual exertions have been wanting on our part to fulfil the contract with the public, or even to answer their most sanguine expectations. But at the close of the sixth year of the contract we have not received more than one-sixth part of our pay.";

The unhappy situation of the deranged officers was set forth in vigorous language, and the remonstrance declared: "This we consider as designed to be our future lot, and that we shall all be like asses of burden who, after having drudged through the heat of the day, to save expense, are turned out to graze the streets for support, till their masters see fit to make use of them again.

" . . . There are recent examples of millions being suddenly raised for carrying on the war, by the voluntary contribution of individuals, in countries where they had nothing to fight for, but aggrandizement, dominion, and conquest. But in this country, whose very existence, as an independent nation, depends ultimately upon the exertions of the present time, not a single dollar after eight campaigns, has been subscribed in support of the cause — by individuals, — tho abounding in wealth, — tho rolling in state, — tho swimming in luxury." [1]

Apparently the Massachusetts officers at first intended to act alone; but they changed their plan, and invited the officers of other States to join them in their application to Congress. Delegates were again appointed, consultations held, and in December a memorial was drawn up in behalf of the officers of New Hampshire, Massachusetts, Connecticut, New York, and New Jersey, and of "their brethren the soldiers." [2]

---

[1] November 22, 1782, *Knox MSS*. x. 118. For the other remonstrances, see *Ibid*. 101–115.

[2] The Rhode Island line was not with the main army, but their officers signified their assent later. The lines of other States were too far off to be consulted.

In this memorial of December, 1782, the officers set forth the failure of Congress to perform their engagements, and the hardships which the army had suffered in consequence. They said that it was with peculiar pain that, at this late period of the war, they addressed Congress on matters of a pecuniary nature; but that they had waited year after year in the vain hope of relief, and now many were unable to endure longer. "In this exigence, we apply to Congress . . . as our head and sovereign." They declared that large sums were due the army; that the securities given by the States in part payment of these debts had so depreciated as to be of little value; and that many officers had been unable to retain even this trifling recompense, for they had been obliged to sell their certificates to keep their families from actual starvation.

"We complain," they said, "that shadows have been offered to us while the substance has been gleaned by others.

"Our situation compels us to search for the cause of our extreme poverty. The citizens murmur at the greatness of their taxes, and are astonished that no part reaches the army. The numerous demands, which are between the first collectors and the soldiers, swallow up the whole.

"Our distresses are now brought to a point. We have borne all that men can bear—our property is expended—our private resources are at an end, and our friends are wearied out and disgusted with our incessant applications. We therefore most seriously and earnestly beg, that a supply of money may be forwarded to the army as soon as possible. The uneasiness of the soldiers, for want of pay, is great and dangerous; any further experiments on their patience may have fatal effects.

"The promised subsistence or ration of provisions consisted of certain articles specified in kind and quantity. This ration, without regard, that we can conceive, to the health of the troops, has been frequently altered, as necessity or conveniency suggested, generally losing by the change some part of its substance. On an average, not more than seven or eight tenths have been issued; the retained parts were, for a short time, paid for; but the business became troublesome to those who were to execute it. For this, or some other reasons, all regard to the

JOINT MEMORIAL TO CONGRESS.   151

dues, as they respected the soldiers, has been discontinued (now and then a trifling gratuity excepted). As these dues respected the officers, they were compensated during one year and part of another, by an extra ration; as to the retained rations, the account for several years remains unsettled; there is a large balance due upon it, and a considerable sum for that of forage.

"The clothing was another part of the soldiers' hire. The arrearages on that score, for the year 1777, were paid off in Continental money, when the dollar was worth about fourpence; the arrearages for the following years are unliquidated, and we apprehend scarcely thought of but by the army. Whenever there has been a real want of means, any defect in system, or neglect in execution, in the departments of the army, we have invariably been the sufferers, by hunger and nakedness, and by languishing in an hospital.

"We beg leave to urge an immediate adjustment of all dues; that as great a part as possible be paid, and the remainder put on such a footing as will restore cheerfulness to the army, revive confidence in the justice and generosity of its constituents, and contribute to the very desirable effect of reëstablishing public credit."

The officers spoke briefly of the unfortunate situation of those who had been deranged, and then passed on to the unpopularity of the grant of half-pay. They declared that they hoped that, for the honor of human nature, no one was so hardened in ingratitude as to deny the justice of this reward for their losses and sufferings. They had reason to believe, they said, that the objection was generally against the mode of payment only; and they offered, for the sake of harmony, to accept a commutation. They begged Congress to include in such an arrangement full provision for disabled officers and soldiers, and for the widows and orphans of those who had lost their lives in the service. They also requested that a mode be pointed out for the eventual payment of the bounty of eighty dollars, promised to soldiers who should serve to the end of the war. In conclusion, the officers said that it would be criminal in them to conceal the great and increasing dissatisfaction in the army, and they entreated that Congress, "to convince the army and the world that the independence of America shall not be placed on the ruin of any particular class of her citizens, will point out a mode for immediate redress." [1]

A committee of three — Major-General McDougall of New York, Lieutenant-Colonel Brooks of Massachusetts, and Colonel Ogden of New Jersey — was chosen to present the memorial to Congress. McDougall had been a "Son of Liberty" and an early and violent opponent of the policy of Parliament. Washington had a high opinion of him; and Lafayette, when in 1778 he had expected to head an invasion of Canada, desired McDougall as second in command on account of his "rigid and imperturbable virtue." [2] Brooks had served in the army for a number of years; he had been employed as assistant inspector under Steuben, and in that position had rendered valuable service. Ogden was a good officer, but less distinguished.

After a long delay in starting, due to the length of time required to raise the money for travelling expenses, and after another delay on the road on account of bad weather, the committee at last reached Philadelphia.[3] They spent some time talking with different members of Congress, and did not formally present the memorial until January 6, 1783. Congress was inclined to regard with disfavor the choosing of delegates and presenting of memorials by officers of the army, considering such acts as an improper mingling of civil and military functions; but Washington had written to Joseph Jones that on the present occasion it was advisable to adopt "soothing measures." He said that the officers had stood between the army and the public, and had risked their lives to quell mutinies; and that, should they now become as discontented as the soldiers, the consequences could not be foretold.[4] Jones doubtless communicated the substance of Washington's letter to other members, and

[1] December, 1782, *Journals of Congress*, viii. 225–228, April 29, 1783.
[2] Washington to President of Congress, October 7, 1777, Washington, *Writings* (Ford), vi. 102–103; Lafayette to President of Congress, January 31, 1778, Tower, *La Fayette in the American Revolution*, i. 278.
[3] McDougall to Knox, January 9, 1783, *Knox MSS.* xi. 36.
[4] Gouverneur Morris to Washington, October 26, 1778, Sparks, *Gouverneur Morris*, i. 174–177; Washington to Jones, December 14, 1782, Washington, *Writings* (Ford), x. 117–119.

Congress received the memorial without objection and referred it to a "grand committee," — that is, a committee consisting of one member from each State.[1]

The committee met promptly and agreed to confer with the financier on the following evening. Morris told them that any present payment of the army was impossible; and that, even if practicable, it would, he thought, be unwise, for it would seem to proceed from the fears rather than from the spontaneous generosity of Congress, and would therefore invite similar demands in the future. A general discussion of affairs then took place, and it was decided that the committee should confer with the officers three days later, Morris to be present. The day proved a stormy one, however, and, notwithstanding the importance of the meeting, there were several absentees. The chairman announced that General McDougall was disabled by rheumatism, and that the deputies had little money and were anxious to get back to camp as soon as possible; they therefore hoped, he said, that the committee would adjourn to McDougall's lodging at the Indian Queen Tavern. The suggestion was at first well received; but a member reminded his colleagues that such an act was not becoming in so dignified a body as a committee of States, especially as a conference with delegates from the army was out of the regular course of business, and the interview was postponed until January 13th, the weather serving as a convenient pretext for adjournment.

The conference took place on the day appointed. The senior deputy, General McDougall, began by acknowledging the attention shown in the appointment of so large a committee. He then passed on to the claims of the officers, dwelling particularly on three points — a present instalment of arrears, security for the remainder, and provision for half-pay. He insisted on the absolute necessity of the first of these, and described with great force the wrongs which the army had suffered. Particular cases of hardship were mentioned, and much stress was laid on the irritation of the army and the need of immediate action. Colonel Ogden declared that he would not wish to return as the

[1] For an account of all the proceedings and discussions, see Madison's report, Elliot, *Debates*, v. 20-64.

messenger of disappointment. Asked to specify the results of a failure to make a partial payment at once, the deputies were unable to do so: but they said that the most intelligent of the soldiers had been seen conferring privately with the sergeants; that there was reason to fear a mutiny or worse; that the situation of the officers, compelled to punish breaches of duty caused by previous breaches on the part of the public, was very painful; and that the lower officers at least would not exert themselves as vigorously as formerly to suppress an outbreak.

McDougall and Brooks both declared that the officers were almost ready to resort to extreme measures, and that this was partly due to the irritation felt at seeing the civil officers regularly receiving their salaries and the military as regularly left unpaid. The deputies said that the members of the legislatures never adjourned without securing their own salaries. To this, one of the committee replied that the legislators received little more than subsistence, which the army also obtained.

The deputies expressed both surprise and indignation at the reluctance of the States to provide a revenue for the central government. McDougall went out of his way to say with peculiar emphasis that the most intelligent and thoughtful part of the army were affected by the weakness of the central government, for they feared that, should it dissolve, the benefits won by the Revolution would be impaired, and that in the dissensions which might follow disunion the officers would be arrayed against each other.

The deputies spoke with much bitterness of the opposition to half-pay. They said that the officers had exposed their lives in defence of their country, and that seven years of military service had unfitted them for their former professions and occupations. Half-pay was, therefore, merely a reasonable provision for their future maintenance; it had, moreover, been solemnly promised by Congress and was a part of the officers' wages. They indignantly complained that officers not receiving a cent of the public money were yet abused as pensioners.[1]

[1] To appreciate the obloquy implied in the term "pensioner," one should remember Dr. Johnson's definition of a pension as " an allowance made to any

The officers then called the attention of the committee to the offer in the memorial to accept a commutation; and the conference closed. After the officers had withdrawn, Hamilton, Madison, and Rutledge were appointed a sub-committee to report arrangements in concert with Morris.

On January 25, 1783, a report, drawn by Hamilton, was presented to Congress by the grand committee. It provided that, "conformably to measures already taken,"[1] the superintendent of finance should, as soon as the condition of the treasury permitted, furnish pay in such amounts as he thought proper; and that the States should be recommended immediately to settle accounts with their respective lines up to August 1, 1780. The committee also submitted the declaration that "the troops of the United States, in common with all the creditors of the same, have an undoubted right to expect" security for the payment of the sums owed them; "and that Congress will make every effort in their power to obtain, from the respective States, general and substantial funds adequate to the object of funding the whole debt of the United States; and that Congress ought to enter upon an

one without an equivalent; in England, it is generally understood to mean pay given to a state hireling for treason to his country." Pensions were also very unpopular because they were regarded as undemocratic and as an encouragement to idleness. When the subject of half-pay was first discussed in Congress, Governor Livingston wrote to Laurens: "If whatever is is right, *a fortiori*, whatever is by act of Congress must unquestionably be right. But in my private judgment, I should be totally against the plan of allowing the officers half-pay after the war. It is a very pernicious precedent in Republican States; will load us with an immense debt, and render the pensioners themselves in a great measure useless to their country. If they must have a compensation, I think they had better have a sum certain to enable them to enter into business, and become serviceable to the community." (April 27, 1778, Sedgwick, *Livingston*, 281.) Root of Connecticut said in Congress: "That the genius of their people would not brook the paying of annual pensions, that they could not bear to see men strutting about their streets in the port of masters who had a right to demand of the people a part of their annual labor and toil to support them in idleness. That they chose rather to pay their officers at once after the war and then see them descend into the class of citizens." (July 31, 1782, *Thomson Papers*, in New York Historical Society, *Collections*, 1878, p. 76.)

[1] This clause was inserted to show, as was the fact, that measures had been taken to procure money for the army before the arrival of the deputies.

immediate and full consideration of the nature of such funds, and the most likely mode of obtaining them."

The committee proposed that those desiring half-pay for life should receive it; and that those wishing to commute should, one year after the peace, be granted [   ] years' full pay in certificates of indebtedness, bearing interest at six per cent. The allowance to widows and orphans was to remain unchanged. Settlement of claims for rations, for clothing, and for compensation due for the same was to be postponed until further information could be obtained.

The order for a present payment, and the call for a State settlement of accounts, passed unanimously; so also did the promise to ask the States to grant a substantial[1] revenue to Congress, "even Rhode Island concurring," says Madison in his journal of the debates. It was then moved that a commutation of six years' full pay be offered in lieu of half-pay for life. New England and New Jersey voted "No," the other six States present "Aye"; and the motion was lost for lack of the nine affirmative votes necessary to pass a tax or an appropriation. Congress, impressed by the magnitude of the sum involved, then referred the report to a committee of five. The subject of obtaining the security promised to the army and the other public creditors was then taken up, and after long debate it was voted in committee of the whole to ask the States to allow Congress to lay a tariff of five per cent *ad valorem* for twenty-five years, unless the war debts were sooner discharged.

On February 13, while the matter was still pending, Congress received a copy of the king's speech on opening Parliament, which indicated a speedy conclusion of peace. The news was very welcome. "The most judicious members of Congress," however, says Madison, "suffered a great diminution of their joy from the impossibility of discharging the arrears and claims of the army, and their apprehensions of new difficulties from that quarter."

[1] The word "general" occurring in the report of the committee was omitted in the resolution as passed. It was thought that the term might be interpreted to mean, not payable by all the States, but to be levied on all articles of taxation. Is it uncharitable to suppose that Hamilton, when he wrote the report, used the word for this very reason?

February 18, 1783, Congress went into committee of the whole on the subject of funds. Delegates Rutledge and Mercer moved that the proceeds of the proposed tariff be applied exclusively to the payment, first of the interest, and then of the principal, of the debts due the army. Probably the opponents of a permanent revenue wished to limit the impost as much as possible, and so tried to play off the claims of the army against a general funding system. The reasons they assigned, however, were that the merits of the army were superior to those of other creditors; that the troops must be paid, and this was the only means; that it would be useless to attempt extensive changes in the mode of raising money; and that, if too much were asked, nothing would be obtained.

These arguments met with small favor, however. The merits of the army were admitted; but it was said that a discrimination in the payment of the public debt should be made only in cases of the last necessity, and that at least the interest on the whole debt should be paid before any of the principal was discharged. It was urged, too, that a discrimination in favor of the army would offend the civil creditors, and that without their influence it would be impossible to induce the States to permit Congress to lay a tariff. Madison said that if separate funds were to be appropriated to separate debts, it would probably be thought best to assign the customs duties, which were little felt, to the payment of foreigners, "leaving more obnoxious revenues for those creditors who would excite the sympathy of their countrymen, and could stimulate them to do justice." A vote was twice taken on a proposal to discriminate, and in both instances every State except South Carolina answered "No."

On February 25 a motion was made to refer the claims of the officers to the several States. It was argued that this was the only practicable arrangement, and that some States considered the grant of half-pay as a "fetch," and not within the "spirit" of the authority conferred by the States on Congress.[1] In

---

[1] In a debate the preceding summer, one member claimed that this grant of half-pay was not even allowed by the letter of Congress's powers. The Articles of Confederation forbade any tax or appropriation without the consent of nine States, and the grant of half-pay for life had not received nine votes.

reply, it was urged that the grant was already made; that one concession to particularism would encourage others; that a reference to the States would be illegal, since it would apportion the public debt in a manner not sanctioned by the Articles of Confederation; and that it would be unfair to officers from States opposed to half-pay. The motion to refer failed, but two days later the attempt was renewed. Mercer of Virginia raised his warning voice, and plaintively told Congress that the commutation, with the funding of other debts, tended "to establish and perpetuate a moneyed interest in the United States; that this moneyed interest would gain the ascendence of the landed interest; would resort to places of luxury and splendor, and, by their example and influence, become dangerous to our republican constitutions."[1]

This speech drew forth a sharp reply from Madison. He pointed out that the commutation was a concession to persons who objected to pensions, but that these very men made it obnoxious by calling it a perpetuity. If a payment of the capital was suggested, he said, it was rightly opposed as impossible; if funding the debt was proposed, "it was exclaimed against as establishing a dangerous moneyed interest, as corrupting the public manners, as administering poison to our republican constitutions." Madison said that he was opposed to perpetuating public burdens, but that they must in some way be discharged, and that "the consequences predicted therefrom could not be more heterogeneous to our republican character and constitution than a violation of the maxims of good faith and common honesty."

The motion to refer again failed, and Congress spent some time in discussing a plan of commutation. On March 10 a committee to whom the subject had been referred brought

At the time half-pay was promised Congress had passed the Articles, but the States had not yet ratified them; and Clark of New Jersey declared that Congress, by adopting the Articles, had bound themselves, though not the States. See *Thomson Papers*, in New York Historical Society, *Collections*, 1878, pp. 72, 77.

[1] It is, however, just to Mr. Mercer to say that he made his prejudices yield to the public necessities, and finally agreed not to continue his opposition outside of Congress.

in a report, which, as amended, gave five years' full pay, to be accepted or rejected by the officers of each State, by the different corps unconnected with any State; and by all other officers entitled to half-pay. The decision of each of these bodies bound a dissenting minority. Some members, however, who were willing to commute wished that the army as a whole should accept or reject the commutation; and the report was not agreed to.

The matter remained in this situation a week, when a letter dated March 12, 1783, was received from Washington, in camp at Newburg, New York, inclosing copies of two anonymous papers, the so-called Newburg Addresses, which had appeared about the tenth and twelfth of March, passionately exhorting the officers to compel Congress to do them justice. Congress was already much troubled by the condition of foreign affairs and by the disorder of the finances; and the addition of this new danger, says Madison, " gave peculiar awe and solemnity to the present moment, and oppressed the minds of Congress with an anxiety and distress which had been scarcely felt in any period of the Revolution." But the seriousness of the present crisis did not prevent an ill-natured move on the part of a few members, who, in the hope of mortifying the men who had defeated their plans for strengthening the authority of Congress, procured the reference of the papers just received to those staunch opponents either of half-pay or of funds, Gilman, Dyer, Clark, Rutledge, and Mercer.[1]

Congress might well be alarmed, for the Addresses were a part of a carefully laid plot which had friends in Philadelphia and in the government itself. Since, however, they were severely condemned by Washington, by the general public, and even by the officers themselves, those who were concerned in the movement were anxious to conceal their participation, or at least to represent their acts in as favorable a way as they could; and it is therefore impossible to give a full account of the affair.

The author of the Addresses was Major John Armstrong, an

---

[1] Madison's report, Elliot, *Debates*, v. 66. For the text of the Addresses and papers relating to them, see Washington, *Writings* (Sparks), viii. Appendix xii.; and Appendix A below.

aide-de-camp of General Gates. Gates himself was to have posed as the leader of the movement; but he seems to have been more or less of a figurehead, put up at the last moment by the real leaders when they found that they could expect no assistance whatever from Washington. The ultimate purpose of Armstrong and his friends will probably never be known. Perhaps it was not clearly defined in even their own minds. Nearly forty years after the appearance of the Addresses, Judge Johnson of the United States Supreme Court published a life of General Greene, in which he declared that the papers were part of a formidable conspiracy to establish a military despotism. Armstrong was still living, and he wrote a scathing review of the book, ridiculing Johnson's arguments and giving what he claimed to be the true story of the Newburg Addresses. This story, Armstrong said, would "conclusively show, that the last of Mr. Johnson's imaginary conspiracies,[1] so far from being an attempt to close the war in usurpation and despotism, was an honest and manly, though perhaps indiscreet, endeavor to support public credit, and do justice to a long-suffering, patient, and gallant soldiery."

Armstrong declared that the officers were called together merely for the purpose of "passing a series of resolutions, which, in the hands of their committee [the committee sent to Philadelphia], and of their auxiliaries in Congress, would furnish a new and powerful lever for operating on" the States which had refused to consent to the impost. He quoted from a letter written to him by Gates on June 22, 1783, in which Gates mentioned that Gordon, the historian, had been begging for information concerning the Newburg Addresses. "As he is an old friend, and an honest man," said Gates, "I have answered frankly: that . . . the letters . . . were intended to produce a strong remonstrance to Congress in favor of the object prayed for in a former one; and that the conjecture, that it was meant to offer the crown to Cæsar [Washington], was without any foundation; referring him to his townsman or neighbor, Dr. Eustis, for further information, as well as for the correctness of this."

[1] The first was the Conway Cabal.

Armstrong's statements should not be unreservedly accepted, for his honesty is not above suspicion. Moreover, in the very article which he wrote to prove the good intentions of the officers, he admitted that Colonel Stewart "saw all grades, and communicated freely with *all;* and whether justly or not, was under the most solemn conviction, that the creed of the army, *without a single exception*, was settled on three points: 1st. that they would look to the national government alone for compensation; 2d. that in prosecuting their claims, they would make common cause with the civil creditors of the Union; and 3d. that they would neither solicit nor accept furloughs, till the issue of the new appeal [the proposition for an impost], to be made to the wisdom and justice of the States, should be distinctly known and officially promulgated."[1]

Furthermore, the Addresses themselves recommended that, unless a favorable answer were given to the memorial, the army should refuse further service and resist to the death any attempt to disband it. This seems bad enough; but Dr. Eustis told Surgeon Thacher that, after the Addresses had failed of their purpose, Armstrong wrote something "much worse," but that his friends persuaded him to refrain from publishing it.[2] The means which the officers intended to employ were clearly revolutionary, and there may be a doubt whether their object was as laudable as Armstrong asserted.

The central government was becoming feebler and feebler, and some of the officers had been turning their thoughts toward monarchy. In the spring of 1782, Colonel Lewis Nicola wrote to Washington that there was little hope that Congress would do the army justice, that experience proved that republics were unstable, and that a limited monarchy was the best form of government; and he plainly intimated his desire that Washington should be made king. But his proposal met with a stern rebuke. "Be assured, sir," Washington replied, "no occurrence in the course of the war has given me more painful sensations, than your information of there being such ideas existing in the army,

---

[1] *United States Magazine and Literary and Political Repository*, January, 1823, pp. 37-41.

[2] Thacher to Pickering, January 5, 1826, Pickering, *Pickering*, i. 436.

as you have expressed, and [such as] I must view with abhorrence and reprehend with severity. For the present the communication of them will rest in my own bosom, unless some further agitation of the matter shall make a disclosure necessary.

"I am much at a loss to conceive what part of my conduct could have given encouragement to an Address, which to me seems big with the greatest mischiefs, that can befall my country. . . . Let me conjure you, then, if you have any regard for your country, concern for yourself or posterity, or respect for me, to banish these thoughts from your mind, and never communicate, as from yourself or any one else, a sentiment of the like nature." [1]

On the whole, we may dismiss as unlikely Judge Johnson's theory of a plot of the officers to establish monarchy. Possibly some officers thought that Gates would accept the position which Washington had refused; but Armstrong, in a private letter to Gates, speaks of monarchy as a great evil which might result from a failure of the States to perform their obligations.[2] Much more probably, many of the officers hoped to compel Congress and the States to retain them in service permanently. A memorandum among the papers of Rufus King, whose information came indirectly from Armstrong himself, contains the following statement: —

"It appears that the arrival of peace and the approaching dissolution of the army formed a singular crisis in the military annals of America — a return to private life was to a majority of the American officers a prospect of obscurity if not of actual misery. The American governments were not favorable to their claims. Their respectability would be lost by separation and their pretensions derided. They were without wealth or family influence and their military situation was more inviting and pleasant than any that they could expect or hope. Their object was to perpetuate that situation or procure one more eligible for this purpose." [3]

The civilian members of the conspiracy cared little for the

---

[1] Washington to Nicola, May 22, 1782, Washington, *Writings* (Ford), x. 21–23, and note.

[2] See Appendix A, below, pp. 208–209.

[3] King, *King*, i. 621–622.

claims of the officers: they aimed at political reform; they hoped that the fear of a military revolt would induce the States to increase the powers of Congress; should this plan fail, they probably wished Congress, supported by the army, to assume additional powers themselves. Their leader is not certainly known; the rumor of the camp gave the doubtful honor to Gouverneur Morris, the assistant superintendent of finance, and coupled with his name that of his chief, Robert Morris.

There is no direct evidence of the participation of Robert Morris in the conspiracy; and he wrote Washington an indignant letter, declaring that, instead of drawing the army to mutiny and sedition, he had remained in office much against his will merely to secure the peaceful disbandment of the troops. On the other hand, there was a widespread belief among the officers that he was concerned in the affair; and in 1788 Armstrong told a friend that Morris was said to have offered to find means of feeding the army.[1] Perhaps Morris encouraged the officers, but hoped that the mere apprehension of violence would induce the States to make concessions; or that, if force proved necessary, means would be found to give it a quasi-legal sanction.

The connection of Gouverneur Morris with the conspiracy is rendered extremely probable by his own correspondence. On January 1, 1783, he wrote to Jay: "The army have swords in their hands. You know enough of the history of mankind to know much more than I have said, and possibly much more than they themselves yet think of. I will add, however, that I am glad to see things in their present train. Depend on it, good will arise from the situation to which we are hastening. And this you may rely on, that my efforts will not be wanting. I pledge myself to you on the present occasion, and although I think it probable, that much of convulsion will ensue, yet it must terminate in giving to government that power, without which government is but a name."[2] Morris told Greene: "I am most perfectly convinced that (with the due exception of miracles) there is no probability the States will ever make such grants [to provide a revenue to discharge all debts], *unless the army be united and determined in the pursuit of it; and unless*

---

[1] King, *King*, i. 621–622. [2] Sparks, *Gouverneur Morris*, i. 249.

they be firmly supported, and as firmly support the other public creditors. That this may happen must be the entire wish of every intelligently just man, and of every real friend to our glorious revolution."[1]

To Knox, Morris wrote: "It has given me much pain to see the army looking wildly for a redress of grievances to their particular States. Separate provisions and no provisions are tantamount in my idea for any laws which they can repeal they will repeal as soon as they find it expedient. The same principle of convenience which will lead them to take care of the army and leave other creditors unnoticed will operate effectually against the army when it is disbanded after a peace. During the war they find you useful and after a peace they will wish to get rid of you and then they will see you starve rather than pay a six-penny tax. These my dear friend are sentiments which experience has compelled me to adopt against my will. And I declare to God it is my sincere opinion that the best legislature on the continent will do things which the worst man among them would in his private capacity be ashamed of. It is therefore not my persuasion but my conviction that the only wise mode is for the army to connect themselves with the public creditors of every kind both foreign and domestic and unremittingly to urge the grant of general permanent funds adequate to the whole interest and which increasing with our numbers and wealth will consequently absorb the principal. The army may now influence the legislatures and if you will permit me a metaphor from your own profession after you have carried the post the public creditors will garrison it for you."[2]

Both Knox and Greene, though ready, as the Du Coudray incident had shown,[3] to leave the service rather than submit to unfair treatment, refused to be drawn into the unlawful and dangerous course hinted at by Gouverneur Morris. Knox wrote that the army had always been Continental, that "a hoop to the barrel," and "cement to the union" were favorite toasts; and he said that the army would gladly help to strengthen the government, but that it "must be directed in the mode by

---

[1] Gouverneur Morris to Greene, February 11, 1783, Johnson, *Greene*, ii. 395.
[2] February 7, 1783 *Knox MSS*. xi. 109.   [3] See above, p. 56.

proper authority." He asked: "As the present constitution is so defective, why do not you great men call the people together, and tell them so? That is, to have a convention of the States to form a better constitution? This appears to us, who have a superficial view only, to be the most efficacious remedy."[1]

Greene put the very pertinent question to his correspondent, "When soldiers advance without authority, who can halt them?"[2] To this Morris replied: "I entirely agree with you in sentiment as to the consequences, which must follow from any unconstitutional procedure of the military. The boundary between their humble petitions, and their most forcible demands, is shadowy and indescribable. *I did hope from their influence;* and I know, that if Congress had taken manly and decisive measures, America would have been united and happy. I was content, on this ground, again to labor and to hazard; but, neither time nor circumstances *will permit anything now.*"[3]

It can hardly be doubted that Gouverneur Morris wished the army to present requests so urgent as to have the effect, if not the form, of threats. In his last letter to Greene he seems, indeed, to disapprove of the use of force; but Morris might naturally endeavor to minimize the illegality and danger of his plans; and even here he speaks of "labor" and "hazard," and wishes that Congress "had taken manly and decisive measures." This suggests a *coup d'état*, though a peaceful one; while the letter to Jay, pledging his efforts and welcoming the danger of convulsion, indicates that if force had proved necessary he would not have hesitated to use it.

It may be urged that the scheme was too violent to have been seriously entertained by a person of orderly and conservative instincts like Morris; but the utter collapse of national authority was making men desperate. During the debate on half-pay, two members of Congress declared that they did not wish the army

[1] Knox to Gouverneur Morris, February 21, 1783, Sparks, *Gouverneur Morris*, i. 256.
[2] Greene to Gouverneur Morris, April 3, 1783, *Ibid.* 251.
[3] Morris to Greene, May 18, 1783, Johnson, *Greene*, ii. 397.

to disband until justice were done it; and, after Washington's patriotism had defeated the conspiracy, Smith wrote to Boudinot, the president of Congress: "Talk of your Cato, your Brutus and your Cassius, — they are all mere fools to him [Washington]. In short, he is too good for an ingrate, base, degenerate world. Verily, I don't know whether it would not have been best for us all had he laid hold of the helm; for I am confoundedly afraid the stupid crew will sink the ship when escaped the storm and got into safe port."

Alexander Hamilton disapproved of an appeal to arms, less because he thought it wrong than because he deemed it useless. He wrote to Washington: "The army would moulder by its own weight, and for want of the means of keeping together; the soldiery would abandon their officers; there would be no chance of success, without having recourse to means that would reverse our revolution. I make these observations, not that I imagine your Excellency can want motives to continue your influence in the path of moderation, but merely to show why I cannot myself enter into the views of coercion, which some gentlemen entertain; for, I confess, could force avail, I should almost wish to see it employed. I have an indifferent opinion of the honesty of this country, and ill forebodings as to its future system."[1]

Hamilton was, however, willing to threaten what he thought it unsafe to attempt. In an earlier letter to Washington he had said: —

"The claims of the army, urged with moderation, but with firmness, may operate on those weak minds which are influenced by their apprehensions more than by their judgments, so as to produce a concurrence in the measures which the exigencies of affairs demand. They may add weight to the applications of Congress to the several States. So far a useful turn may be given to them. But the difficulty will be to keep a complaining and suffering army within the bounds of moderation.

"This your Excellency's influence must effect. In order to it, it will be advisable not to discountenance their endeavor to procure redress, but rather, by the intervention of confiden-

[1] March 25, 1783, Sparks, *Correspondence of the Revolution*, iv. 13.

tial and prudent persons, to *take the direction of them.* This, however, must not appear; it is of moment to the public tranquillity that your Excellency should preserve the confidence of the army without losing that of the people. This will enable you, in case of extremity, to guide the torrent, and to bring order, perhaps even good, out of confusion. It is a part that requires address, but it is one which your own situation as well as the welfare of the community points out."[1]

The conspirators spared no pains to insure success. The public was prepared for an outbreak by rumors that the officers had resolved not to disband.[2] The delegates from the army at Philadelphia were willing to accept a mere recommendation by Congress that the several States should commute the officers' claims; but they were persuaded that a Continental provision could alone secure their half-pay, and Brooks and Ogden, and probably McDougall, were drawn into the intrigue. An attempt was made to lessen the influence of Washington, and to induce the officers to regard General Gates as their true leader. The conspirators talked of Washington's reserve and his austerity of temper, both of which were said to have increased of late; and they made the most of the unpopularity of certain gentlemen who had been recently appointed on his staff.[3] Some officers were thus alienated without suspecting whither they were being led. Letters were written to different officers, and plans were discussed for supplying the army.

In February, 1783, Brooks returned to camp to prepare the officers for a demonstration. He carried a written report from the committee, which gave hopes that their application would meet with success;[4] but in private conversation he spoke of the prospect of relief from Congress as gloomy. His words made much impression. Major Wright wrote sadly to his friend, Colonel Webb, " I think with you that every honest good citizen are our friends, but the honest and good compose but a very

---
[1] February 7, 1783, Sparks, *Correspondence of the Revolution*, iii. 550–551.
[2] Washington to Joseph Jones, March 12, 1783, Washington, *Writings* (Ford), x. 175, note 1.
[3] Elliot, *Debates*, v. 55.
[4] Washington, *Writings* (Sparks), viii. 552–554.

small part of the world at this day." Major Shaw complained that the mountain had "brought forth a mouse," but said that the prospect of peace had had a soothing effect at camp.[1]

By March, 1783, the train was laid, and Colonel Walter Stewart was chosen to apply the match. During the winter Stewart had gone to Philadelphia on sick leave; and he remained there after his recovery, in spite of the efforts of the commander-in-chief to get him back to camp.[2] Notwithstanding the attempts of the conspirators to undermine the influence of Washington, Stewart was directed to sound him, and, if he thought it prudent, to reveal a part of their plans and request him to assume the leadership. But Stewart soon became convinced that no aid could be expected from Washington.[3]

Gates was then approached, and he consented to put himself at the head of the movement. Reports were circulated among the officers that it was universally expected that the troops would not disband until justice was done them; that the public creditors looked to them for assistance, and were willing to join them in the field if necessary; and that some members of Congress wished the army to take decisive measures in order to compel the delinquent States to do justice.[4] When the minds of the officers were supposed to be sufficiently excited, an anonymous call was issued, requesting a meeting of the general and field-officers, together with a delegate from each company and from the medical staff. "But to this end," says Armstrong in telling the story forty years later, "there was yet wanting the interposition of a hand, which should touch with some ability the several chords of sympathy and feeling that belonged to the case, and thus secure to the deliberations and their result, that tone and energy, without which, they would be a dead letter. The choice fell upon Major Armstrong, a very young man (the aide de camp of General Gates), who, yielding to the solicitations

---

[1] Wright to Webb, February 28, 1783, Ford, *Correspondence of Samuel B. Webb*, iii. 4; Shaw to Eliot, February 23, 1783, Quincy, *Shaw*, 101.

[2] Washington to Steuben, February 18, 1783, *Sparks MSS.* xv. 321.

[3] King, *King*, i. 622.

[4] Washington to Jones, March 12, 1783, Washington, *Writings* (Ford), x. 175.

of his friends, in a few hours produced an address, which was believed to be peculiarly adapted to its object."[1]

This Address, March 10, 1783, was, indeed, well contrived to inflame the passions of the officers. After a highly wrought description of their merits, their sufferings, and the fate which the ingratitude of their country had prepared for them, Armstrong urged them, if their determination were in any proportion to their wrongs, to carry their appeal "from the justice to the fears of government. Change," he said, "the milk-and-water style of your last memorial. . . . Tell them [Congress] . . . that the slightest mark of indignity from Congress now must operate like the grave, and part you forever; that, in any political event, the army has its alternative. If peace, that nothing shall separate you from your arms but death; if war, that courting the auspices, and inviting the direction of your illustrious leader, you will retire to some unsettled country, smile in your turn, 'and mock when their fear cometh on.'" This compliment to Washington is the more noticeable, because another phrase was thought to be aimed at him in particular, — "suspect the man, who would advise to more moderation and longer forbearance."[2]

The originals of the call and the Address were carried to the adjutant-general's office, "where were every morning assembled aides-de-camp, majors of brigades, and adjutants of regiments, all of whom, that chose to do so, took copies and circulated them."[3] The Address produced a great effect. Washington said that in elegance and in force of expression it had "rarely been equalled in the English language." Pickering called it a "truly Junian" composition;[4] and all recognized in the unknown author a writer of extraordinary power. Unfortunately, many officers did not confine their admiration to Armstrong's rhetoric, but applauded his sentiments as well. There was great peril that men who meant to go no farther than remonstrances verg-

---

[1] *United States Magazine, and Literary and Political Repository*, January, 1823, p. 41.
[2] Washington, *Writings* (Sparks), viii. 555–558; Appendix A, below.
[3] Washington, *Writings* (Sparks), viii. 565.
[4] Washington to Harrison, March 19, 1783, Washington, *Writings* (Ford), x. 190; Pickering to Hodgdon, March 16, 1783, Pickering, *Pickering*, i. 440.

ing on threats would be insensibly led into treason. Pickering wrote to his wife: "If the business is conducted with prudence, it may have the best effects in promoting the success of those salutary measures, proposed and proposing by Congress, for the purpose of establishing such permanent revenues as will insure the payment of the army and other public creditors. In this view the meeting has my hearty concurrence. But should rashness govern the proceedings, the consequences may be such as are dreadful even in idea. God forbid the event should be so calamitous!"[1]

Yet, notwithstanding his seeming moderation, Pickering desired that Congress be informed that the army did not wish to be disbanded until its accounts were settled and funds established to pay it. "In this measure," Pickering said, "I extended my views beyond the army. I cast my eye on the numerous public creditors, who at present have but a *hope* that they will ever be paid. I considered the reputation of my country as at stake in this great question of establishing funds to pay the public debts. I did not desire the army to disband until this essential, all-important point were gained. The wish of the army to this effect being communicated, I knew that Congress and the governments of the States would make some useful and necessary reflections on it."[2] Probably the quartermaster-general hardly realized that the soldier who begins with covertly threatening the civil power may end by openly coercing it.

Fortunately, Washington was at least partially aware of the plans of Stewart and his friends.[3] Knowing the excited feelings of the officers, he did not venture an absolute prohibition of the meeting; but he gained time for sober second thought by an order condemning the anonymous call, but requesting a

[1] March 14, 1783, Pickering, *Pickering*, l. 407.
[2] Pickering to Mrs. Pickering, March 16, 1783, *Ibid.* 442.
[3] How Washington obtained this knowledge is uncertain. One account says that Brooks was the informer; another mentions Knox, and hints that in repeating to Washington what he had learned he broke the strict rules of honor. Possibly Brooks had taken Knox into his confidence, expecting, but not exacting, secrecy; and Knox believed that the danger to the country required him to lay the matter before the commander-in-chief.

MEETING OF MARCH 15, 1783.   171

meeting, similar to that so irregularly summoned, four days later.[1] Meantime he used to the utmost his personal influence with individual officers, and induced many to abandon their rash and disloyal scheme.[2]

The anonymous author thereupon issued a second and shorter Address, in which he boldly declared that the order showed Washington's sympathy with the movement. He also urged that, if his advice was good, the fact that it was anonymous should work no prejudice, and promised to reveal himself if suspicion fell on another.[3]

The meeting was held in a sort of assembly hall, which had been recently erected under somewhat peculiar circumstances. Chaplain Evans desired to have a building in which to hold divine service, and a number of the officers felt the need of a large room in which they could have dancing parties. Thus, the church and the world joined forces, and the "New Building," as it was officially styled, was the result. Mr. Evans wished to call it the "Temple of Honor and Virtue," but modesty or desire for brevity led the officers to drop the latter part of the designation, and the building was commonly spoken of as the "Temple."[4]

After the officers gathered, Washington unexpectedly appeared. "Every eye was fixed upon the illustrious man, and attention to their beloved general held the assembly mute."[5] Washington said that he had committed his thoughts to writing that he might express them with more perspicuity and connection, and then proceeded to read an address to the officers. He began by referring to the unmilitary character of the anonymous summons, and the manifest intention of appealing to passion rather than to reason. He explained that on this account he had opposed an irregular and hasty meeting; but he said that his conduct in the past would show that he was not

---

[1] Washington, *Writings* (Sparks), viii. 558.
[2] Gordon, *History of the American War*, iv. 356.
[3] Washington, *Writings* (Sparks), viii. 558–560; Appendix A, below.
[4] Pickering, *Pickering*, i. 399; Lossing, *Field-Book of the Revolution*, ii. 117–118.
[5] Shaw to Eliot, April, 1783, Quincy, *Shaw*, 103.

indifferent to the interests of the army, and he asserted that the advice given in the Anonymous Addresses proved that their author, whoever he might be, was a foe to the army, perhaps an emissary from New York. Washington expressed his own confidence in the justice of Congress, and solemnly promised to aid the officers in every way consistent with his duty. His written address concluded with an earnest entreaty that the officers would not do anything which would lessen their dignity and sully their glory, but that they would, by giving "one more distinguished proof of unexampled patriotism, and patient virtue," cause posterity to say, "Had this day been wanting, the world had never seen the last stage of perfection, to which human nature is capable of attaining."[1]

Washington then added that, as a corroborative proof of the good disposition of Congress, he would read a letter which he had received from one of their number, a gentleman who had always shown himself a fast friend of the army. The letter, he explained, was not even remotely intended for this use, but it contained sentiments so pertinent to the occasion that he thought himself justified in communicating them.[2] The letter described the plans and efforts of Congress to obtain a revenue; declared that, were a discrimination in paying the public debts just, one would be made in favor of the army; explained that the delay in answering the officers' petition was due to the slowness natural to a body like Congress, in which so many different interests were represented; and referred to the dependence of Congress on the States. The writer also pointed out that when the military once assume undue power, retreat becomes difficult, and they may be carried farther than at first they mean to go. He mentioned a report that attempts were being made to lessen Washington's popularity, and expressed his fears for the country if these attempts should be successful.[3]

[1] Washington, *Writings* (Sparks), viii. 560–563; Appendix A, below.
[2] Pickering to Hodgdon, March 16, 1783, Pickering, *Pickering*, i. 438.
[3] Jones to Washington, February 27, 1783, Sparks, *Correspondence of the Revolution*, iii. 554–560. Washington did not think it wise to give the letter in full. Besides omitting considerable matter relating to Vermont which had

The letter doubtless produced a good effect. Major Shaw, and even Timothy Pickering, described it as "sensible"; but an incident during the reading of it was much more impressive than the letter itself. After the first paragraph, Washington drew out his spectacles with the remark, that he had grown gray in the service and now found himself growing blind. "There was something so natural, so unaffected, in this appeal," says Major Shaw, "as rendered it superior to the most studied oratory; it forced its way to the heart, and you might see sensibility moisten every eye."[1]

Having laid his opinions before the assembly, Washington withdrew, and Gates took the chair.[2] On the motion of Knox, seconded by Rufus Putnam, thanks were unanimously voted to the commander-in-chief for his "excellent address," and he was assured that "the officers reciprocate his affectionate expressions with the greatest sincerity of which the human heart is capable." The memorial to Congress, the resolutions of that body acknowledging the right of the soldiers to security and promising to try to obtain a revenue, and the report of the committee to Philadelphia were read. It was then voted that a committee of three — a general, a field-officer, and a captain — should draw up resolutions and report in half an hour. General Knox, Lieutenant-Colonel Brooks, and Captain Howard were chosen.

Three resolutions were reported, and, after undergoing some

---

no bearing on the present case, he left out these sentences: "Whether to temporize, or oppose with steady, unremitting firmness what is supposed to be in agitation, of dangerous tendency, or that may be agitated, must be left to your own sense of propriety and better judgment. . . . That we shall have peace soon is almost reduced to a certainty; but my fears are, it will not be attended with those blessings generally expected. There are so many great questions, very interesting to particular States, unsettled, that it is difficult to avoid uneasy impressions for the consequences" (Pickering, *Pickering*, i. 444–445, note).

[1] Shaw to Eliot, April, 1783, Quincy, *Shaw*, 103–104.
[2] The general order requesting the meeting had designated the senior officer present as chairman. The senior major-general was Gates, and Washington, who had heard reports that, notwithstanding the appearance of perfect friendship and cordiality, the "old leaven" of the time of the Conway Cabal was still working, took the opportunity of thus quietly removing his old rival from the floor.

changes, were passed.¹ The first asserted the patriotism of the officers, and their resolve to preserve their reputation unstained in spite of any distress and danger. The second affirmed their confidence in the justice of Congress and their country, and their conviction that the army would not be disbanded before its accounts were adjusted and adequate funds provided for securing the amount due, including the commutation for half-pay. The third requested the commander-in-chief to write to Congress and ask for a more speedy decision on the late memorial. The third resolution also declared that a prompt reply "would produce immediate tranquillity in the minds of the army, and prevent any further machinations of designing men to sow discord between the civil and military powers of the United States." ²

There was no debate. Pickering made a strong speech disapproving the Anonymous Address, but setting forth the sufferings of the army; and his words made considerable impression. It is said that, if a man of firmness and of moderate eloquence had risen to support him, the effect produced by Washington's speech would have been lost.³ The historian, Gordon, who was closely connected with Gates, says, "It was happy for the army and country, that, when his Excellency had finished and withdrawn, no one rose and observed, 'that General Washington was about to quit the military line laden with honor, and that he had a considerable estate to support him with dignity, but that their case was very different.'"⁴ No one, however, was hardy enough to say this, and the three resolutions passed unanimously.

Thanks were voted to the committee sent to Congress; a copy of the proceedings was ordered to be forwarded to General McDougall, and he was requested to continue at Philadelphia until the business was accomplished. A resolution was also

---

¹ What these changes were is not known; only the final form of the resolutions has been preserved.

² Washington, *Writings* (Sparks), viii. 564-565; Pickering, *Pickering*, i. 438-440.

³ King, *King*, i. 622.

⁴ Gordon, *History of the American War*, iv. 357-358.

offered, "That the officers of the American army view with abhorrence, and reject with disdain, the infamous propositions contained in a late anonymous address to the officers of the army, and resent with indignation the secret attempts of some unknown persons to collect the officers together in a manner totally subversive of all discipline, and good order."[1] This resolution is recorded as passing unanimously, that is, there was no open opposition by speech or vote. Timothy Pickering believed the censure far too severe for the offence; but, discouraged by his former ill success, he refrained from offending Washington and his friends, and contented himself with silently abstaining from voting. Pickering made up, however, for this unwonted self-restraint by pouring forth his contempt for the "*mobile vulgus*" in his letters to his wife and to a friend in Philadelphia.[2]

Even Pickering praised Washington's speech, and many of the officers were profoundly touched by it. General Schuyler, in a letter written two days after the meeting, says: "Never, through all the war, did his Excellency achieve a greater victory than on this occasion — a victory over jealousy, just discontent, and great opportunities. The whole assembly were in tears at the conclusion of his address. I rode with General Knox to his quarters in absolute silence, because of the solemn impression on our minds. I have no doubt that posterity will repeat the closing words of his Excellency's address, — 'Had this day been wanting, the world had never seen the last stage of perfection to which human nature is capable of attaining.'"[3]

Major Shaw applied these same words to Washington, in writing to a friend: "I rejoice in the opportunities I have had of seeing this great man in a variety of situations; — calm and intrepid where the battle raged, patient and persevering under the pressure of misfortune, moderate and possessing himself in the full career of victory. Great as these qualifications deservedly render him, he never appeared to me more truly so,

---

[1] Washington, *Writings* (Sparks), viii. 565.
[2] Pickering, *Pickering*, i. 437-443.
[3] Pickering to Hodgdon, March 16, 1783, Pickering, *Pickering*, i. 437-438; Schuyler to Van Rensselaer, March 17, 1783, Lossing, *Schuyler*, ii. 427, note.

than at the assembly we have been speaking of. On other occasions he has been supported by the exertions of an army and the countenance of his friends; but in this he stood single and alone. There was no saying where the passions of an army, which were not a little inflamed, might lead; but it was generally allowed that longer forbearance was dangerous, and moderation had ceased to be a virtue. Under these circumstances he appeared, not at the head of his troops, but as it were in opposition to them; and for a dreadful moment the interests of the army and its general seemed to be in competition! He spoke, — every doubt was dispelled, and the tide of patriotism rolled again in its wonted course. Illustrious man! what he says of the army may with equal justice be applied to his own character. 'Had this day been wanting, the world had never seen the last stage of perfection to which human nature is capable of attaining.'" [1]

March 18 the following notice appeared in general orders: "The commander-in-chief is highly satisfied with the report of the proceedings of the officers assembled on the 15th instant, in obedience to the orders of the 11th. He begs his inability to communicate an adequate idea of the pleasing feelings, which have been excited in his breast by the affectionate sentiments expressed towards him on that occasion, may be considered as an apology for his silence." [2]

On the same day Washington wrote to the president of Congress, inclosing a copy of the resolutions passed by the officers and warmly urging a compliance with their wishes. Quoting a passage from the Anonymous Address which pictured the miserable fate awaiting the officers, he says that, if this be true, "then shall I have learned what ingratitude is, then shall I have realized a tale, which will embitter every moment of my future life. But I am under no such apprehensions. A country, rescued by their arms from impending ruin, will never leave unpaid the debt of gratitude." [3] Washington also wrote an unofficial letter to Joseph Jones, impressing on him the need

[1] Shaw to Eliot, April, 1783, Quincy, *Shaw*, 104.
[2] Washington, *Writings* (Sparks), viii. 565.
[3] Washington, *Writings* (Ford), x. 178-181.

of taking such measures as would prevent renewed disturbance. He said that, although force could not help the officers, passion might easily carry them away; and that the mere attempt at violence would stain the honor of America.[1]

Washington's exhortations found Congress in a pliant mood. The extremity of the danger had affected even the Connecticut delegates, for, on March 20, Dyer made a proposition concerning half-pay substantially the same as one which his own vote had defeated ten days before. It was referred to a committee, and while still in their hands Washington's report arrived. "The dissipation of the cloud which seemed to have been gathering," says Madison, "afforded great pleasure on the whole, to Congress; but it was observable that the part which the general had found it necessary, and thought it his duty, to take, would give birth to events much more serious, if they should not be obviated by the establishment of such funds as the general, as well as the army, had declared to be necessary."[2]

The same day that the letter was received, the committee to whom Dyer's proposal had been referred submitted a report advising that a sum in gross be given to the officers. First came an explanatory preamble, stating that the opposition to a system of pensions was one reason for the commutation. Objection was made, but Dyer entreated that the preamble be allowed to stand as it would help to reconcile Connecticut to the measure; and his wishes were indulged. The commutation was five years' full pay, in cash or six per cent securities, at the option of Congress. This commutation was to be accepted or rejected by the separate lines, by the hospital department, by the retired officers from the several States, and by all not included in these divisions, each body deciding for and binding the individuals in it. In the case of retired officers, their acceptance cancelled all dues accruing since leaving the service. It was made the duty of the financier, as soon as the acceptance of the above-mentioned divisions should be made known, to take measures for the settling of accounts, and to issue six per cent certificates of indebtedness.

[1] March 18, 1783, Washington, *Writings* (Ford), x. 182–184.
[2] Elliot, *Debates*, v. 73.

On the roll-call, Georgia was not represented; New Hampshire and New Jersey voted "No"; Rhode Island also voted "No," but, as only one delegate was present, the vote of the State was lost.¹ Massachusetts, Connecticut, New York, Pennsylvania, Delaware, Maryland, Virginia, North Carolina, South Carolina, voted "Aye." Nine States had voted in the affirmative and the resolution was passed. The commutation appears to have been generally accepted; many of the younger officers, indeed, were unwilling to take it, but they were overborne by the older men, and by those who were in pressing need of immediate relief.²

¹ *Journals of Congress*, viii. 161–164, March 22, 1783; Elliot, *Debates*, v. 73.
² *Congressional Globe*, 34 Cong. 3 sess. 335, January 15, 1857.

CHAPTER IX.

MUTINY OF 1783 AND DISBANDMENT OF THE ARMY.

A PRELIMINARY treaty of peace between the United States and Great Britain was concluded at Versailles, January 23, 1783; the news reached Philadelphia March 23, but Congress took no action until they received an official notification from the American envoys. They then, on April 11, issued orders for a cessation of hostilities, but gave no directions concerning the discharge of the men enlisted for the war. The soldiers, however, had become suspicious that Congress was planning to detain them after the expiration of their enlistments; and Washington feared that they would not distinguish between a cessation of hostilities and a definitive peace, and would become still more discontented. For this reason he thought of suppressing the resolution of Congress; but all the generals advised against such a course, and he directed that the cessation of hostilities be solemnly proclaimed on the following day, April 19.[1] In his order he warmly thanked and praised the "patriot army," and reminded them that nothing now remained "but for the actors of this mighty scene to preserve a perfect unvarying consistency of character through the very last act, to close the drama with applause, and to retire from the military theatre with the same approbation of angels and men, which has crowned all their former virtuous actions."[2]

At the same time Washington wrote to Congress, begging them to decide what should be done with the soldiers enlisted

[1] There was a delay of one day, so that the conclusion of the war might be announced exactly eight years after it had begun.
[2] April 18, 1783, Washington, *Writings* (Sparks), viii. 568.

for the war. The Connecticut non-commissioned officers were claiming half-pay, and "how far their ideas, if not suppressed by some lucky expedient, may proceed," he said, "it is beyond my power to divine." Washington suggested that it would have a good effect if the men enlisted for the war were allowed to retain their arms and accoutrements. Congress promptly gave the desired permission, and also allowed Washington to grant furloughs or discharges at his pleasure; and in May they ordered him to give furloughs to all privates enlisted for the war and to a proportionate number of officers.[1]

In the execution of this order a new difficulty presented itself. When the officers had first suggested that the army should not be disbanded until funds for paying it were established, they did not suppose that peace was so near, and they did not now expect that Congress would go to the expense of maintaining the army for months merely to gratify their wish; but they did look for at least a partial payment of the sums due them before they were sent home.[2] Certificates for an instalment of three months' pay had been promised, but they had not arrived; nor were the accounts yet settled. When the order for issuing furloughs became known, the officers commanding regiments and corps joined in an appeal to Washington which was almost frantic in its earnestness. They assured him of their deep respect and affection, and entreated him not to dismiss them and their men unpaid and with claims unsettled. Washington replied that certificates for three months' pay, maturing in six months, would be issued, and that a messenger had been sent to hasten their despatch;[3] and the accounts, he hoped, would be settled in a few days. He said that, as the delay would be short, and as furloughs were a matter of favor, the officers and soldiers might accept them or not as they pleased. The desire for home proved so strong, however, that when the

---

[1] Washington to President of Congress, April 18, 1783, Washington, *Writings* (Ford), x. 225–230.

[2] Washington to Bland, April 4, 1783, *Ibid.* 206–212.

[3] For some of these notes Morris was personally responsible. This fact has been denied, but descendants of Morris have in their possession notes signed by him in his private capacity.

moment of choice came not many officers, and only a few soldiers whose homes were within the enemy's lines, refused the furlough. On June 13 most of the soldiers quietly left camp, but a body of three-year men was retained until the British should evacuate New York. This lack of ceremony in what was practically the disbanding of the army caused some unfavorable comment.[1] It was probably due in part to the fact that technically the men were only on leave; but Washington may also have thought that, since some of the officers felt that they had been too easily persuaded to accept unfavorable terms in the preceding March, a farewell gathering might give opportunity for a public protest or for something worse.

The main army had quietly disbanded; but some Pennsylvanians rose in open mutiny, lowering the reputation of the country abroad, and very probably depriving their own State of the privilege of furnishing the national capital.[2] A body of men had been raised in Pennsylvania in the latter part of 1782, and were now stationed at Lancaster and Philadelphia. On June 13, 1783, the soldiers at the latter place presented through their sergeants an insolent memorial to Lincoln, the Secretary at War. Lincoln immediately sent a part of the discontented troops to Lancaster with orders that furloughs should be offered them there, and that if they were refused the men should be marched to Carlisle. He also despatched an officer to stop a detachment from the Southern army which was returning by water to Philadelphia; the messenger missed the vessel, however, and the men were landed. Meantime, supposing these precautions sufficient, the Secretary carried out a plan, which he had previously formed, of going to Virginia, and left the War Office in charge of his assistant, Major Jackson. But he was mistaken in supposing that the danger of serious trouble had ceased when the soldiers were removed from the capital. At Lancaster eighty of the men

---

[1] Heath to Washington, June 5, and Washington to Heath, June 7, 1783, *Remembrancer*, xvi. 221–224; Washington to President of Congress, June 24, 1783, Washington, *Writings* (Ford), x. 272–273; Pickering, *Pickering*, i. 473.

[2] For general references to this Pennsylvania mutiny, see Hazard, *Register of Pennsylvania*, ii. 275–278, 328–333; Hamilton, *Works* (Lodge), viii. 124–144.

mutinied and set out for Philadelphia, — to have their accounts settled, they said. When Congress heard the news, they appointed Hamilton, Ellsworth (the future chief justice), and Richard Peters, as a committee to confer with the Executive Council. The Council talked much of the reported good behavior of the soldiers, of the unreliability of the city militia, and of the impossibility of collecting a sufficient force in time to stop the mutineers. A member of the committee remarked that "in all cases in which he could not determine precisely what to do it was a maxim with him to do nothing;" and it was decided to send Major Jackson to try the effects of persuasion.

Congress was much displeased at this moderation, and some of the members declared that, if Philadelphia would not protect them, it was time to go elsewhere; but the only action they took was to send for General St. Clair, who was near the city.[1] Major Jackson's oratory proved unsuccessful; the soldiers entered Philadelphia the next day, and took up their quarters in the barracks. Congress met and transacted business as usual; then, as it was Friday, adjourned, according to custom, until Monday.

On Saturday, June 21, the soldiers made a demonstration. They placed guards at the magazines and public offices, and beset the state-house, where the Executive Council were sitting.[2] Hearing that the soldiers were plotting mischief, President Boudinot at once called a meeting of Congress; but, while one member was still needed to make a quorum, the soldiers arrived. They did not disturb Congress, but they sent a curt memorial to the Council, demanding leave to appoint commissioned officers to take command, with full power to pursue such measures as they should judge most expedient to procure justice. They threatened, if this were not granted in twenty minutes, to "instantly let in these injured soldiers upon you." Sentinels were also

[1] Elliot, *Debates*, v. 92.

[2] Pickering, *Pickering*, i. 474-475, note. There is a tradition that an attempt was made on the treasury. The story is that one party marched to the financier's office; Morris had prudently withdrawn, but an assistant received his uninvited guests very courteously, told them that there was no money there, but that they were at perfect liberty to examine the books. His offer was declined, and the men proceeded to join the main body (Watson, *Annals of Philadelphia*, ii. 331).

placed before the doors of the state-house and under the windows of the council chamber, though both ingress and egress were permitted.

The Council refused to be intimidated. They waited about an hour, and then sent to ask if the message were approved by the soldiers. Some leaders replied that it was, and that the Council should soon hear more from them. Congress refused to transact any business while under duress; but directed General St. Clair to try to get the soldiers back to the barracks; whereupon, with the consent of Dickinson, president of the Council, and Boudinot, St. Clair promised them leave to select three officers to confer with the Council. Meanwhile the attitude of the mutineers became more threatening. Liquor was obtained from a neighboring tavern, and the soldiers shouted out threats against members and pointed their muskets at the windows. At three, the usual hour for adjournment, the members dispersed and, though some of the soldiers offered a mock obstruction, no real effort was made to detain them.[1] General St. Clair, Colonel Potter, and others harangued the soldiers, who consented to appoint a committee to confer with the Council. They could not agree, however, on the persons whom they should choose to represent them; and in the wrangle a sergeant led his men off, and the rest followed his example. But for the seizure of the magazine, which the soldiers still guarded, the affair seemed very much like a farce.[2]

In the evening Congress met in special session. Insulted by their own troops, and irritated by the recollection of former differences with the government of Pennsylvania, the members were in no conciliatory mood. They passed a resolution that effectual measures ought to be taken to support the public authority, and directed the committee formerly appointed to confer with the Council. The Council declared that it would

---

[1] Elliot, *Debates*, v. 93.

[2] Alexander Garden, who was in Philadelphia at the time, asserts that Hamilton addressed the soldiers, but with so little success that he advised Congress "to think of eternity, since he confidently believed, that within the space of the hour not an individual of their body would be left alive" (Garden, *Anecdotes*, ii. 423-424). Madison, however, who was on the spot, makes no mention of this in his journal.

be unsafe to summon the militia, as Congress desired, unless assurances of a firm and adequate support were first obtained. They promised to consult the colonels and to do their best, but said that the affair was not so much a Pennsylvania insurrection as a mutiny of Continental troops, and that Congress might send to Washington for assistance.

At eight o'clock Monday morning the soldiers elected six officers to confer with the Council, promising "in the presence of Almighty God" to support them in compulsive measures, and threatening them with death if they flinched; but, as the officers refused powers so insolently worded, some slight modifications were made. The committee of Congress applied again to the Council, who again refused to call out the militia, asserting, with some reason, that the soldiers might consider it a breach of faith after the permission to appoint commissioners.

On Tuesday morning the Council were supplied with another argument, for the field-officers of the militia reported that the citizens were unwilling to act against the soldiers. Hamilton called on the Council to correct some misinformation which he had given, and when he had done his errand, President Dickinson took him aside and in a private conversation asked him, as a man of military experience, to say whether it would not be dangerous to attempt to collect militia in the face of men "already embodied, accustomed to arms, and ready to act at a moment's warning." But Hamilton was of the opinion that "nothing can be more contemptible than a body of men used to be commanded and to obey, when deprived of the example and direction of their officers. They are infinitely less to be dreaded than an equal number of men who have never been broken to command, nor exchanged their natural courage for that artificial kind which is the effect of discipline and habit. Soldiers transfer their confidence from themselves to their officers, face danger by the force of example, the dread of punishment, and the sense of necessity. Take away these inducements and leave them to themselves they are no longer resolute, than till they are opposed." Hamilton said that these soldiers were isolated, and were without efficient leadership; that they would be awed by the thought of armed resistance to the government; and that if the Council would take resolute action, the mutineers would submit.[1] Hamilton added, however, that, as the removal of Congress might injure the government abroad and cause dissension at home, he would undertake the heavy responsibility of delaying action; that he had, indeed, already refused to concur in a written report which would have been immediately followed by the departure of Congress. But he soon heard that the officers chosen to represent the mutineers were acting suspiciously, and that the soldiers were becoming drunk. He then hesitated no longer; the committee recommended that Congress leave the city, and the members quietly slipped away. Boudinot left behind a formal proclamation summoning them to meet at Princeton, New Jersey, on Friday.

Meantime a report of an intended attack on the bank came to the ears of the authorities, and proved more potent than all the arguments of Hamilton. A council attended by several field-officers met that evening at President Dickinson's, where measures were taken to form a guard, and it was resolved to try to get out of the magazines such ammunition as was ready for use, under the pretext of removing powder which was private property.

The next day, Wednesday, brought matters to a crisis. The plan of securing ammunition proved successful. It was reported that the soldiers' rations would be stopped on Friday; and, fearing violence, the Council ordered out a guard of one hundred militia privates with their officers, and took other precautions. While the clerk was copying the resolutions, two captains appeared with the demands of the men. The Council refused to consider them until the soldiers received their officers and made full satisfaction to Congress. The delegates replied that the soldiers did not think they had offended Congress, as the purpose of their visit to the state-house on the preceding Saturday was merely to apply to the Council; and they begged the authorities to prepare for the worst. The guard was accordingly ordered to be increased to five hundred men, and the members of the Council dispersed to raise the militia and to call all citizens to arms. Fortunately, there was no bloodshed, or even tumult. The soldiers were terrified by the firmness of

[1] Hamilton to Dickinson, Hamilton, *Works* (Lodge), viii. 140-141.

the Council, the support given them by the officers, and a report that Washington with all his army and the New Jersey militia was marching on the city. Two of the committee — Carberry and Sullivan — wrote to a third, "Consult your own safety; we cannot get to you," and took to flight. It is said that they reached Chester and there embarked for England.[1] An officer and some citizens addressed the soldiers, and the men (except some of those from Lancaster) agreed to submit.

Leaving those who still held out to guard their muskets, the main body paraded unarmed before Dickinson's house, where the president addressed them. He began, according to a letter he wrote to Congress, by reminding them of their "unprecedented and heinous fault." Dickinson next commanded the mutineers to put themselves under the command of their officers, and at the end of twenty-four hours to compel the men from Lancaster to lay down their arms and set out for that town. The first order was obeyed; the second was rendered superfluous by the recalcitrants submitting at noon. Soon afterward the mutineers began their march; and Dickinson sent the good news to the president of Congress before he slept, the French minister kindly consenting to act as an express.[2]

Meanwhile a strong detachment was on its way from West Point to restore order and protect Congress. Boudinot had written to Washington immediately after the interrupted session of Saturday, the 21st, but his letter did not reach headquarters until the 24th. On receiving the news, Washington at once detached three regiments of infantry and one of artillery, over fifteen hundred men in all, under the command of the senior officer, Major-General Howe, whose prompt measures had crushed the New Jersey mutiny.[3] Though the rising had now been suppressed, it was felt safer to let him proceed, perhaps to

[1] Carberry afterward returned to the United States, and during Washington's administration became an applicant for federal office. His friends united in a petition urging that his participation in the mutiny should be regarded as a youthful indiscretion.

[2] Dickinson to President of Congress, June 25, 1783, Stillé, *Dickinson*, 245–246.

[3] Washington to President of Congress, June 24, 1783, Washington, *Writings* (Ford), x. 270–271. See above, p. 139.

be present at the trials. Carberry and Sullivan had escaped; but other officers who had served on the committee were tried by court-martial, as were a few of the soldiers; the officers were acquitted. It is said that, as the government wished to get rid of the army as quietly as possible, it considered severity ill-timed and so gave a hint to Howe. Several of the soldiers were convicted; some suffered corporal punishment, and two were sentenced to death. These were led, as they supposed, to execution; but at the last moment a pardon was announced.[1]

The fugitive Congress remained in New Jersey, where they had been most cordially received. Previous to his departure from Philadelphia, President Boudinot wrote to his brother Elisha: "I wish you could get your troop of horse to offer their aid. . . . I wish Jersey to show her readiness on this occasion, as it may fix Congress as to their permanent residence."[2] New Jersey was equal to the opportunity, and magistrates and people overwhelmed Congress with civilities. Governor Livingston, to whom President Boudinot applied, wrote promptly to express his own mortification at the mutiny, and the readiness of the people of New Jersey to protect Congress "if that august body shall think proper to honor this State with their presence." For his own part, he said, he would hold himself not a little honored by being personally engaged in defending the representatives of the United States against insult and indignity.[3] The college authorities at Princeton offered the use of the hall and library, and every other accommodation in their power. The people of Princeton, of Trenton and vicinity, the magistrates, militia, and citizens of "New Ark," and the officers of the militia of the three neighboring counties presented loyal addresses, to which Congress made due response. The people of Trenton seem to have expressed themselves with much vigor, for the president was directed to reply that "Congress highly applaud the proper resentment the citizens of Trenton . . . have discovered against disturbers of the public peace and violators of the dignity of the

---

[1] Scharf and Westcott, *Philadelphia*, i. 430; Denny, *Military Journal*, 53.
[2] June 23, 1783, Boudinot, *Boudinot*, i. 337.
[3] Livingston to Boudinot, June 24, 1783, Sedgwick, *Livingston*, 380.

Union."[1] Quarters in the college were accepted, and soon there was a rush of sedan chairs and a style of living which to the simple people of Princeton seemed quite luxurious.

Deserted Philadelphia was sullen and angry. The general belief was that the leaders in the removal of Congress had acted from interest and the rest from timidity, or, as some thought, passion. A contributor to the *Remembrancer* ended his account by remarking that, "if the king of England was to withdraw every time he conceives himself affronted, he would long before now have been in Hanover." The editor added, "and it is very remarkable, that our American tumults (if they may be called tumults) are the most orderly, quiet, harmless, and peaceable of any in the world." In another issue, a "spectator" congratulated every friend of humanity on the peaceable settlement of the affair, cited various examples of moderation, and asked: "Why should not rulers of republics, by negotiating revolts, prevent unnecessary bloodshed among their citizens? They are the fathers of the people, and should be as tender of their lives, as of the lives of their children."[2] Even the account of the mutiny by Scharf and Westcott, in their *History of Philadelphia*, written a century after the event, shows some resentment. The authors say: "The action of Congress throughout the affair was hasty, undignified, and ill-advised. The movement was not directed against that body at all, but against the State authorities, and the flight to Princeton was simply an act of folly. But, like most acts of folly, it was persisted in with an assumption of dignity that was ridiculous in so grave a body. . . . Probably ashamed to return to a city from which it had fled so precipitately in the face of purely imaginary danger, that body adjourned on the first of November to meet at Annapolis."[3]

Opinion in Philadelphia was not wholly unfavorable to Congress. A writer in the *Remembrancer,* while blaming Boudinot's proclamation of adjournment, which was expressed in a somewhat offensive form, defended the action of Congress in leaving the city. He pointed out that small disturbances often grew to

---

[1] *Journals of Congress*, viii. 288–289, 294–296, July 2, 4, and 26, 1783.

[2] June 28 and July 9, 1783, *Remembrancer*, xvi. 274, 278.

[3] Scharf and Westcott, *Philadelphia*, i. 430.

great ones, citing as an example the recent "No Popery," or Lord George Gordon, riots in London.[1] In a few weeks overtures were made to Congress inviting their return. Many citizens signed an address setting forth the loyalty and services of Philadelphia and promising to try to protect Congress. The Council journal for Monday, August 4, 1783, contains this entry: "The delegates from this State to Congress were admitted into the council chamber, and made the following representation: 'That Wednesday was assigned for the ultimate determination of Congress whether they would return to this city or not; that they believed the affirmative determination on this question would be very acceptable to the people of this city, and that they had some reason to believe that an invitation from Council would probably give it that desirable cast.'

"*Resolved*, That the delegates from Pennsylvania be at liberty to assure Congress that their return to this city would be a very acceptable event to the Council of this State."[2]

If a literal copy was sent, such an indirect and coolly formal invitation must have repelled, rather than attracted, "that august body." The Assembly was somewhat more cordial than the Council. They offered Congress the use of the state-house, and promised to take measures to enable the executive of the State to "protect the honor and dignity of Congress, and of those persons who compose the Executive Council." They also asked Congress to define the jurisdiction which they desired at the seat of government.[3]

Congress still refused to return. They had been brought into closer relations with the government of Pennsylvania than with that of any other State, and they thought that on more than one previous occasion they had had reason to complain of neglect. Joseph Jones wrote to Madison that Congress should not be satisfied with a mere request to return; that the people of Philadelphia should express their disapprobation of the remissness of the Council, and should promise to protect the dignity of the

[1] July 5, 1783, *Remembrancer*, xvi. 277.
[2] *Pennsylvania Colonial Records*, xiii. 637.
[3] Scharf and Westcott, *Philadelphia*, i. 430.

federal government. Whipple of New Hampshire, an ex-member of Congress, wrote that he was sorry for their manner of leaving Philadelphia, but that now that they had left he hoped they would never return. Gouverneur Morris thought that Congress should be near Philadelphia because the bank was there, but that they should have jurisdiction wherever they were; only the lack of temptation, he said, had saved them heretofore from being insulted by an " ungoverned State." [1]

Both parties were ready to attribute the action of those who disagreed with them to unworthy motives. Boudinot thought that the reluctance of Dickinson and his colleagues to act was due to fear of the October elections. Dickinson, in a message to the legislature, hinted that Boudinot wished to provoke insult in order to have an excuse for getting Congress into New Jersey. We may, however, acquit both Dickinson and Boudinot of consciously sacrificing the public welfare to personal or local interests. When we remember the sympathy manifested by the citizens for the mutineers of 1781, when we consider how well Dickinson knew the temper of the people, when we remember that the militia officers reported a call of men unadvisable, we may say of Dickinson that he does not deserve serious blame. There were, indeed, plausible reasons for the action of the Council. The position of the soldiers was a strong one; they were armed and at least partially trained, and they held the public magazine. It may be true that honor should have been preferred to safety; yet a bloody fight in the streets of the capital, and perhaps the seizure or even murder of some high officials, would have disgraced the United States. Negotiations gave a pretext for delay; and meanwhile dissensions might break out among the soldiers, or help come from West Point.

A qualified approval of the action of Dickinson and the Council does not necessarily imply a censure of Congress. It was proper that they should impress on the Council the gravity

[1] *Journals of Congress*, viii. 296, July 28, 1783; Jones to Madison, July 28, 1783, Ford, *Letters of Joseph Jones*, 130; Whipple to Lee, September 15, 1783, Lee, *Arthur Lee*, ii. 280; Morris to Jay, September 25, 1783, John Jay, *Correspondence and Public Papers*, iii. 87.

of the situation; and they did not leave until the third day after the mutiny, when there were alarming reports from the barracks, and reason to suspect the fidelity of some of the committee of officers. It was said that there was danger that other soldiers, recently disbanded, might join the mutineers. These signs of danger were not indeed the only causes of the flight to Princeton: Congress was sensitive; Boudinot wished the capital to be located in New Jersey, and would unconsciously set a high standard for Philadelphia; and Hamilton was by nature a friend of strong government. But Congress did not again sit in Philadelphia till 1790, and then only for a short term of years. The excitement over the mutiny soon died down, and the mutineers lost their opportunity of harm when the army was disbanded.

On November 25 the British evacuated New York; and Washington, believing that there was no further need of his services, determined to resign his commission. On December 4 he bade a touching farewell to his officers,[1] and then set out for Annapolis, where Congress was sitting. His journey south-

[1] The historian Gordon thus describes the scene: "On Thursday noon, the principal officers of the army assembled at Frances's (alias Black Sam's) tavern, to take a final leave of their much-loved commander-in-chief. After a while, General Washington came in, and calling for a glass of wine, thus addressed them. 'With an heart full of love and gratitude, I now take leave of you. I most devoutly wish, that your latter days may be as prosperous and happy, as your former ones have been glorious and honorable.' Having drank, he said, 'I cannot come to each of you to take my leave; but shall be obliged to you, if each will come and take me by the hand.' General Knox being nearest turned to him; Washington, with tears rolling down his cheeks, grasped Knox's hand, and then kissed him; he did the same by every succeeding officer, and by some other gentlemen who were present. The passions of human nature were never more tenderly agitated, than in this interesting and distressful scene. The whole company were in tears. When Washington left the room, and passed through the corps of light infantry about two o'clock on his way to Whitehall, the others followed, walking in a solemn, mute, and mournful procession, with heads hanging down and dejected countenances, till he embarked in his barge for Powle's Hook. When he had entered, he turned, took off his hat, and with that bid them a silent adieu. They paid him the same affectionate compliment, and the barge pushing off, returned from Whitehall in like manner as they had advanced" (Gordon, *History of the American War*, iv. 383-384).

ward was a continual triumph; the people and the governments of the States through which he passed vied with each other in expressions of respect and esteem. On reaching Annapolis, Washington asked Congress whether they wished him to tender his resignation in person or by letter. Congress decided in favor of the former method, and on December 23 gave him a public audience.

Washington's speech was very brief. He congratulated Congress on the establishment of independence, expressed his particular obligations to the gentlemen who had formed his military family, and recommended to the special favor and patronage of Congress such of them as might desire to continue in service. In conclusion he said: —

"I consider it an indispensable duty to close this last solemn act of my official life, by commending the interests of our dearest country to the protection of Almighty God, and those who have the superintendence of them to His holy keeping.

"Having now finished the work assigned me, I retire from the great theatre of action; and, bidding an affectionate farewell to this august body, under whose orders I have so long acted, I here offer my commission, and take my leave of all the employments of public life." [1]

In reply, the president of Congress (no other than Washington's old enemy, Mifflin) lauded Washington's character, and prayed in the name of Congress "that your days may be happy as they have been illustrious; and that He will finally give you that reward which this world cannot give."[2]

The resignation of Washington left General Knox in command of the army. Knox continued the work of disbandment, and was able to report, on January 3, 1784, that his force had been reduced to less than seven hundred men. Occupation might have been found for them in protecting the Western frontier; but there was strong opposition to any standing army whatever, the right of Congress to maintain one in time of peace was doubted, and hence, on June 2, 1784, Congress voted that all troops be discharged except eighty privates and a pro-

[1] Washington, *Writings* (Ford), x. 338–339.
[2] *Journals of Congress*, ix. 14, December 23, 1783.

portionate number of officers, who were kept to guard the public stores.[1]

The story of the administration of the Revolutionary army should, perhaps, in strictness end here; but a word or two concerning the public provision afterward made for the officers and men may not be without interest.

The disbanded soldiers mingled quietly with the mass of the citizens. Liberal inducements had been offered by the States and by local authorities to secure enlistment, and it is said that men who received large bounties shortly before the end of the war returned home richer than when they left. But the times were hard, and the number of ex-soldiers seeking employment lowered wages. Some were obliged to depend on children or friends for support, or to go from town to town telling stories of the war and obtaining subsistence from the liberality of their hearers, and from doing such odd jobs as they could obtain.[2]

The officers also found themselves in a very unpleasant situation, for half-pay was extremely unpopular. Some, indeed, of those who disliked the measure were mindful of the claims of public faith. Samuel Adams, though he disapproved of it, was of the opinion that the promise of commutation should be kept. He said that Congress possessed the right to maintain an army to carry on the war, and that by the nature of the case they were the sole judges of the necessary means; that they had acted on the advice of the commander-in-chief, and with due deliberation; and that the several States were bound in justice and honor to fulfil the promises of their representatives.[3]

On the other hand, it was asserted that Congress had no right to make such a grant, and that the officers had not acted in good faith, but had taken advantage of the public danger to obtain by deceit and intimidation an indorsement of their schemes from General Washington. The commutation was

---

[1] Brooks, *Knox*, 186; *Journals of Congress*, ix. 290–291, June 2, 1784.

[2] Austin, *Gerry*, i. 394, note; Bolton, *The Private Soldier under Washington*, 246–247.

[3] Samuel Adams to Noah Webster, April 30, 1784, Wells, *Samuel Adams*, iii. 209.

declared to be the result of a conspiracy of the officers, many public creditors, and a few members of Congress who themselves hoped for pensions in the future. It was said that the country was already overburdened, and that, if the five million dollars at which the commutation was estimated were added to the public debt, men must sell "the houses from over their heads and the clothes from off their backs" to help build up an aristocracy.

Nor was the opposition confined to words. Massachusetts declared that she could not at present consent to grant Congress the power to lay a tariff, because she disapproved of the principle of the half-pay and commutation acts.[1] In Connecticut a convention was called to oppose commutation, representatives from over two-thirds of the towns attended, and for a while it seemed as if there might be a revolution.[2]

After the popular excitement subsided the officers were still unable to obtain their dues. The government could not pay even the interest on its debts; and the officers were in such pressing need of money that they were frequently obliged to sell their certificates at a ruinous discount, the price falling, it is said, as low as twelve and one-half cents on the dollar.

In 1790, the government under the Constitution having gone into operation, there was a general refunding of the public debt, and new stock was issued to holders of public securities, providing for the ultimate payment both of the principal and the overdue interest. But the officers who had already parted with their certificates received no benefit: an attempt was made in Congress to divide the new stock between the present and the original holders; but it was urged that both honor and a regard for the future credit of the United States required a literal compliance with the promise to pay the actual holder at the time of presentation, and the officers were left without relief.[3] For twenty years nothing was done; then, in 1810, an attempt was again made to obtain assistance from Congress,

---

[1] Another reason assigned for the refusal was that the salaries paid to ministers and other civil officers of the United States were too high.

[2] Stuart, *Trumbull*, 594-597; McMaster, *United States*, i. 178; Austin, *Gerry*, i. 395.

[3] Rives, *Madison*, iii. 78-88.

but without success. The efforts were renewed from time to time; and in 1828 an act was passed granting full pay for life, not, however, to exceed the amount of a captain's pay (four hundred and eighty dollars per annum) from March 3, 1826, to all officers who by the resolution of October 21, 1780, were entitled to half-pay for life. A similar pension was also given to the non-commissioned officers and soldiers who by the resolution of May 15, 1778, were promised a bounty of eighty dollars. Pensions had already been given to every officer and soldier "who was in need of the assistance of his country for support," and in 1832 all who had served two years or more were allowed a pension of full pay according to rank, but no one was to receive more than a captain's pay; those who had served six months or more, but less than two years, were allowed a smaller pension in proportion to the length of their service. In 1836 the provisions of this act were extended to soldiers' widows who had married before the expiration of their husbands' last enlistment. This time-limitation on the marriage was afterward relaxed, and was finally removed altogether.[1]

In 1864, when the number of Revolutionary soldiers on the pension roll had been reduced to twelve, Congress passed an act allowing each of them an additional pension of one hundred dollars a year. In the following year, when only five survived, a further pension of three hundred dollars was granted them. Congress also directed that, immediately on the approval of the act, a copy of the same, signed by the speaker of the House, the president of the Senate, and the President of the United States, be sent to each of the persons named in the act. A little later, two other soldiers not on the roll were given a pension of five hundred a year.[2] It is not to be supposed that these men had rendered any peculiar service, or that Congress felt that the Revolutionary soldiers had hitherto been ungenerously treated; Congress simply wished to bestow on the few remaining men who had fought for independence "the parting benediction of a grateful people."

[1] Glasson, *History of Military Pension Legislation in the United States*, 40, 44, 49.
[2] *Ibid.* 49-50; United States, *Statutes at Large*, xiii. 39.

The story of the administration of the Revolutionary army is not one in which an American can take pride. The people were often indifferent, the officers captious and quarrelsome, and Congress inefficient and negligent. Such failings were perhaps natural. The country was poor, and in the rural districts the burdens of the war were hard to bear. The officers were left unpaid for months at a time, and were subjected to the most galling mortifications. Members of Congress had little experience in the management of great affairs, and were obliged to pay careful attention to the wishes of their constituents. Recent historians have told us much of the errors of the men of the Revolution; perhaps they have been a little forgetful of their sufferings and their achievements.

APPENDICES.

APPENDIX A.

THE NEWBURG ADDRESSES AND PAPERS CONNECTED THEREWITH.

1. FIRST ANONYMOUS ADDRESS TO THE OFFICERS OF THE ARMY, MARCH 10, 1783.[1]

GENTLEMEN, —

A fellow-soldier, whose interest and affections bind him strongly to you, whose past sufferings have been as great, and whose future fortunes may be as desperate as yours, would beg leave to address you.

Age has its claims, and rank is not without its pretensions to advice; but, though unsupported by both, he flatters himself, that the plain language of sincerity and experience will neither be unheard nor unregarded.

Like many of you he loved private life, and left it with regret. He left it, determined to retire from the field with the necessity that called him to it, and not till then; not till the enemies of his country, the slaves of power, and the hirelings of injustice were compelled to abandon their schemes, and acknowledge America as terrible in arms as she had been humble in remonstrance. With this object in view he has long shared in your toils, and mingled in your dangers; he has felt the cold hand of poverty without a murmur, and has seen the insolence of wealth without a sigh. But too much under the direction of his wishes, and sometimes weak enough to mistake desire for opinion, he has till lately, very lately, believed in the justice of his country. He hoped, that, as the clouds of adversity scattered, and as the sunshine of peace and better fortune broke in upon us, the coldness and severity of government would relax; and that more than justice, that gratitude, would blaze forth upon those hands, which had upheld her in the darkest stages of her passage from impending servitude to acknowledged independence.

But faith has its limits as well as temper; and there are points, beyond

[1] Washington, *Writings* (Sparks), viii. 555-558.

which neither can be stretched without sinking into cowardice or plunging into credulity. This, my friends, I conceive to be your situation; hurried to the very verge of both, another step would ruin you forever. To be tame and unprovoked, when injuries press hard upon you, is more than weakness; but to look up for kinder usage, without one manly effort of your own, would fix your character, and show the world how richly you deserve those chains you broke. To guard against this evil, let us take a review of the ground upon which we now stand, and from thence carry our thoughts forward for a moment into the unexplored field of expedient.

After a pursuit of seven long years, the object for which we set out is at length brought within our reach. Yes, my friends, that suffering courage of yours was active once; it has conducted the United States of America through a doubtful and bloody war; it has placed her in the chair of independency, and peace returns again to bless — whom? A country willing to redress your wrongs, cherish your worth, and reward your services? A country courting your return to private life, with tears of gratitude and smiles of admiration, longing to divide with you that independency which your gallantry has given, and those riches which your wounds have preserved? Is this the case? Or is it rather a country, that tramples upon your rights, disdains your cries, and insults your distresses? Have you not more than once suggested your wishes, and made known your wants to Congress, wants and wishes, which gratitude and policy should have anticipated, rather than evaded? And have you not lately, in the meek language of entreating memorials, begged from their justice what you could no longer expect from their favor? How have you been answered? Let the letter, which you are called to consider to-morrow, make reply!

If this then be your treatment, while the swords you wear are necessary for the defence of America, what have you to expect from peace, when your voice shall sink, and your strength dissipate by division; when those very swords, the instruments and companions of your glory, shall be taken from your sides, and no remaining mark of military distinction left but your wants, infirmities, and scars? Can you then consent to be the only sufferers by this revolution, and, retiring from the field, grow old in poverty, wretchedness, and contempt? Can you consent to wade through the vile mire of dependency, and owe the miserable remnant of that life to charity, which has hitherto been spent in honor? If you can, go, and carry with you the jest of Tories, and the scorn of Whigs; the ridicule, and what is worse, the pity of the world! Go, starve and be forgotten! But if your spirits should revolt at this; if you have sense enough to discover and spirit sufficient to oppose tyranny, under whatever garb it may assume, whether it be the plain coat of republicanism, or the splendid robe of royalty; if you have yet learned to discriminate between a people and a cause, between men and principles; awake, attend to your situation, and redress yourselves! If the present moment be lost, every future effort is in vain; and your threats then will be as empty as your entreaties now.

I would advise you, therefore, to come to some final opinion upon what you can bear, and what you will suffer. If your determination be in any proportion to your wrongs, carry your appeal from the justice to the fears of government. Change the milk-and-water style of your last memorial. Assume a bolder tone, decent, but lively, spirited, and determined; and suspect the man, who would advise to more moderation and longer forbearance. Let two or three men, who can feel as well as write, be appointed to draw up your *last remonstrance*, for I would no longer give it the suing, soft, unsuccessful epithet of *memorial*. Let it represent in language, that will neither dishonor you by its rudeness, nor betray you by its fears, what has been promised by Congress, and what has been performed; how long and how patiently you have suffered; how little you have asked, and how much of that little has been denied. Tell them, that, though you were the first, and would wish to be last, to encounter danger, though despair itself can never drive you into dishonor, it may drive you from the field; that the wound, often irritated and never healed, may at length become incurable; and that the slightest mark of indignity from Congress now must operate like the grave, and part you for ever; that, in any political event, the army has its alternative. If peace, that nothing shall separate you from your arms but death; if war, that courting the auspices, and inviting the direction of your illustrious leader, you will retire to some unsettled country, smile in your turn, "and mock when their fear cometh on." But let it represent, also, that should they comply with the request of your late memorial, it would make you more happy and them more respectable; that, while war should continue, you would follow their standard into the field; and when it came to an end, you would withdraw into the shade of private life, and give the world another subject of wonder and applause; an army victorious over its enemies, victorious over itself.

2. SECOND ANONYMOUS ADDRESS TO THE OFFICERS OF THE ARMY, MARCH 12, 1783.[1]

GENTLEMEN, —

The author of a late address, anxious to deserve, though he should fail to engage your esteem, and determined at every risk to unfold your duty and discharge his own, would beg leave to solicit the further indulgence of a few moments' attention.

Aware of the coyness with which his last letter would be received, he feels himself neither disappointed nor displeased with the caution it has met. He well knew, that it spoke a language, which till now had been heard only in whispers; and that it contained some sentiments, which confidence itself would have breathed with distrust. But their lives have been short, and their observation imperfect indeed, who have yet to learn, that alarms may be false; that the best designs are sometimes obliged to assume the worst aspect; and that, however synonymous surprise and disaster may be in military phrase, in moral and political meaning they convey ideas as different as they are distinct. Suspicion, detestable as it is in private life, is the loveliest trait of political characters. It prompts you to inquiry, bars the door against design, and opens every avenue to truth. It was the first to oppose a tyrant here, and still stands sentinel over the liberties of America. With this belief, it would ill become me to stifle the voice of this honest guardian; a guardian, who (authorized by circumstances digested into proof) has herself given birth to the address you have read, and now goes forth among you, with a request to all, that it may be treated fairly; that it be considered, before it be abused, and condemned, before it be tortured, convinced that, in a search after error, truth will appear; that apathy itself will grow warm in the pursuit, and, though it will be the last to adopt her advice, it will be the first to act upon it.

The General Orders of yesterday, which the weak may mistake for disapprobation, and the designing dare to represent as such, wears in my opinion a very different complexion, and carries with it a very opposite tendency.

Till now, the Commander-in-chief has regarded the steps you have taken for redress with good wishes alone; his ostensible silence has authorized your meetings, and his private opinion has sanctified your claims. Had he disliked the object in view, would not the same sense of duty, which forbade you from meeting on the third day of the week, have for-

[1] Washington, *Writings* (Sparks), viii. 558-560.

bidden you from meeting on the seventh? Is not the same subject held up for your discussion, and has it not passed the seal of office, and taken all the solemnity of an order? This will give system to your proceedings, and stability to your resolves. It will ripen speculation into fact; and, while it adds to the unanimity, it cannot possibly lessen the independency of your sentiments. It may be necessary to add upon this subject, that, from the injunction with which the General Orders close, every man is at liberty to conclude, that the report to be made to Head-Quarters is intended for Congress. Hence will arise another motive for that energy, which has been recommended. For can you give the lie to the pathetic descriptions of your representations, and the more alarming predictions of your friends?

To such, as make a want of signature an objection to opinion, I reply, that it matters very little who is the author of sentiments, which grow out of your feelings, and apply to your wants; that in this instance diffidence suggested what experience enjoins; and that, while I continue to move on the high road of argument and advice, which is open to all, I shall continue to be the sole confidant of my own secret. But should the time come, when it shall be necessary to depart from this general line, and hold up any individual among you as an object of the resentment or contempt of the rest, I thus publicly pledge my honor as a soldier, and veracity as a man, that I will then assume a visible existence, and give my name to the army, with as little reserve as I now give my opinions.

3. WASHINGTON'S ADDRESS TO THE OFFICERS, MARCH 15, 1783.[1]

GENTLEMEN, —

By an anonymous summons an attempt has been made to convene you together. How inconsistent with the rules of propriety, how unmilitary, and how subversive of all good order and discipline, let the good sense of the army decide.

In the moment of this summons, another anonymous production was sent into circulation; addressed more to the feelings and passions, than to the reason and judgment of the army. The author of the piece is entitled to much credit for the goodness of his pen, and I could wish he had as much credit for the rectitude of his heart; for, as men see through different optics, and are induced by the reflecting faculties of

---

[1] Washington, *Writings*, viii. 560–563.

the mind to use different means to obtain the same end, the author of the address should have had more charity, than to mark for suspicion the man, who should recommend moderation and longer forbearance, or in other words, who should not think as he thinks, and act as he advises. But he had another plan in view, in which candor and liberality of sentiment, regard to justice, and love of country, have no part; and he was right to insinuate the darkest suspicion, to effect the blackest designs.

That the address is drawn with great art, and is designed to answer the most insidious purposes, that it is calculated to impress the mind with an idea of premeditated injustice in the sovereign power of the United States, and rouse all those resentments, which must unavoidably flow from such a belief; that the secret mover of this scheme, whoever he may be, intended to take advantage of the passions, while they were warmed by the recollection of past distresses, without giving time for cool, deliberate thinking, and that composure of mind, which is so necessary to give dignity and stability to measures, is rendered too obvious, by the mode of conducting the business, to need other proof than a reference to the proceeding.

Thus much, Gentlemen, I have thought it incumbent on me to observe to you, to show upon what principles I opposed the irregular and hasty meeting, which was proposed to be held on Tuesday last, and not because I wanted a disposition to give you every opportunity, consistent with your own honor and the dignity of the army, to make known your grievances. If my conduct heretofore has not evinced to you, that I have been a faithful friend to the army, my declaration of it at this time would be equally unavailing and improper. But, as I was among the first, who embarked in the cause of our common country; as I have never left your side one moment, but when called from you on public duty; as I have been the constant companion and witness of your distresses, and not among the last to feel and acknowledge your merits; as I have ever considered my own military reputation as inseparably connected with that of the army; as my heart has ever expanded with joy, when I have heard its praises, and my indignation has arisen, when the mouth of detraction has been opened against it; it can scarcely be supposed, at this late stage of the war, that I am indifferent to its interests. But how are they to be promoted? The way is plain, says the anonymous addresser; if war continues, remove into the unsettled country; there establish yourselves, and leave an ungrateful country to defend itself. But whom are they to defend? Our wives, our children, our farms and other property, which we leave behind us? Or, in the state of hostile separation, are we to take the two first (the latter cannot be removed) to perish in a wilderness with hunger, cold, and nakedness? If peace takes place, never sheathe your swords, says he, until you have obtained full and ample justice. This dreadful alternative, of either deserting our country in the extremest hour of distress, or turning our arms against it, which is the apparent object, unless Congress can be compelled into instant compliance, has something so shocking in it, that humanity revolts at the idea. My God! What can this writer have in view by recommending such measures? Can he be a friend to the army? Can he be a friend to this country? Rather is he not an insidious foe? Some emissary, perhaps from New York, plotting the ruin of both by sowing the seeds of discord and separation between the civil and military powers of the continent? And what a compliment does he pay to our understandings, when he recommends measures, in either alternative, impracticable in their nature?

But here, Gentlemen, I will drop the curtain, because it would be as imprudent in me to assign my reasons for this opinion, as it would be insulting to your conception to suppose you stood in need of them. A moment's reflection will convince every dispassionate mind of the physical impossibility of carrying either proposal into execution.

There might, Gentlemen, be an impropriety in my taking notice, in this address to you, of an anonymous production; but the manner in which that performance has been introduced to the army, the effect it was intended to have, together with some other circumstances, will amply justify my observations on the tendency of that writing. With respect to the advice given by the author to suspect the man, who shall recommend moderate measures and longer forbearance, I spurn it, as every man who regards that liberty, and reveres that justice, for which we contend, undoubtedly must. For, if men are to be precluded from offering their sentiments on a matter, which may involve the most serious and alarming consequences, that can invite the consideration of mankind, reason is of no use to us; the freedom of speech may be taken away, and, dumb and silent, we may be led away like sheep to the slaughter.

I cannot, in justice to my own belief, and what I have great reason to conceive is the intention of Congress, conclude this address, without giving it as my decided opinion, that that honorable body entertain exalted sentiments of the services of the army, and, from a full conviction of its merits and sufferings, will do it complete justice. That their endeavors to discover and establish funds for this purpose have been unwearied, and will not cease, till they have succeeded, I have no doubt; but, like all other large bodies, where there is a variety of different interests to reconcile, their deliberations are slow. Why then should we distrust them; and, in consequence of that distrust, adopt measures, which may cast a shade over that glory, which has been so justly acquired, and tarnish the reputation of an army, which is celebrated through all Europe for its fortitude and patriotism? And for what is this done? To bring the object we seek nearer? No! Most certainly, in my opinion, it will cast it at a greater distance.

For myself (and I take no merit in giving the assurance, being induced to it from principles of gratitude, veracity, and justice), a grateful sense of the confidence you have ever placed in me, a recollection of the cheerful assistance and prompt obedience I have experienced from you, under every vicissitude of fortune, and the sincere affection I feel for an army I have so long had the honor to command, oblige me to declare in this public and solemn manner, that, in the attainment of complete justice for all your toils and dangers, and in the gratification of every wish, so far as may be done consistently with the great duty I owe to my country, and those powers we are bound to respect, you may freely command my services to the utmost extent of my abilities.

While I give you these assurances, and pledge myself in the most unequivocal manner to exert whatever ability I am possessed of in your favor, let me entreat you, Gentlemen, on your part, not to take any measures, which, in the calm light of reason, will lessen the dignity and sully the glory you have hitherto maintained. Let me request you to rely on the plighted faith of your country, and place a full confidence in the purity of the intentions of Congress, that, previous to your dissolution as an army, they will cause all your accounts to be fairly liquidated, as directed in their resolutions, which were published to you two days ago, and that they will adopt the most effectual measures in their power to render ample justice to you for your faithful and meritorious services. And let me conjure you in the name of our common country, as you value your own sacred honor, as you respect the rights of humanity, and as you regard the military and national character of America, to express your utmost horror and detestation of the man, who wishes, under any specious pretences, to overturn the liberties of our country, and who wickedly attempts to open the flood-gates of civil discord, and deluge our rising empire in blood.

By thus determining and thus acting, you will pursue the plain and direct road to the attainment of your wishes; you will defeat the insidious designs of our enemies, who are compelled to resort from open force to secret artifice; you will give one more distinguished proof of unexampled patriotism and patient virtue, rising superior to the pressure of the most complicated sufferings; and you will, by the dignity of your conduct, afford occasion for posterity to say, when speaking of the glorious example you have exhibited to mankind, " Had this day been wanting, the world had never seen the last stage of perfection, to which human nature is capable of attaining."

4. DRAFT OF A REPLY TO THE ANONYMOUS ADDRESSES, MARCH 15, 1783.[1]

GENTLEMEN

You have lately been addressed by an anonymous writer who stiles himself your *fellow Soldier*, & from his age and rank, tells you he 'expects to be *heard* and *regarded*.'

That the sufferings, patience, and perseverance of the American Armys is *without* a *parallel*, that language must fail in *painting their virtues*, and the Fable of the Poets fall short of American realities. That the Army deserve *every thing their Country* can give. *Nay, with reverance, everything* Heaven can bestow is readily acknowledged, — how to obtain this reward then, or at least, what is the best mode to be pursued in order to obtain *justice?*, I take to be the inquiery of us all, and the design of the Meeting on Saturday next.

Our fellow Soldier after having worked his own, and endeavored to raise your passions to the *highest pitch;* tells you to " carry your appeal from the justice, to the fears of Government, tell them, (says he) that the slightest mark of indignity from Congress *now*, must part us *like the Grave, forever*. That in any political event the Army has its alternative, if peace, that nothing can separate you from your *Arms* but *Death*, if War, that you will retire to some yet unsettled Country, smile in your turn, and mock when their fear cometh on."

This my friends you will agree is an extraordinary step, and deserves, a cold and dispassionate consideration *before we make it*. As one then who is as desirous as any of you to obtain *justice*, whose interest, Coun-

---

[1] *Knox MSS*. xii. 22. On the back of the manuscript is the following indorsement, probably written by General Knox, " B. Gen[l]. Rufus Putnams examination of certain anonymous papers — March 15 — 83."

try, & *connections* are the same with yours, I beg leave to mention some of the objections which lie in my mind against the proposed plan.

Congress *will* or they will not be frightened into a compliance with your demands, if Congress complies, as some have suggested they will, and grants you all you *ask, can* you then disband with *safety*, what *security* will you have that those promises shall be *fulfilled?* Will Congress be more likely to make good those you shall *extort* from them, *than* those they have voluntarily *made? Will* the several States think them more binding, or will they be more likely to grant funds to Congress than now? Is it not possible, that not only the States, but even Congress may then declare, not only our half Pay, and the Debts they owe us, forfeited, but our lives also, for having levied War against the Community.

So that should we succeed according to our utmost wishes, should the high tone remonstrance proposed frighten Congress into our measures, and the several States grant such funds as Congress may require? you could with less safety lay down your Arms then, than now, Nay you could not *then* with any *propriety* quit the field, for having once made a separation between the Civil and Military power, *between Congress* & her *Army*, you have *then* passed the *Rubicon*. — So that upon the plan proposed, if we would secure to ourselves the fulfillment of those promises *we extort*, (for none I presume suppose that Congress have the Money to give us), it will be necessary to keep the field till the debts are discharged, *when* that will *be* and the prospect there is of prevailing with the *Soldier* to tarry for such prudential purposes, I leave every one to conjecture.

But what if Congress does not comply with our demands, shall we then *recede?*, if we do, will it not be with disgrace?, Can we with honor give up our Arms after we have told Congress that we will not?, if not let us consider the matter well before we address Congress in the language proposed, for if this is once done, we must be subjected to the *disgrace* and *mortification* of receding from the measure, must then *submit* to be disbanded with a *lost reputation*, and *forfeited honor*, or involve our Country in the *horrors* of a Civil War. — If we can prevail with the Soldiery to join us, or find other people mad enough to engage in our schemes, which is another matter; We ought to inquire very particularly about before we give in to the measure our anonymous Brother proposes, and must therefore request him to answer the following questions,

Sir, is the present Army sufficient to Dragoon the Country into our measures, provided they United to oppose us. — if not, how are you to augment your Army?, but if our present numbers are sufficient, how are you to secure them to [engage?] in your service?. will the three years Men who came out upon large bounties and their wages secured by private contract at *home*, tarry a moment after they are told by Congress they may go, and perhaps a proclamation declaring them traitors to their Country, if they do not instantly quit your Standard & join that of Congress?— Have you any assurance that the Men engaged during the *War* with Great Britain will tarry an hour after Peace takes place, and Congress declares them discharged?. But if you can persuade the present Soldiery to engage in your War, how long will they serve *without pay?*. Or can you pay them, if not [able] to pay, have you Monies to support them?, if not, how are they to be fed?, have Congress Magazines of provisions, a Military Chest, or Funds of any kind sufficient for the purpose on which you intend to seize?. No, it is presumed we shall obtain supplies on *credit*, that cannot be! for with all the *credit* and exertions of the United States we have but *just* escaped starving, how *vain* then is the idea that the Officers of the Army who have been so many Years telling the World how *poor* they are, should be able to obtain a sufficient credit to support an Army, designed to *subjugate*, or overturn the present Constitution of America— Have you then any alternative for subsisting your Army but that of plundering your Country?

No, Horrid alternative this! nor will I believe it possible under any circumstances *whatever*, you can adopt the measure.— But should we my friends by the *arts* of *designing Men*, be persuaded that the public creditors in general will join us, and the Soldiery will agree to follow our fortunes, and by these, or any *other* means be surprised into so rash an undertaking and prove *unfortunate?* — Pray consider what our situation will then be?. — if we would act the prudent part, we must look to the *end*, as well as the beginning, We have hitherto supposed a possibility of succeeding some how or other, and that you will *overturn* the present Government, and by force of Arms establish some other *form*. — But if we take into consideration all the circumstances *which* we *ought to do* on this *occasion*, there is a moral certainty we shall *fail*. Nay, 'tis impossible in the nature of things that we can succeed. — For if we have no means of subsisting an Army but by *plunder*, if we are to have no supplies but what are to be obtained by the point of the Bayonet, I leave *you* to determine, *how long* you will persuade this, or any other Army to follow your fortunes. and when the Soldiery forsake you, what will be your situation?, *despised* and *insulted*, by an *enraged* populace, *exposed* to the *revenging* hand of *justice* — You will then flee to *Caves* & *Dens* to hide yourselves from the *face* of *day*, and of Man — you will then *truly* be, "the jest of Tories, and the scorn of Whigs," But there will be none to *pity* you, — But are we in such *desperate* circumstances?, Have we been *abused*, and *insulted* by Congress as is pretended? — By the report of the Committe which will be laid before you on Saturday, & the resolutions of Congress of the 25th Jany last, it appears that Mr Morris is directed to give you all the cash in his power.

That Congress have also pointed out a mode for the settlement of your Accounts, that you shall have the same securities as other public Creditors, and that Congress will make every effort in their power to obtain from the respective States substantial *funds* adequate to the object, of Funding the whole debt, and that the other matter contained in your Memorial is refered to a Committe of five.

Now what can Congress do more to give you satisfaction?, you will not require of them impossibilities, — it's true, they may Commute your half Pay, but they are under no obligation to do it, you have no demand for it at present, nor are Congress under any obligation to change the mode of reward, therefore, if that matter should be decided contrary to our wishes, we shall have no ground of complaint on that account. — Our business then I conceive lies within a very narrow compass — Viz. a warm & affectionate address to our *Illustrious Chief* — pointing out the disadvantages that will arise to the Army if they should be disbanded before their Acco^{ts} are settled, or in case the War continues, that justice & policy require there should not be a moments delay — Beseeching his Excell^y that he would use his influence to have the business set about immediately.

5. EXTRACT OF A LETTER FROM ARMSTRONG TO GATES, APRIL 29, 1783.[1]

Ogden is now here from the army — and, as he conceals nothing, he tells us a great deal. Among other things, it is said, that the army look back with horror and regret upon the mistaken step they have taken, and like contemptible penitents, who have sinned beyond the prospect of salvation, wish to have it to do over again. It is now, however, too late — the soldiery are anxious to disperse — no ties, no promises, will hold them longer — and with them will every loitering hope of ours break also — Adieu, then, to national character, to arrears and all — and wel-

[1] *Sparks MSS.* xxii. 162-164.

come fraud, rapine, and all the extreme distresses of another civil war. For can it be otherwise? Will the Whigs, who have lent their money — and will the men, who have lent their time and blood to America, sit down quietly under their wants — and their wretchedness? No — a dissolution of all *debts*, of all *credits* — of every principle of union and society, must and will follow — And, suffer me to ask — where will it stop? God, in his anger, gave them a King — and we want a scourge. All our hopes rest upon the impost; and that was damned, like the last, in the womb of Congress. Well, I believe, upon the whole — we shall bear our burthen of "outrageous fortune," as well as the most serene and great among them — But, I could have been as happy in not giving this instance of my fortitude. One secret, however, Ogden tells me — but which shall be no longer so. Mr. Brooks was sent from hence, with orders to break of [f] sentiments like those contained in the anonymous Address to the Officers, and to prepare their minds for some manly, vigorous association with the other public creditors — but the timid wretch discovered it to the only man, from whom he was to have kept it, and concealed it from those, to whom he had expressly engaged to make it known — To be more explicit, he betrayed it to the Commander in Chief — who, agreeably to the original plan was not [to] have been consulted till some later period. Such a villain! I would have written again — had I not seen the impotency of the army, and the assurance of Congress — They see our weakness and laugh at our resentments. My efforts, therefore, might have not only been unavailing, but injurious — The last got into the paper, God knows how. I knew nothing of it, and could wish it had been prevented; for, as it stands, it now groans under, not only my sins, but those of Mr. Bailey and his devils too — I mean the blunders.

APPENDIX B.

LIST OF AUTHORITIES CITED.

ADAMS, JOHN. Works; with a Life of the Author. Edited by Charles Francis Adams. 10 vols. Boston, 1856.

ADAMS, JOHN and ABIGAIL. Familiar Letters during the Revolution; with a Memoir of Mrs. Adams. Edited by Charles Francis Adams. New York, 1876.

AMORY, THOMAS C[OFFIN]. The Military Services and Public Life of Major-General John Sullivan of the American Revolutionary Army. Boston and Albany, 1868.

AUSTIN, JAMES T[RECOTHICK]. The Life of Elbridge Gerry; with Contemporary Letters, to the Close of the American Revolution. 2 vols. Boston, 1828-1829.

BALCH, THOMAS WILLING. The French in America during the War of Independence of the United States, 1777-1783. A translation . . . of Les Français en Amérique pendant la Guerre de l'Indépendance des États-Unis, par Thomas Balch. 2 vols. Philadelphia, 1891-1895.

BANCROFT, GEORGE. History of the United States of America, from the Discovery of the Continent. The Author's Last Revision. 6 vols. New York, 1883-1885.

BOLTON, CHARLES KNOWLES. The Private Soldier under Washington. New York, 1902.

BOUDINOT, J[ANE] J., compiler. The Life, Public Services, Addresses, and Letters of Elias Boudinot, LL.D., President of the Continental Congress. 2 vols. Boston and New York, 1896.

BOWDOIN, JAMES, and TEMPLE, JOHN. The Bowdoin and Temple Papers [1756-1782]. Massachusetts Historical Society, *Collections*, 6th series, vol. ix. Boston, 1897.

BROOKS, NOAH. Henry Knox, a Soldier of the Revolution, Major-General in the Continental Army, etc. New York and London, 1900.

BRYANT, WILLIAM CULLEN, and GAY, SYDNEY HOWARD. A Popular History of the United States. 4 vols. New York, 1876-1881.

CLARK, JOSEPH. Diary, from May, 1778, to November, 1779. New Jersey Historical Society, *Proceedings*, vii. 93-110. Newark, 1855.

COFFIN, CHARLES. The Life and Services of Major General John Thomas. New York, 1844.

DEANE, SILAS. The Deane Papers [1774-1790]. New York Historical Society, *Collections*, 1886-1890. 5 vols. New York, 1887-1891.

DEARBORN, HENRY. Journals, 1776-1783. Cambridge, 1887.

DEMING, HENRY CHAMPION. An Oration upon the Life and Services of General David Wooster, delivered at Danbury, April 27, 1854. Hartford, 1854.

DENNY, EBENEZER. Military Journal; with an Introductory Memoir. Philadelphia, 1859.

DONIOL, HENRI. Histoire de la Participation de la France à l'Établissement des États-Unis d'Amérique: Correspondance Diplomatique et Documents. 5 vols. Paris, 1886-1892.

DRAKE, FRANCIS S[AMUEL]. Life and Correspondence of Henry Knox, Major-General in the American Revolutionary Army. Boston, 1873.

DUER, WILLIAM ALEXANDER. The Life of William Alexander, Earl of Stirling; with Selections from his Correspondence. New York, 1847.

DURAND, JOHN, editor. New Materials for the History of the American Revolution; translated from Documents in the French Archives. New York, 1889.

ESSEX INSTITUTE. Historical Collections. 37 vols. Salem, 1859-1901.

FORCE, PETER, and CLARKE, M. ST. CLAIR, editors. American Archives: consisting of a Collection of Authentick Records, State Papers, Debates, and Letters and other Notices of Publick Affairs. 4th and 5th series. 9 vols. Washington, 1837-1853.

FORD, PAUL LEICESTER. The True George Washington. Philadelphia, 1896.

GARDEN, ALEXANDER. Anecdotes of the American Revolution, illustrative of the Talents and Virtues of the Heroes of the Revolution who acted the most Conspicuous Parts therein. 3 vols. Brooklyn, 1865.

GLASSON, WILLIAM HENRY. History of Military Pension Legislation in the United States. New York, 1900.

GORDON, WILLIAM. The History of the Rise, Progress and Establishment of the Independence of the United States of America: including an Account of the Late War; and of the Thirteen Colonies, from their Origin to that Period. 4 vols. London, 1788.

GRAYDON, ALEXANDER. Memoirs of His Own Time; with Reminiscences of the Men and Events of the Revolution. Edited by J. S. Littell. Philadelphia, 1846.

GREENE, GEORGE WASHINGTON. Historical View of the American Revolution. Boston, 1865.

GREENE, GEORGE WASHINGTON. The Life of Nathanael Greene, Major-General in the Army of the Revolution. 3 vols. New York, 1867-1871.

HALE, EDWARD E., and EDWARD E., JR., editors. Franklin in France; from Original Documents, most of which are now published for the first time. 2 vols. Boston, 1887-1888.

HAMILTON, ALEXANDER. Works. Edited by Henry Cabot Lodge. 9 vols. New York and London, 1885-1886.

HAZARD, SAMUEL, editor. The Register of Pennsylvania; devoted to the Preservation of Facts and Documents and Every Other Kind of Useful Information respecting the State of Pennsylvania. 16 vols. Philadelphia, 1828-1836.

HEATH, WILLIAM. Letters from Washington to Heath [1775-1783]. Massachusetts Historical Society, *Collections*, 5th series, iv. 1-285. Boston, 1878.

HEITMAN F[RANCIS] B[ERNARD]. Historical Register of the Officers of the Continental Army during the War of the Revolution. Washington, 1893.

HILDRETH, RICHARD. The History of the United States of America. 6 vols. New York, 1880-1882.

HISTORICAL MAGAZINE (The), and Notes and Queries concerning the Antiquities, History, and Biography of America. 23 vols. in 17. Boston, etc., 1857-1875.

HOLMES, ABIEL. American Annals; or a Chronological History of America from its Discovery in MCCCCXCII. to MDCCCVI. 2 vols. Cambridge, 1805.

HUBLEY, BERNARD. The History of the American Revolution. Vol. I. Northumberland, Penn., 1805.

IRVING, WASHINGTON. Life of George Washington. 5 vols. New York, 1856-1859.

JOHNSON, WILLIAM. Sketches of the Life and Correspondence of Nathanael Greene, Major-General of the Armies of the United States, in the War of the Revolution. 2 vols. Charleston, 1822.

JOHNSTON, HENRY P[HELPS], editor. The Record of Connecticut Men in the Military and Naval Service during the War of the Revolution, 1775-1783. Hartford, 1889.

JONES, JOSEPH. Letters, 1777-1787. [Edited by Worthington Chauncey Ford.] Washington, 1889.

KAPP, FRIEDRICH. The Life of John Kalb, Major-General in the Revolutionary Army. New York, 1884.

KAPP, FRIEDRICH. The Life of Major-General Frederick William von Steuben. 2 vols. New York, 1859.

KING, CHARLES R[AY], editor. The Life and Correspondence of Rufus King. 6 vols. New York, 1894-1900.

KNOX, HENRY. MSS. Papers. In Library of the New England Historic Genealogical Society, Boston.

LEE, CHARLES. The Lee Papers [1754-1811]. New York Historical Society, *Collections*, 1871-1874. 4 vols. New York, 1872-1875.

LEE, RICHARD HENRY. Life of Arthur Lee. 2 vols. Boston, 1829.

LEE, RICHARD HENRY. Memoir of the Life of Richard Henry Lee, and his Correspondence. 2 vols. in 1. Philadelphia, 1825.

LESTER, C[HARLES] EDWARDS. Our First Hundred Years: the Life of the Republic of the United States of America illustrated in its four great periods: Colonization, Consolidation, Development, Achievement. New York, 1875.

LINN, JOHN BLAIR, and EGLE, WILLIAM H[ENRY], editors. Diary of the Revolt in the Pennsylvania Line. *Pennsylvania Archives*, 2d series, xi. 631-674. Harrisburg, 1880.

LODGE, HENRY CABOT. George Washington. (American Statesmen Series.) 2 vols. Boston and New York, 1889.

LOSSING, BENSON J[OHN]. The Life and Times of Philip Schuyler. 2 vols. New York, 1883.

LOSSING, BENSON J[OHN]. The Pictorial Field-Book of the Revolution. 2 vols. New York, 1851-1852.

LOWELL, EDWARD J[ACKSON]. The Eve of the French Revolution. Boston and New York, 1892.

MCMASTER, JOHN BACH. A History of the People of the United States, from the Revolution to the Civil War. 5 vols. New York, 1896-1900.

MADISON, JAMES, reporter. Debates on the Adoption of the Federal Constitution, in the Convention held at Philadelphia, in 1787; with a Diary of the Debates of the Congress of the Confederation. (Jonathan Elliot, *Debates*, vol. v.) Washington, 1845.

MAGAZINE OF AMERICAN HISTORY, with Notes and Queries. 29 vols. New York and Chicago, 1877-1893.

MARSHALL, JOHN. The Life of George Washington, Commander-in-Chief of the American Forces. 5 vols. Philadelphia, 1804-1807.

MASSACHUSETTS. Massachusetts Soldiers and Sailors of the Revolutionary War. 10 vols. Boston, 1896-1902.

MASSACHUSETTS HISTORICAL SOCIETY. Collections. 5th and 6th series. 20 vols. Boston, 1871-1899.

MASSACHUSETTS HISTORICAL SOCIETY. Proceedings, 1791-1902. 35 vols. Boston, 1879-1902.

MOORE, FRANK. Diary of the American Revolution; from Newspapers and Original Documents. 2 vols. New York and London, 1860.

MUHLENBERG, HENRY A[UGUSTUS]. The Life of Major-General Peter Muhlenberg, of the Revolutionary Army. Philadelphia, 1849.

NEW HAMPSHIRE. Provincial Papers. Documents and Records relating to the Province of New-Hampshire, from the Earliest Period of its Settlement: 1623-1776. Edited by Nathaniel Bouton. 7 vols. Concord, etc., 1867-1873.

NEW JERSEY HISTORICAL SOCIETY. Proceedings. 1st series. 10 vols. Newark, 1847-1867.

NEW YORK HISTORICAL SOCIETY. Collections, 1868-1894. (Publication Fund Series.) 27 vols. New York, 1868-1895.

PARTON, JAMES. Life and Times of Benjamin Franklin. 2 vols. Boston, 1867.

PELLEW, GEORGE. John Jay. (American Statesmen Series.) Boston and New York, 1890.

PENNSYLVANIA. Minutes of the Supreme Executive Council of Pennsylvania, from its Organization to the Termination of the Revolution. ("Colonial Records," vols. xi.-xvi.) 6 vols. Harrisburg, 1852-1853.

APPENDIX B.

PENNSYLVANIA ARCHIVES. 2d series. Edited by John Blair Linn and William Henry Egle. 19 vols. Harrisburg, 1874-1893.

PICKERING, OCTAVIUS, and UPHAM, CHARLES W[ENTWORTH]. The Life of Timothy Pickering. 4 vols. Boston, 1867-1873.

PONTGIBAUD, CHARLES ALBERT, COMTE DE MORÉ. A French Volunteer of the War of Independence (the Chevalier de Pontgibaud). Translated and edited by Robert B. Douglas. Paris, 1897.

REED, WILLIAM B[RADFORD]. Life and Correspondence of Joseph Reed. 2 vols. Philadelphia, 1847.

REMEMBRANCER (The); or Impartial Repository of Public Events. 17 vols. London, 1775-1784.

RHODE ISLAND. Records of the Colony of Rhode Island and Providence Plantations, in New England. Edited by John Russell Bartlett. 10 vols. Providence, 1856-1865.

RIVES, WILLIAM C[ABELL]. History of the Life and Times of James Madison. 3 vols. Boston, 1859-1868.

ROOSEVELT, THEODORE. Gouverneur Morris. (American Statesmen Series.) Boston and New York, 1888.

SCHARF, J[OHN] THOMAS. History of Maryland, from the Earliest Period to the Present Day. 3 vols. Baltimore, 1879.

SCHARF, J[OHN] THOMAS, and WESTCOTT, THOMPSON. History of Philadelphia, 1609-1884. 3 vols. Philadelphia, 1884.

SEDGWICK, THEODORE, JR. A Memoir of the Life of William Livingston. New York, 1833.

SEGUR, COUNT LOUIS PHILIPPE DE. Memoirs and Recollections. Boston and New York, 1825.

SHAW, SAMUEL. Journals; with a Life of the Author. Edited by Josiah Quincy. Boston, 1847.

SMITH, WILLIAM HENRY. The St. Clair Papers: The Life and Public Services of Arthur St. Clair. 2 vols. Cincinnati, 1882.

SPARKS, JARED, editor. Correspondence of the American Revolution; being Letters of eminent Men to George Washington, from the Time of his taking Command of the Army to the End of his Presidency. 4 vols. Boston, 1853.

SPARKS, JARED. The Life of Gouverneur Morris, with Selections from his Correspondence and Miscellaneous Papers. 3 vols. Boston, 1832.

SPARKS, JARED. Sparks MSS. In Harvard University Library.

STILLÉ, CHARLES J[ANEWAY]. The Life and Times of John Dickinson, 1732-1808. Philadelphia, 1891.

STILLÉ, CHARLES J[ANEWAY]. Major-General Anthony Wayne and the Pennsylvania Line in the Continental Army. Philadelphia, 1893.

STRYKER, WILLIAM S[CUDDER]. Official Register of the Officers and Men of New Jersey in the Revolutionary War. Trenton, 1872.

STUART, I[SAAC] W[ILLIAM]. Life of Jonathan Trumbull, Sen., Governor of Connecticut. Boston, 1859.

LIST OF AUTHORITIES.

SUMNER, WILLIAM GRAHAM. The Financier and the Finances of the American Revolution. 2 vols. New York, 1891.

THACHER, JAMES. A Military Journal during the American Revolutionary War. Boston, 1827.

THOMSON, CHARLES. The Thomson Papers [1765–1816]. New York Historical Society, *Collections*, 1878. New York, 1879.

TOMES, ROBERT. The Battles of America by Sea and Land; a Complete Naval and Military History of the Country. 4 parts in 3 vols. New York [1861].

TOWER, CHARLEMAGNE, JR. The Marquis de Lafayette in the American Revolution; with some Account of the Attitude of France toward the War of Independence. 2 vols. Philadelphia, 1895.

UNITED STATES. Congressional Globes; containing Sketches of the Debates and Proceedings. 109 vols. Washington, 1835–1873.

UNITED STATES. Journals of Congress; containing the Proceedings [1774–1788]. 13 vols. Philadelphia [1777–1801].

UNITED STATES. MSS. Papers of the Board of War. In the Department of State, Washington.

UNITED STATES. Secret Journals of the Acts and Proceedings of Congress [1775–1778]. 4 vols. Boston, 1820.

UNITED STATES. Statutes at Large [1789–1902]. 32 vols. Boston and Washington, 1850–1903.

UNITED STATES MAGAZINE (The), and Literary and Political Repository, January, 1823. New York [1823].

UPHAM, C[HARLES] W[ENTWORTH], editor. The Life of George Washington, First President of the United States, written by himself; comprising his Memoirs and Correspondence, etc. 2 vols. London, 1852.

WALDO, ALBIGENCE. Diary kept at Valley Forge. *Historical Magazine*, v. 129–134, 169–172. New York, 1861.

WASHINGTON, GEORGE. Writings. Edited by Worthington Chauncey Ford. 14 vols. New York and London, 1889–1893.

WASHINGTON, GEORGE. Writings, . . . with a Life of the Author. Edited by Jared Sparks. 12 vols. Boston, 1837.

WATSON, JOHN F[ANNING]. Annals of Philadelphia and Pennsylvania in the Olden Time. 2 vols. Philadelphia, 1845.

WEBB, SAMUEL BLACHLEY. Correspondence and Journals [1772–1806]. Edited by Worthington Chauncey Ford. 3 vols. New York, 1893–1894.

WELLS, WILLIAM V[INCENT]. The Life and Public Services of Samuel Adams. 3 vols. Boston, 1865.

WHARTON, FRANCIS, editor. The Revolutionary Diplomatic Correspondence of the United States. 6 vols. Washington, 1889.

WILKINSON, GENERAL JAMES. Memoirs of My Own Times. 3 vols. Philadelphia, 1816.

WILSON, JAMES GRANT, editor. The Memorial History of the City of New York. 4 vols. New York, 1892–1893.

INDEX.

ADAMS, John, on qualifications of a general, 7; moves that Congress adopt the army and appoint a general, 8; remarks of, on Hancock's wish to be commander-in-chief, 9 note; attitude of, on appointment of Lee and Gates, 10; member of committee to draw up instructions for Washington, 11; writes to Gerry approving of Washington's appointment, 12; describes situation of Congress, 18; member of the Board of War, 19; opinion of, on jealousy concerning rank, 37; discusses appointment of Southerners in the New England army, 39; defends principle of promotions by Congress, 41–42; assigns reasons for certain promotions, 43; gives reasons for defects of American officers, 43; asks Knox for a plan of a military academy, 43; comment of, in diary, on Du Coudray's death, 58; unwilling to propose giving a bounty, 72; opinion of, concerning bounties, 72; promises to consent to liberal commutation, 145.

Adams, Samuel, seconds motion for appointing general, 8–9; receives Conway cordially, 33; defends right of Congress to grant half-pay, 193.

America, military situation of, 4.

Americans, qualities and experience of, as soldiers, 1, 3.

Appointments, Congressional *versus* colonial, 39; discussed in Congress, 39–41; victory for colonial, 41, 42–43; opinions of Washington and Gerry on character of State, 43; recommendation by Congress to States concerning, 43; Congress gives Washington powers in regard to, 44.

Aristocratic feeling, instances of, 7.

Armand, Colonel, Marquis de la Rouerie, account of, 64.

Armstrong, Major John, author of Newburg Addresses, 159–160; articles by, in *United States Magazine*, 160; purposes of, 160, 162; writes Newburg Address, 168–169.

Army, Continental, besieges Boston, 1; Washington takes command of, 13; confusion and lack of discipline in, 13; reforms introduced by Washington in, 14–15; reënlistment of, 15–17; jealousy between militia and, 36; jealousy of, in Congress diminishes, 85; at Valley Forge, 92–96; blames Congress for its sufferings, 94; supplied with clothing, 99; renewed suffering of, 104; lack of food for, in 1780, 105–106; distress of, at the close of 1780, 111–112; condition of, at close of war, 114–117; in the Carolinas, sufferings of, 118–120; in Virginia, lack of supplies for, 120–121; discussion of methods of supplying, 122–124; furloughs given to, 180–181; disbanded, 192–193.

Artificers, sufferings of, 102.

BALME, Colonel Mottin de la, appointed inspector-general of cavalry, 57 note.

Banks, John, makes contracts for supplying army, 120; becomes bankrupt, 120.

Barber, Colonel Francis, conduct of, in New Jersey mutiny, 139.

Blane, Ephraim, appointed commissary-general, 104.

Boudinot, Elias, talks with a Pennsylvania mutineer, 129; summons Congress, 182; sends to Washington for help, 186; writes brother that he hopes Congress will be well received in New Jersey, 187.

Bounty, soldiers demand, 71; Southerners object to, 71; Washington recommends, 72; Congress grant a small, 72; declared insufficient by Knox and

217

INDEX.

Washington, 72; Congress increase, 73; Washington opposes, in specie, 75; of a month's pay given, 77; of eighty dollars promised for service throughout the war, 84; another, given, 127.

Bread, said to be bad, 88; quality of, improves, 89.

Brigadier-generals, appointed, 11; Washington suggests each State furnish its own, 45; new system of appointment of, 45–46.

Broglie, Comte de, hopes to supersede Washington, 58.

Brooks, Lieutenant-Colonel John, blames commissary-general, 94; goes to Boston on committee, 144; hopes to win over legislature, 145; appointed one of committee to Congress, 152; account of, 152; drawn into the Newburg conspiracy, 167; returns to camp, 167; may have told plans of conspirators to Knox, 170 note; one of committee on Newburg Addresses, 173.

Buchanan, William, appointed commissary-general, 89.

Burke, Thomas, refuses to attend a session of Congress, 21–22.

Butler, Colonel Richard, accompanies Wayne to Princeton, 129.

CADWALLADER, Brigadier-General John, wounds Conway in duel, 34.

Carberry, Captain Henry, flies to England, 186; returns and seeks office, 186 note.

Carroll, Charles, expresses admiration for Washington, 33.

Chase, Samuel, attacks the system of State appointments, 40.

Civil servants, distresses of, 102–103.

Claiborne, Quartermaster, unable to furnish supplies, 121.

Clark, Abraham, criticises Washington, 25; writes to Stirling on half-pay, 83; gives arguments against half-pay for life, 85; attitude of, in regard to system of specific supplies, 104 note.

Clark, Joseph, extracts from diary of, 94, 95.

Clinton, Governor George, Schuyler comments on election of, 7; borrows money for the troops, 124.

Clinton, Sir Henry, sends offers to mutineers, 134.

Clothier-general, office of, established, 86; powers of, increased, 113. *See also* Mease.

Clothing, offered as a bounty, 73; sold to army, 86; States endeavor to purchase, 86; of Maryland troops, 86–87; of Connecticut troops, 87; inconveniences in importing, 87–88; competition of States for, 88; difficulties in obtaining, 99; department reorganized, 100; recommendations of the Board of War concerning, 100–101; arrival of, from France, 101–102; States relieved from supplying army with, 113; contract for furnishing army with, 116; Colonel Jackson complains of lack of, 116–117; Washington says army is well supplied with, 116, 117; Southern army ill supplied with, 118–120.

Commander-in-chief, choice of, 6–9.

Commissary-general, office of, established, 86; department of, reorganized, 89; Trumbull resigns as, 89; Buchanan incompetent, 89; detained at Philadelphia, 97; department of, reorganized, 97–98; Wadsworth appointed, 98; Wadsworth resigns as, 103–104; Ephraim Blane appointed, 104. *See also* Blane, Buchanan, Wadsworth.

Committee, grand, appointed, 153; confer with officers, 153; report, 155–156; Congress discuss report of, 156.

Committees sent to camp, description of, 20.

Commutation, officers offer to accept, 151; proposed by grand committee, 156; report on, disagreed to, 159; promised by Congress, 177–178; accepted by officers, 178; opposition to, in Connecticut and Massachusetts, 194; officers receive small benefit from, 194.

Congress, Continental, confronted with actual war, 1; problem before, 4; moral courage of, 5; try to avoid a general conflict, 5; prepare to meet conflict, 6; appoint Washington and other generals, 8–11; difficult position of, 18; John Adams describes situation of, 18; lack of power of, 18; reluctance to command, 18; jealousy of,

INDEX.   219

for their own authority, 19; establish War Office, 19; reorganize War Office, 20; send committees to camp, 20; deterioration of character of, 20–21; Laurens comments on, 21; long debates in, 21; unable to compel attendance, 21–22; condition of, in 1779, 22; support Washington, 23; become dissatisfied with Washington, 23–24; strength of opposition to Washington in, 26–27; appoint Gates chairman of the Board of War, 27; return Wilkinson's letter, 31; discuss methods of appointing officers, 39–40; yield to States, 40–41; opinion and action of, in regard to promotions, 41, 43, 44, 46; confer extraordinary powers on Washington, 44; forbid rank to be conferred on civil staff, 45; receive foreign officers cordially, 50; engage engineers, 54; rebuke Sullivan, Knox, and Greene, 56; withdraw from their position, 57; appoint Du Coudray inspector of military manufactures, 57; bury Du Coudray at public expense, 57; appoint Lafayette and Kalb major-generals, 59, 61; give directions concerning foreign officers, 66; offer bounties, 72, 73; question of powers of, 74; give month's extra pay to army, 77; increase pay of subalterns, 78; increase pay of officers below the rank of general, 79; discuss half-pay, 80; grant half-pay for seven years, 83; repeal vote for granting half-pay for life, 84; give bounty of eighty dollars to soldiers, 84; give half-pay for life, 85; appoint officers for supplying army, 86; purchase clothing for re-sale to soldiers, 86; advise States to regulate sales of clothing, 87; import clothing, 87–88; reorganize system of supplying the army, 88; mistakes of, 89; try to remedy defects, 89; order Washington to seize provisions, 90; reasons for action of, 91; appoint day of thanksgiving, 91; bad management of, 96–97; reorganize quartermaster and commissary departments, 97–98; reorganize clothing department, 100; recommend States to provide clothing for their troops, 101; vindicate Greene and Wadsworth, 103; establish system of specific supplies, 104; inefficiency of, 107; reorganize quartermaster department, 107; displeased by letter of Greene, 108; general discussion of policy of, in regard to supplying the army, 122–123; respect of Pennsylvania mutineers for, 126; vote bounties to certain soldiers, 127; mutineers say they will apply to, 129; Washington wishes to remain in Philadelphia, 131; appoint a committee to confer with Pennsylvania Council, 131; unable to obtain money, 143; said in, that no State can release itself from obligation to discharge half-pay, 146; dislike officers choosing delegates, 152; receive officers' memorial graciously, 153; appoint grand committee, 153; discuss commutation, 156, refuse to refer commutation to States, 157–158; refer Newburg Addresses to committee, 159; promise commutation, 177–178; order cessation of hostilities, 179; order war soldiers furloughed, 180; angry at slackness of Council, 182, 183; beset by soldiers, 183; adjourn to Princeton, 185; flattering reception of, 187–188; refuse to return to Philadelphia, 189; discussion of wisdom of, in leaving Philadelphia, 190–191; receive Washington's resignation, 192; disband the army, 192–193.

Connecticut, praised by Washington for keeping her troops supplied with clothing, 87; non-commissioned officers of, demand half-pay, 180; opposition of, to half-pay, 194.

Connecticut legislature, directs Trumbull to write to Congress in behalf of Wooster and Spencer, 38.

Conway Cabal, subject of, interesting but obscure, 24; objects of, 24; persons connected with, 25; officers generally hold aloof from, 26; more successful in Congress, 26–27; grows strong, 27, 29; collapses, 31–32. *See also* Gates, Lafayette, Mifflin, Washington.

Conway, Major-General Thomas, appointed inspector-general, 27; promised a position by Deane, 27; character of, 27; appointed brigadier, 27; demands promotion, 27–28; Washington remonstrates against promotion of, 28;

offers to resign, 29; appointed major-general, 29; letter of, to Gates, 29; intercourse with Washington, 29, 30; treatment of, by Washington, 31; writes another letter of resignation to Congress, 33; Congress accept resignation of, 33; tries to withdraw his resignation, 33; writes Gates his opinion of Congress, 33; wounded in duel, 34; apologizes to Washington, 34.

Cox, John, appointed assistant quartermaster-general, 97.

Crafts, Colonel, quarrels with Colonel Jackson about rank, 36.

Cushing, Thomas, opposes appointment of Washington, 9; hopes Washington and Lee will be well received in Massachusetts, 12.

DAYTON, Colonel Elias, conduct of, during New Jersey mutiny, 138–139.

Deane, Silas, defends principle of State appointment, 39, 40; invites Conway to enter American service, 27; annoyed by applications from foreigners, 47; engages four engineers, 54; makes contract with Du Coudray, 55; makes contracts with Kalb, and Lafayette, and Mauroy, 58; suggests a foreigner for commander-in-chief, 58.

Dearborn, Major Henry, extracts from diary of, 92.

De Borre, Brigadier-General, Prud'Homme, account of, 63–64.

Dickinson, John, president of Council of Pennsylvania, 183; discusses matters with Hamilton, 184–185; rebukes mutineers, 186; sends to Congress news of submission of soldiers, 186; conduct of, discussed, 190.

Duane, James, writes to Montgomery about his rank, 35; defends appointments by Congress, 40.

Du Buysson, Lieutenant-Colonel, describes his reception in America, 59.

Du Coudray, Major-General Tronson, recommended as director of artillery, 54; character of, 54–55; contract signed with, 55; reaches America, 55; objections to appointment of, 55; unpopular in France, 56; appointed inspector of military manufactures, 57;

drowned, 57; Adams's comment on death of, 57.

Duportail, Major-General Louis Lebique, renders good service, note 54.

Dyer, Eliphalet, defends the principle of State appointments, 39, 40; member of committee on Newburg Addresses, 159; attitude of, on commutation, 177.

ELLSWORTH, Oliver, appointed on committee to confer with Council of Pennsylvania, 182.

Emerson, Chaplain William, describes camp at Cambridge, 13.

Engineers, American need of, 54; four engaged, 54; Du Coudray claims command of, 56 note.

Enlistments, difficulty of securing, 72; evils of short, 73; bounties offered for, 72–73, 127; disputes concerning the, of the Pennsylvanians, 126–127.

Eustis, Surgeon William, Gates refers Gordon to, 160; makes damaging statement concerning Armstrong, 161.

Evans, Chaplain, instrumental in the erection of the "Temple," 171.

FINANCE, superintendent of, office of, established, 113; Robert Morris appointed, 113; powers given to, 113. See also Morris (Robert).

Fleury, Lieutenant-Colonel Louis de, account of, 64–65; describes appearance of Maryland troops, 86–87.

France, relations of, with America, 48; American prejudices against, 60–61.

Franklin, Benjamin, annoyed by applications of foreigners for commissions, 47.

French officers, see Officers (foreign).

Fuel, lack of, 88.

Funding system, discussed in Congress, 157.

GALVAN, Major, given a command in the South, 68.

Garanger, Captain, unable to obtain employment, 54.

Garden, Alexander, quoted, 183 note.

Gates, Major-General Horatio, offers his services, 10; adjutant-general, 10; made popular by success against Burgoyne, 24; chairman of Board of War,

27; accuses Hamilton of breaking open his desk, 29-30; corresponds with Washington concerning Conway's letter, 30; quarrels with Wilkinson, 31; denies that he wished to supersede Washington, 31-32; probably the tool of others, 32; sent to join army, 32; gives opinion on employment of foreign officers, 65-66; figurehead in affair of Newburg Addresses, 160; letter of, quoted by Armstrong, 160; consents to lead Newburg conspiracy, 168; chairman of officers' meeting, 173.

Generals, American, lack of experience of, 3; comparison of experienced, with inexperienced, 3; issue address to the army, 16; given only the half-pay of a colonel, 83; given half-pay in proportion to their pay, 85. *See also* Officers (American), and generals by name.

George III., proclaims Americans rebels, 5; speech of, to Parliament indicates peace, 156.

Gerry, Elbridge, suggests Washington as commander-in-chief, 8; can find no evidence of existence of plan to remove Washington, 32; opposes acceptance of Conway's resignation, 32; on character of State appointments, 43; gives Washington arguments against half-pay, 79.

Gilman, John Taylor, member of committee on Newburg Addresses, 159.

Gimat, Lieutenant-Colonel, employed in South, 68.

Glover, Brigadier-General John, extract from letter of, 101-102.

Gordon, William, corresponds with Washington, 28; Gates gives information to, 160; comments on address of Washington, 174.

Great Britain, military advantages of, 4.

Greene, Major-General Nathanael, appointed brigadier-general, 11; will not permit any legislature to humiliate him, 36; views of rank when in command of an army, 36 note; objects to special promotion, 41; accuses Congress of discriminating against New England officers, 42; assures Congress of Washington's moderation and fidelity, 44; protests against displacing Knox by Du Coudray, 56; offers to resign, 56; rebuked, 56-57; defends himself, 57; suggests substitute for meat, 92; appointed quartermaster-general, 97; assistants and salary of, 97-98; praised by Washington, 98; unpopular, 103; offers to resign as quartermaster-general, 103; vindicated by Congress, 103; displeased with plan for remodelling quartermaster department, 107; letter of, resigning as quartermaster-general, 107-108; anger of Congress with, 108; Washington interposes in behalf of, 109-110; reasons for resignation of, as quartermaster-general, 110; thanked by Washington, 111; describes condition in army, 118, 119, 120; endorses Banks's notes, 120; refuses to mix in military plot, 165. *See also* Quartermaster-General.

HALF-PAY, demanded by officers, 79; Washington's opinions in regard to, 79-80; Congress postpone action on, 80; discussed in Congress, 80; granted for seven years, 83-84; advocated for life by Washington, 84, 85; given to widows and orphans, 85; granted for life by Congress, 85. *See also* Commutation, Officers.

Hamilton, Alexander, laments degeneracy of Congress, 20; suspected by Gates of breaking open his desk, 29-30; member of sub-committee of grand committee, 155; writes report of grand committee, 155; advises Washington to use discontent of army to influence States, 166-167; appointed on committee to confer with Pennsylvania Council, 182; reported speech of, to Congress, 183 note; gives his opinion of mutinous soldiers, 184-185; consents to departure of Congress from Philadelphia, 185.

Hancock, John, president of Congress, 6; desires to be commander-in-chief, 8-9; informs Washington of his appointment, 9; governor of Massachusetts, 144; promises to support claims of officers, 145.

Harrison, Benjamin, member of the Board

INDEX.

of War, 19; assures Washington of the support of Congress, 23.

Harvard College, court-martial sits in chapel of, 15.

Harvard, town of, remonstrates against increase of officers' pay, 78.

Heath, Major-General William, appointed brigadier-general, 11; placed above Thomas, 37; hurt at favor shown to Lafayette, 68; receives letters from Washington on condition of army, 116, 117; ordered to prepare a detachment to suppress New Jersey mutiny, 139.

Henry, Patrick, praises Washington, 6; anonymous letter to, 24; sends letter to Washington, 25.

Hort, Commissary William, blamed by Greene, 119.

Howard, Captain Vashel D., one of committee on Newburg Addresses, 173.

Howe, Major-General Robert, suppresses New Jersey mutiny, 139-140; commands troops sent to Philadelphia, 186.

INDEPENDENCE, Americans reluctant to declare, 5.

Inspector-general, establishment of office of, 27; Conway appointed, 27. *See also* Conway, Steuben.

Irish, urged to desert, 125; number of, in Pennsylvania troops, 125.

JACKSON, Colonel Henry, involved in dispute about rank at a funeral, 36; complains of lack of clothing for the troops, 116-117.

Jackson, Major William, attempts to stop mutineers, 182.

Jay, John, tells his son of opposition to Washington, 26; defends appointments by Congress, 40; letter of Gouverneur Morris to, 163.

Jealousy, between colonies, 16; of all government, 19; between regulars and militia, 36; of military power decreases in Congress, 85.

Johnson, Judge William, gives account of Newburg Addresses, 160.

Jones, Joseph, corresponds with Washington, 109; letters of Washington to, 152, 176-177; letter of, read to officers, 172; opinion of, as to return of Congress to Philadelphia, 189.

KALB, "Baron" de, on lavish grant of military titles, 45; sent on secret mission to America, 48 note; promised by Deane rank of major-general, 58; character and aims of, 58; makes demands on Congress, 61; appointed major-general, 61; compares his position with Lafayette's, 62 note; compared with Steuben, 62.

King, Rufus, memorandum of, concerning plans of officers, 162.

Knox, Major-General Henry, approves course of Washington and Lee, 14; disapproves of State appointments, 43; in command of artillery, 55; offers resignation, 56; rebuked by Congress, 56-57; informs wife that he will not apologize to Congress, 57; opinion of, of bounty offered by Congress, 72; urges increase of officers' pay, 78; complains of beef, 115; unable to go with committee to Boston, 144; writes to Governor Hancock, 144-145; refuses to mix in military plot, 164; suggests convention to change Articles of Confederation, 165; said to have informed Washington of conspirators' plans, 170 note; moves thanks to Washington, 173; one of committee on Newburg Addresses, 173; effect of Washington's speech on, 175; superintends disbandment of the army, 192.

Knox, Mrs. Henry, gives opinion of Du Coudray, 55; expresses joy at prospect of husband's return, 55 note.

Kosciusko, Thaddeus, good services of, 51.

LAFAYETTE, Major-General Marquis de, refuses to join Conway Cabal, 26; statement of, concerning the purpose of Cabal, 32; promised by Deane the rank of major-general, 58; coldly received in Philadelphia, 59; appointed major-general, 59; claims of, 59 note; services of, 60-61; Kalb compares his position with that of, 62 note; praised by Washington, 67; compared with Steuben, 67; favor shown to, 67; describes suf-

fering at Valley Forge, 93; ordered out of Princeton by mutineers, 130.
Land, offered as a bounty, 73.
Laurens, Henry, speaks severely of degeneracy of Congress, 21; forwards to Washington anonymous letter sent him, 25; copies quotation from Conway's letter, 30; beset by foreign officers, 46; opposes half-pay, 81; gives reasons to Washington and Livingston for his opposition to half-pay, 81-82.
Lee, Major-General Charles, aids in reorganizing Maryland militia, 2; offers his services to the American cause, 10; appointed second major-general, 11; feels entitled to higher rank, 11; address to, by Massachusetts Congress, 13; helps strengthen discipline, 14; desired by the Conway Cabal for commander-in-chief, 32.
Lee, Francis Lightfoot, opposes acceprance of Conway's resignation, 33.
Lee, Richard Henry, member of committee to draw up instructions for Washington, 11; censures Mr. "*Clearly-out-of-order*," 22; praises Washington, 23; admires Gates, 26; told by Washington that Conway's appointment would be disastrous, 28; receives Conway cordially, 33.
Lincoln, Major-General Benjamin, appointed Secretary at War, 20; warned by Washington against excessive economy, 142-143; takes measures to prevent mutiny, 181.
Lisle, Major Romand de, dissatisfied with his rank, 52.
Livingston, Governor William, receives letters from Laurens on half-pay, 81-82; comments on Pennsylvania mutiny, 137; objects to half-pay, 155 note; would feel honored in protecting Congress, 187.
Local prejudices, Washington finds it impossible to destroy, 44-45.
Lovell, James, criticises Conway's letter, 28-29; votes against half-pay, 84.
Ludwig, Christopher, account of, 88-89.
Luzerne, Chevalier de, receives letter from Sullivan on Pennsylvania mutiny, 137.

McDOUGALL, Major-General Alexander, one of the committee to go to Philadelphia, 152; account of, 152; states grievances of officers, 153-154; probably drawn into conspiracy, 167; requested to remain at Philadelphia, 174.
McWilliams, Major William, repeats Wilkinson's quotation from Conway's letter, 29.
Madison, James, member of sub-committee of grand committee, 155; describes feelings of Congress, 156; objects to limitation of tariff, 157; replies to Mercer, 158; describes effect of Newburg Addresses, 159; describes effect of letter from Washington, 177.
Major-generals, appointed, 11. *See also* generals by name.
Marines, manner of raising, 123.
Maryland, remonstrates against land grants, 74; troops of, destitute of clothing, 86-87.
Massachusetts, legislature of, ask Congress to take control of army, 6; welcome Washington and Lee, 13; interpose in behalf of Thomas, 37; opposition to half-pay in, 145; postpone petition of officers, 145-146; decline to allow Congress to levy a tariff, 194.
Massachusetts, officers from, complain of preference shown to foreign officers, 68; apply to State to make provision for them, 144; appoint delegates to draw up memorial to Congress, 147; grievances of, 146, 147-149; invite cooperation of other officers, 149.
Mauroy, Vicomte de, promised rank of major-general by Deane, 58; dismissed with thanks, 61.
Mease, James, conduct of, as clothier-general, 123.
Memorial of officers to Congress, presentation of, 152; reception of, 153.
Mercer, John Francis, wishes to limit tariff, 157; member of committee on Newburg Addresses, 159.
Mifflin, Major-General Thomas, member of Conway Cabal, 26; begs Gates to take care of his papers, 29; allowed to join the army, 32; conduct as quartermaster-general, 96-97; praises Washington, 192.
Military academy, John Adams asks Knox for plans for, 43.

Military policy, true, of the Americans, 4.
Militia, characteristics of American, 1; of Massachusetts, criticised by Timothy Pickering, 1-2; efforts to improve, 2-3; jealousy between Continentals and, 36; Washington on defects of, 72-73.
Money, Continental, depreciation of, 75.
Montgomery, Major-General Richard, wishes gentlemen could be induced to serve, 7; willing to accept whatever rank Congress judge best, 35.
Month, question of pay by calendar or lunar, 76.
Morris, Gouverneur, compares Congress to Continental money, 20-21; gives Washington information concerning Congress, 32 note; expresses gratification at Conway's resignation, 33; concerned in affair of Newburg Addresses, 163; letters of, to Jay, Knox, and Greene, 163-165; thinks Congress should have jurisdiction at their residence, 190.
Morris, Lewis, magnanimous conduct of, 35; describes encampment on rice plantations, 118-119.
Morris, Robert, appointed superintendent of finance, 113; uses his credit for public benefit, 113; supplies army by contract, 113; makes new contract, 115; has agent in South, 120; declares present payment of officers impossible, 153; question of connection of, with Newburg Addresses, 163; engages his credit for the payment of the army, 180 note.
Mutiny, threatened at Valley Forge, 96; of Connecticut regiments, 106; of New England troops, 124.
Mutiny, New Jersey, outbreak of, 138; progress of, 138-139; sternly suppressed, 139-140.
Mutiny, Pennsylvania (first), outbreak of, 124-125; causes of, 125-128; description of, 128-136; comments on, 137; (second), outbreak of, 182-183; subdued, 185-186. *See also* Pennsylvania.

NEUVILLE, Monsieur de, writes his own recommendation, 52.
Newburg Addresses, appearance of, 159, 171; account of, 169; reception of, by officers, 169-170. *See also* Armstrong,

Gates, Officers (American), Morris (Gouverneur), Morris (Robert).
New England, requested by Washington to reënforce the army in Canada, 23; a desire to insult Washington shown by some delegates from, 24; sends men to oppose Burgoyne, 24; delegates from, favor promotions by the colonies, 40; supposed discrimination against, in appointments, 42; soldiers of, 71; accused by Washington of monopolizing commissions, 71; conference attended by delegates from, 78; a brigade from, revolts, 124.
New Jersey, Convention of, remonstrate against appointment of New Jersey field-officers by Congress, 40; nominate field-officers, 40-41.
New Jersey Gazette, praises behavior of mutineers, 137.
New York, Provincial Congress of, describe qualifications of an American general, 7; complain of inequalities of pay of New York troop, 75-76.
Nicola, Colonel Lewis, wishes Washington to become king, 161.

OFFICERS, American, chosen by soldiers, 14; many unfit for their post, 14; some, court-martialled, 15; some, suspected of discouraging enlistments, 16; subaltern, complain of inequalities of pay, 77; subaltern, have pay increased, 78; demand increase of pay, 78; pay of, compared with pay of British officers, 78; Congress raise pay of, 79; demand half-pay, 79; suffering of families of, 94; accused by Steuben of shirking duty, 95; situation of, in last period of war, 142-143; draw up memorial to Congress, 147-149; unhappy situation of "deranged," 149; memorial of, 150-152; jealous of favor shown to civilians, 154; some, incline toward monarchy, 161; wish to force Congress to keep them in service, 162; favor strengthening central government, 154, 164-165; anonymous call for meeting of, 168, 169; pass resolutions condemning Newburg Addresses, 174; object to being furloughed, 180; condition of, after discharge, 193; commutation of little value to, 194; receive pensions, 195. *See also* Appointments, Commutation, Half-pay, Promotion, Rank.

Officers, foreign, apply for commissions, 47; accustomed to serve in armies of other countries, 48; special reasons of, for seeking American service, 48–50; well received by Congress, 50; often unworthy, 50–51; American jealousy of, 51; attempts to get rid of, 51–52; vanity of, 52; hardships of, 53–54; Gates's opinion of, 65; Congress give directions concerning, 66; Washington remonstrates against undeserved promotion of, 66; remarks on policy of Congress concerning, 70. *See also* Armand, Broglie, De Borre, Du Buysson, Du Coudray, Duportail, Kalb, Kosciusko, Lafayette, Lisle, Plessis, Pulaski, Roche de Fermoy, Woedtke.

Ogden, Colonel Matthias, one of committee to Philadelphia, 152; emphasizes discontent of officers, 153–154; drawn into Newburg conspiracy, 167.

Osgood, Samuel, writes letters on half-pay, 145–146.

PARSONS, Major-General Samuel H., objects to special promotion, 41.

Pay, amount of soldiers', 71; discontent of soldiers with their, 71; considered too high by Southerners, 71; irregularity of, 74; inequalities in, 75–76; question of, by calendar or lunar month, 76; of subalterns raised, 77–78; officers demand increase of, 78; of officers raised, 79. *See also* Commutation, Generals, Half-pay, Money, Officers (American).

Pennsylvania, Assembly of, request Congress to return to Philadelphia, 189.

Pennsylvania, Council of, described, 131 note; send Reed and Potter to conciliate mutineers, 131; refuse to call out militia, 182, 183; threatened by mutineers, 182–184; take vigorous measures, 185–186; express desire for return of Congress, 189.

Pennsylvania Packet, comments of, on mutiny, 137.

Pennsylvania troops, mutiny of, 124; motives of, 125–128; proceed to Princeton, 129; well-organized, 130; demands of, 131–132; remove to Trenton, 134; conduct of, concerning spies, 135–136; behavior of, praised, 137; discharged or furloughed, 140; difficulty of assembling, 141; attempted mutiny of, quelled, 141; present insolent memorial to Council, 181; second mutiny of, 181–182; surround statehouse, 182–183; appoint delegates, 184; make submission, 186. *See also* Mutiny (Pennsylvania).

Pensions, popular dislike of, 154 note; given after the Revolution, 195.

Peters, Richard, secretary and member of the Board of War, 20; one of committee to confer with Pennsylvania Council, 182.

Pettit, Charles, appointed assistant quartermaster-general, 97; complains of slowness of government, 107; differs from Greene concerning the new plan of the quartermaster department, 110.

Philadelphia, people of, blame Congress, 188; many citizens of, present address to Congress, 189.

Pickering, Timothy, describes Massachusetts militia, 1–2; suggests substitute for meat, 92; complains of cost of living, 103; appointed quartermaster-general, 111; gives orders to sell supplies, 112; blamed by Washington, 115; criticised by Shaw, 142; opinion of, on Newburg Address, 169; approves meeting of officers, 170; calls Jones's letter sensible, 173; dislikes resolutions of officers, 175. *See also* Quartermaster-general.

Plessis, Lieutenant-Colonel Du, account of, 65; praised by Washington, 65.

Potter, General, sent to negotiate with mutineers, 131; exonerated by committee, 136.

Prices, rise of, 102.

Privates, careless of the laws of health, 14; given bounty of eighty dollars for war enlistment, 84; condition of, after discharge, 193; receive pensions, 195–196.

Promotions, Congress maintain their right to make, 41; correspondence between Greene and Adams on, 41–42; left to

Q

States, 42–43; system of, recommended by Congress to States, 44; Washington advises Congress on, 45; Congress establish new system of, 45; general conduct of Congress in regard to, 46; of foreign officers, Washington remonstrates against, 66. *See also* Officers, Rank.

Pulaski, Brigadier-General, Count Casimir, account of, 64.

Putnam, Major-General Israel, appointed major-general, 11; appointment of, offends Wooster and Spencer, 38.

Putnam, Brigadier-General Rufus, goes to Boston on a committee, 144; seconds motion of thanks to Washington, 173.

QUARTERMASTER-GENERAL, office of, established, 86; Mifflin resigns as, 97; department of, reorganized, 97; Greene appointed, 97; department of, again reorganized by Congress, 107; Greene resigns as, 111; Pickering appointed, 111. *See also* Greene, Mifflin, Pickering.

RANK, sensitiveness of officers on subject of, 36; quarrels concerning, 36; Congress's views on, 37; John Adams's opinion on, 37; General Thomas dissatisfied with his, 37; Generals Wooster and Spencer dissatisfied with their, 38; lavishly given, 45; Congress restrict allowance of, 45. *See also* Officers, Promotion.

Rations, dispute over extra, 114; compensation for retained, unpaid, 144.

Rum, thirty hogsheads of, distributed among the soldiers, 89–90.

Rush, Dr. Benjamin, thought to be writer of anonymous letter, 25.

Rutledge, Edward, member of committee to draw up instructions for Washington, 11; member of the Board of War, 19.

ST. CLAIR, Major-General Arthur, opinion of, on Pennsylvania enlistments, 126; ordered out of Princeton by the mutineers, 130.

Sands, Comfort, makes contract for feeding army, 113; narrow views of, 114;

gives up contract, 115; has contract for clothing army, 116.

Scammell, Colonel Alexander, disapproves concessions to mutineers, 136.

Scharf and Westcott, quotations from, 188.

Schuyler, Major-General Philip, comments on Clinton's election as governor, 7; appointed major-general, 11; member of a committee sent to camp, 107; describes effect of Washington's address at Newburg, 175.

Sargent, Jonathan D., criticises Washington, 25.

Shaw, Major Samuel, views of, on rank, 36; disapproves of concessions to mutineers, 136; criticises Pickering, 142; criticises the people, 146; thinks committee to Philadelphia accomplished little, 168; praises Jones's letter, 173; describes effect of Washington's address, 173, 175–176.

Sherman, Roger, opposes the appointment of Washington, 9; member of the Board of War, 19.

Shreve, Colonel Israel, conduct of, in New Jersey mutiny, 138.

Spencer, Major-General Joseph, offended at appointment of Putnam, 38.

Spies, sent to Princeton by Clinton, 134; arrested and fate of, discussed, 134–135; hanged, 135; reward for surrender of, refused, 135–136.

States, allowed by Congress to appoint officers, 40–41; purchase clothing, 86; advised by Congress to regulate sales of clothing, 87; given appointment of clothiers, 100; relieved of care of clothing army, 113.

Steuben, Major-General, letter of, concerning foreign officers, 52; compared with Kalb, 62; comes to America, 62–63; services as inspector-general, 63; desires a command in the line, 66; compared with Lafayette, 67; describes condition and conduct of American officers, 94, 95; unable to secure supplies, 121.

Stewart, Colonel Walter, accompanies Wayne to Princeton, 129; meets Reed, 132; sounds the officers, 161; sounds Washington, 168.

Stirling, Major-General Lord, Conway

INDEX. 227

makes disrespectful reference to, 28; reports Wilkinson's quotation of Conway's letter to Washington, 28; remonstrates against an appointment, 41.

Sullivan, Major-General John, ambiguous conduct of, in regard to Cabal, 26; corresponds with Washington on promotion, 45; offers to resign, 56; rebuked by Congress, 56-57; approves concessions to mutineers, 136; praises behavior of mutineers, 137.

Supplies, specific, system of, established by Congress, 104; failure of, 104-105; abolished in the North, 113; continued in the South, 120; suffering in consequence of, 120-121; great defects in system of, 123.

"TEMPLE," the, account of, 171.

Thanksgiving, of December 18, 1777, description of, 91-92.

Thatcher, Surgeon James, on sufferings of troops, 112.

Thomas, Major-General John, appointed brigadier, 11; difficulty concerning rank of, 37-38.

Treasury, Board of, slow, 107; abolished, 113.

Troup, Robert, Wilkinson misrepresents, 31.

Trumbull, Jonathan, Jr., criticises Washington, 25.

Trumbull, Joseph, resigns position as commissary-general, 89.

Tryon, Governor William, procures the formation of militia companies in New York, 3.

VALLEY FORGE, sufferings of army at, 92-96.

Virginia, deference paid to, 7; sends clothing to her troops, 99.

WADSWORTH, Jeremiah, appointed commissary-general, 98; praised by Washington, 98; resignation of, 103-104. *See also* Commissary-general.

Wagon-master, neglects duty, 97.

Waldo, Albigence, extracts from diary of, 94, 95-96.

War, Board of, established, 19; reorganized, 20; abolished, 20; ordered to contract for supplies, 89; care for clothing of army, 99; ask to be relieved from this duty, 100; give advice for procuring clothing, 100-101; intervene in behalf of artificers, 102; call on governors of Maryland and Delaware for provisions, 106; unable to get credit in Philadelphia, 112; correspond with Washington on terms of enlistment of Pennsylvanians, 127.

War, Secretary at, appointed, 20. *See also* Lincoln.

Ward, Major-General Artemas, principal general in New England army, 8; said to be incompetent, 8; objections to superseding, 9; appointed first major-general, 11.

Ward, Samuel, defends the principle of State appointments, 39.

Washington, General George, how regarded, 6; advises that gentlemen be chosen as officers, 7; arguments in favor of choosing commander-in-chief, 6-7; arguments against appointment of, 8; Elbridge Gerry desires appointment of, 8; appointed, 8; accepts, 9; instruction and commission prepared for, 11-12; sets out for Cambridge, 12; John Adams and Cushing write letters introducing, 12; cordial reception of, in Massachusetts, 12-13; takes command of army, 13; improves its discipline, 14; court-martials officers, 15; cares for health of soldiers, 15; prepares to reënlist army, 15; complains of the difficulty of doing so, 15-16; laments degeneracy of Congress, 20; sustained by Congress, 23; treacherous attacks upon, 24-25; criticisms of, 25-26; opposition to, in Congress, 26-27; remonstrates against appointment of Conway as major-general, 28; will not resign, 28 note; writes to Conway, 29; writes to Gates, 30; attitude of, toward Conway, 31; supported by public opinion, 31; apology of Conway to, 34; informs Congress of prevalence of disputes in regard to rank, 36; asks Congress to assert their right to make promotions, 41; asks Congress to increase number of generals, 42; on character of State appointments, 43; given extraordinary powers by Congress, 44; finds it impossible to do away with local prejudices, 44–45; writes to Sullivan and Congress on promotion, 45; complains of demands of foreign officers, 48; rebukes foreign officers for unwarranted claims, 52–53; objects to Du Coudray's appointment, 55; compares Steuben and Lafayette, 67; writes to Heath, giving reasons for employing certain officers, 68; accuses New England of monopolizing commissions, 71; urges Congress to offer bounties, 72–73; urges that signers of Continental bills work faster, 75; opposes giving bounties in coin, 75; opposes inequalities in payment of troops, 76–77; disapproves of giving a month's extra pay to soldiers, 77; recommends increase in pay of subalterns, 77; thinks half-pay unwise, 79; changes his opinion, 79; says that self-interest is the basis of human action, 79; urges Congress to grant half-pay, 80; receives letter from Laurens on half-pay, 81–82; urges Congress to make the grant for life, 84, 85; informs Congress of sufferings of army, 89; directed to seize supplies, 90; explains his conduct to Congress, 90–91; reports conditions at Valley Forge to Congress, 93; criticises management of affairs, 93; remarks of, on the sufferings at Valley Forge, 96; praises Greene and Wadsworth, 98; says the army is well clothed, 99; gives opinion of the system of specific supplies, 104–105; calls on New Jersey for provisions, 105; begs Jones to prevent suspension of Greene, 109–110; thanks Greene for services as quartermaster-general, 111; complains of bad management in clothing army, 111–112; orders a part of the troops discharged on account of lack of clothing, 112; objects to sale of supplies, 112; describes Sands and his methods, 114–115, 116; blames Pickering, 115; corresponds with Board of War on terms of enlistment of Pennsylvanians, 126–127; reasons of, for not going to Philadelphia during the Pennsylvania mutiny, 130–131; fears ill effects from concessions, 136; takes measures to suppress New Jersey mutiny, 139; calls New Jersey mutiny a fortunate event, 140; warns Lincoln against excessive economy, 142–143; refuses to permit Knox to go to Boston, 144; fears trouble among officers, 147; advises that officers be conciliated, 152; informs Congress of Newburg Addresses, 159; rebukes Nicola for suggesting that he make himself king, 161–162; praised in letter to Boudinot, 166; advised by Hamilton on his conduct toward the army, 166–167; attempts to alienate officers from, 167; sounded by Stewart, 168; praises style of Newburg Addresses, 169; calms officers, 170–171; addresses officers, 172; thanked by officers, 173; effect of address of, described by Schuyler and Shaw, 175–176; thanks officers, 176; writes to Philadelphia in their behalf, 176–177; proclaims cessation of hostilities, 179; asks Congress what he shall do with men enlisted for the war, 179–180; excuses officers from accepting furloughs, 180; sends force to Philadelphia, 186; takes leave of officers, 191 note; resigns his commission, 191–192.

Wayne, Major-General Anthony, criticises Washington, 26; remark of, on obtaining clothing, 99; expresses fears of a mutiny, 124; attempts to suppress mutiny, 128–129; sends news to Washington, 129; follows troops, 129; negotiates with mutineers, 131–132; meets Reed, 132; offers reward for delivery of spies, 135; expects Pennsylvanians to reënlist, 140; quells attempt at mutiny, 141.

Webb, Colonel Samuel B., letter from Major Wright to, 167–168.

Wentworth, Governor Benning, recommends codification of New Hampshire militia laws, 2–3.

Whipple, William, opinion as to return of Congress to Philadelphia, 190.

Widows and orphans of officers given half-pay for seven years, 85.

Wild, Ebenezer, extract from journal of, 92.

Wilkinson, Lieutenant-Colonel James, gives extract from Conway's letter, 29;

tries to explain his quotation away, 29; untrustworthy, 30; tries to lay blame on Troup, 31; quarrels with Gates, 31; resigns as secretary of the Board of War, 31.

Williams, Sergeant, appointed "Major-General" by mutineers, 130; Reed has poor opinion of, 133; arrests spies, 134-135; inclined to send them back to New York, 135.

Williams, William, criticises Washington, 25.

Wilson, James, member of the Board of War, 19.

Woedtke, Baron de, a drunkard, 50-51.

Wolcott, Oliver, votes against half-pay, 84.

Wooster, David, appointed brigadier-general, 11; outranked by Putnam, 38.

Wright, Major Joseph Allen, comments on prospects of officers, 167-168.